THE
SECRET
MUSEUM

Molly Oldfield

First published in 2013 by Collins

An imprint of HarperCollins*Publishers*
77–85 Fulham Palace Road
London W6 8JB

www.harpercollins.co.uk

10 9 8 7 6 5 4 3 2 1

Text © Molly Oldfield 2013

The author asserts her moral right to be identified as the author of this work.

A catalogue record for this book is available from the British Library.

ISBN: 978-0-00-745528-7

Publisher – Hannah MacDonald
Editor – Craig Adams
Senior Project Editor – Georgina Atsiaris
Design – Lucy Sykes-Thompson
Illustrations – Hennie Haworth
Picture Research – Giulia Hetherington
Production – Stuart Masheter

Colour reproduction by FMG. Printed and bound in China by R R Donnelley.

THE
SECRET
MUSEUM

Molly Oldfield

CONTENTS

INTRODUCTION

[10]

A Gutenberg Bible
ON VELLUM

[14]

Harrison Schmitt's
SPACE SUIT

[20]

Three pieces of
MARS

[26]

A Bejewelled
CROSS

[56]

A Haida
SHAMAN'S RATTLE

[60]

Francis Crick's
SKETCH OF DNA

[66]

**TABLET K.143, SCHOO
EXERCISE BOOK**
OF ASHURBANIPAL
KING OF ASSYRIA

[72]

Auguste Piccard's
BALLOON GONDOLA

[100]

JASON JUNIOR

[106]

Underwater Painting
BY ZARH PRITCHARD

[111]

Anglerfish
COUPLE

[117]

Flag from the
**BATTLE OF
TRAFALGAR**

[143]

A BLUE WHALE

[149]

Logbook of the
KON-TIKI EXPEDITION

[155]

Wally Herbert's
SLEDGE

[162]

A piece of
**NEWTON'S
APPLE TREE**

[32]

The first
CULTIVATED PEARLS

[38]

Lamourouxia viscosa
SEED FROM MEXICO

[45]

Things beneath the
FLOORBOARDS

[51]

Vladimir Nabokov's
**BUTTERFLY
GENITALIA CABINET**

[78]

Charles Dickens's
**FELINE
LETTER OPENER**

[83]

THE HEART TOKEN

[88]

**ITEM RDMSC
RD 1/1/1**

[94]

The first Giraffe
IN FRANCE

[123]

A GREAT AUK EGG

[128]

A GLASS JELLYFISH

[133]

The interior of
VASA

[137]

SONG 21

[167]

EXU BOCA DE FOGO

[173]

**Livingstone and
STANLEY'S HATS**

[179]

Hawai'ian Feather
HELMET

[184]

The Lienzo
OF TLAPILTEPEC

[188]

Mixtec Turquoise
MOSAIC SHIELD

[193]

ALICIA (1965–67)
Mural by Joan Miró
and Josep
Lloréns Artigas

[198]

An Unopened
BOOK

[203]

BLOOD'S DAGGER

[232]

Tell Halaf
SCULPTURES

[237]

Alfred Nobel's
WILL

[243]

Sketches
OF CHURCHILL

[248]

A Channel Islands
PILLAR BOX

[276]

Buckingham Palace
SWITCHBOARD

[280]

A leaf of
GOAT EYE STAMPS

[285]

The tools that belong
TO QUEEN VICTORIA
DENTIST

[289]

Van Gogh's
SKETCHBOOKS

[314]

Box in a Valise
BY MARCEL
DUCHAMP

[319]

Margaret Fonteyn's
TUTU

[326]

Stanley Peach's
CENTRE COURT
DESIGNS

[333]

The
DIAMOND SUTRA

[210]

Tibetan Abbot's
COSTUME

[216]

Two Golden Bees,
from the
GLASS PALACE IN BURMA

[222]

SLAP-SOLED SHOES

[227]

FRIENDSHIP BOOK

[254]

TORAH ARK CURTAIN

[261]

**The Tower of
the Blue Horses**
BY FRANZ MARC

[265]

Christmas Telegram
FROM AGENT ZIGZAG

[270]

Skull of a
**TAPUIASAURUS
MACEDOI**

[293]

Handaxe
FROM HOXEN

[299]

A Series of
PAINTINGS BY OZIAS

[304]

The Spaulding Collection
OF JAPANESE PRINTS

[309]

**Original Draft of
'Auld Lang Syne',**
ROBERT BURNS

[339]

INDEX

[344]

ACKNOWLEDGEMENTS

[350]

PICTURE CREDITS

[352]

for my
GRANDPARENTS

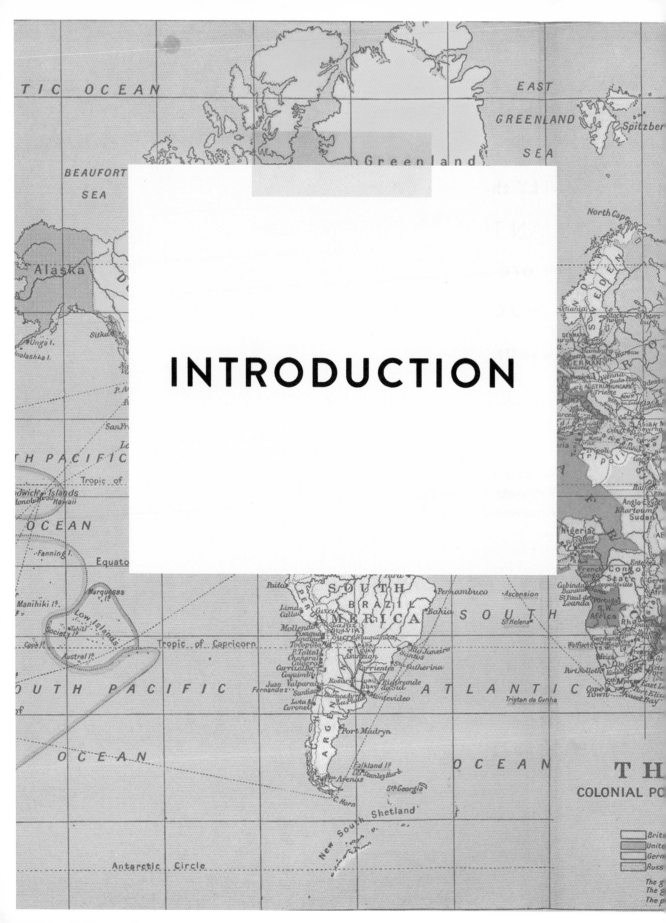

INTRODUCTION

USUALLY there is MORE HIDDEN AWAY

THAN THERE IS ON DISPLAY.

There are all sorts of reasons why.

AS THE SEED OF MY IDEA GREW INTO A SEEDLING,

I BEGAN to UNEARTH SOME of THESE REASONS.

Since 2002 I have been a writer and researcher for the television show *QI*. I also co-write a weekly QI column in the *Saturday Telegraph* and research a Radio 4 programme called *The Museum of Curiosity*. One of the things I'm often asked about *QI* is 'How do you find the script questions?' My answer is that I find a lot of ideas in museums – they're a great place to go to learn, to get fresh ideas and to wander around in beauty. I used to visit the public areas, notebook in hand, scribbling down question ideas without realizing that, behind closed doors, most of each museum's collection is hidden away from public view.

That changed when two fish curators from the Natural History Museum invited me to look around their fishy realm. I went excitedly, thinking it would be fun but really with no idea of quite how surprising and wonderful the behind-the-scenes fish collection would be. We spent three hours pushing open high-security doors and peering into tanks to marvel at specimens like Archie, the giant squid (and his tank mate, the even bigger colossal squid), who is too big to fit in the galleries, and sharks that inspired super-fast Olympic swimwear.

The curators showed me their favourite specimens that live among shelves of glass jars containing fish from every country on Earth. One of those specimens, an anglerfish couple, made it into the pages of this book. The endless shelves full of fish have been collected over the course of a century: Darwin's collection from the *Beagle* is on a shelf not far from some rare fish from Borneo that the current curators had picked up on a fishing trip earlier that month. The space was zinging with possibility and stories, and I caught the bug for backstage.

As I emerged into the light of the museum itself, the seed of the idea for a book landed lightly upon me. I began to wonder if all museums were like this – housing things that only researchers and curators know about? A few days passed, the seed began to unfurl its roots and I decided to call a few more museums to ask them whether they had any treasures behind the scenes that they rarely display. It turned out that they did. The Science Museum told me about a huge ex-RAF airbase in Wiltshire, filled with enormous objects they don't have space to display. The Foundling Museum has a collection of tokens left by the mothers of foundlings, hidden away in an archive. The Van Gogh Museum in Amsterdam cares for van Gogh's sketchbooks, which they have never exhibited. Writing this a year later, looking back, it seems funny that I had to ask the museums the question. Of course, almost all museums have a storage collection filled with objects that are an integral part of the collection but are rarely put out for exhibition.

Usually there is more hidden away than there is on display. There are all sorts of reasons why. As the seed of my idea grew into a seedling, I began to unearth some of these reasons. Sometimes, objects are too precious to exhibit and for their own security need to be kept securely in a vault. This was the case with a bejewelled cross that lives in a museum in Brazil, in a dangerous part of Salvador de Bahia. Very often the treasures are too fragile to show, so it is best to keep them in a climate-controlled, dark environment because lengthy exposure to light would destroy them. At the Peggy Guggenheim Collection in Venice I saw a piece by Duchamp in 'the bunker' that is very rarely put out in the light of the galleries and lives with other fragile treasures, protected by covers which the museum nicknames 'pyjamas'.

Sometimes it's a question of size – there isn't space for enormous objects in a museum and it's impossible to effectively display tiny, microscopic specimens. It's also a matter of not having enough space – there isn't

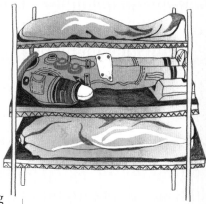

room to show everything. Natural History museums keep between 90 and 99 per cent of their specimens – a vast array of species collected over centuries across the Earth – as reserve collections, behind closed doors, ready for researchers, conservation groups or climate change specialists to delve into. Like the fish collection at the Natural History Museum, this is where the action happens.

No matter what the subject of the museum or why each object is in a reserve collection, everything that isn't on display is valued in its own right and conserved for the future. Usually you can see anything you would like to, if you ask the museum to see it but, if you're at all like me, perhaps you didn't know that all of these treasures were there. Once I realized quite how much lay unexplored away from the public space of each museum I felt compelled to take some of these treasures that lurk in cupboards, basements and vaults and lift them into the light and onto the pages of this book.

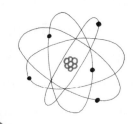

The seedling of this book was fed and watered with the help of curators and conservators at each museum: keepers of the keys to the hidden realms. Each time a door was unlocked and a curator ushered me into the collection they knew so well I found myself in a world of stories, lucky enough to be with the one person on Earth who could best explain the significance of the objects that surrounded us.

I picked things intuitively, selecting those I liked or those that provoked an emotional reaction in me. Sometimes curators suggested precious things in storage that they would rarely display, other times the curator and I roamed freely around the storage areas until I found something that looked interesting, and the curator and I would then research the item's history. If you were to write this book you would no doubt pick totally different treasures, but these are some of the things I discovered that I think are wonderful.

Whatever you're into, there ought to be something here for you: take your pick – what about a spacesuit covered in moon dust? Or maybe three pieces of Mars, kept in storage at the Vatican Observatory? A letter opener made from the paw of Charles Dickens's cat? A friendship book written in by Anne Frank? Perhaps a tutu danced in by Margot Fonteyn?

Delve in and have a look around. I hope you will find ideas, people, stories and treasures that will fascinate and inspire you.

[OBJECT 01]

A GUTENBERG BIBLE
ON VELLUM

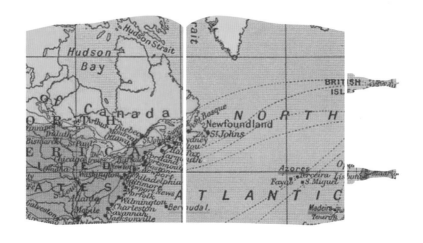

[Location]

The MORGAN LIBRARY and MUSEUM
New York City, USA

The **MORGAN LIBRARY AND MUSEUM**
IS A MUSEUM
IN all SENSES of the WORD:
A LIBRARY,
as the first museums were,

a **TREASURE CHEST** of artefacts,

as MUSEUMS are TODAY,

and a
GIFT TO THE MUSES.

[**Pierpont Morgan (1837–1913)**]
Pierpont Morgan was a brilliant financier and an avid collector of rare and precious things. His son J. P. Morgan, Jr gave his father's extraordinary library to the public in 1924, and now anyone who visits can see a selection of his art, rare books, manuscripts, drawings, prints and ancient artefacts that are on display.

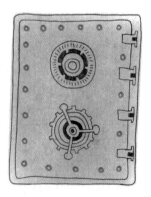

IF THE MUSES LOOK FOR heaven here on Earth, I think they must find it in museums. Originally more like libraries, museums were conceived as 'shrines for the muses', filled with books. It was only in the seventeenth century that they became showpieces for wonderful objects. The Morgan Library and Museum is a museum in all senses of the word: a library, as the first museums were, a treasure chest of artefacts, as museums are today, and a gift to the muses.

The Morgan is in the former home of Pierpont Morgan (1837–1913), one of the most brilliant financiers America has ever seen and a generous and devoted patron of the arts. Each day, hundreds of people wander around Pierpont's sumptuous library, built for $1.2 million, with a mantelpiece and ceiling sourced from Rome. They marvel at the books and artwork on show in his home and his library, which his banking colleagues dubbed 'The Up-town Branch'.

Only a fragment of the work at the Morgan is on display. Most of their treasures are beneath the buzzing city of New York, resting in three floors of quiet, humidity-controlled rooms carved out of the rock. The long rooms are filled with grey, steel-enclosed safes, each one fiercely protective of its delicate contents: ideas that shaped the history of human feeling and thinking, touchstones of our culture.

Few people know they are there, waiting, deep in the calm, beneath Manhattan, but I imagine the muses love to flit around there, exulting in the hidden treasures: the only manuscript of *Paradise Lost*, dictated by the blind poet Milton, notebooks containing lyrics by Bob Dylan (the first moment 'Blowing in the Wind' came to Dylan is scribbled in pencil), neat scores by Mozart and Debussy and messy scores by Beethoven, drawings by Dürer and Picasso and hundreds of ideas produced by some of the most creative people that have ever lived. The muses laugh gleefully, for they have been listened to. The archives of the Morgan are proof that we humans can sometimes hear the quiet calls of the gods of art and find the skill to translate this calling into physical form.

Only the curators of the Morgan go down to the archives. They swap things in and out of display and bring items requested by people who want to see them up to the beautiful Morgan reading room. I came into the reading room to view a Gutenberg Bible, the first book ever printed in the western world. The Morgan owns three copies, more than any other institution in the world. There are only 50 or so copies in existence, and only 12 of those are on vellum. I had a morning to myself with the Morgan's copy of the Gutenberg Bible on vellum.

Inge Dupont, one of the librarians, brought it up out of the vaults of the Morgan and there it was, in two enormous volumes – Old and New Testament. It was sitting on a trolley, which Inge and her colleague wheeled across the reading room to a desk. Together, they heaved the New Testament up on to a lectern. They handed me a piece of acid-free card with which to turn the pages and asked me to turn them holding the bottom right-hand pages only. Then they left me alone with one of the most valuable books in the world. It was sublime. I felt so lucky. I'd seen a copy on paper in the New York Public Library, but it was behind glass. This civilization-changing beauty was here in my hands.

I stood up to read it. Gutenberg created the Bibles so they could be read in monastery refectories, by lots of monks at the same time, so they tend to be enormous. This one was huge, and the vellum pages were stiff to turn, so I had to be standing above the Bible to turn a page. Standing up also seemed appropriate. When the first Gutenberg Bible to come to the United States arrived in New York, the officers at the Customs House were asked to remove their hats on seeing it, for the privilege of viewing a Gutenberg Bible is available to so few.

As I turned the pages, I was in a vortex, transported to Johannes Gutenberg's workshop in Mainz, Germany, in 1454; to a room in which Gutenberg paced up and down, watched by his investors, helped by his assistants, combining ink and calf's leather and his new invention, a printing press which held 270 type moulds of letters, to create 180 Bibles, which would begin a revolution in the way we receive and spread information.

Gutenberg worked hard. In fact, I have reason to believe he slept in his workshop, or at least came to work in the clothes he slept in at home. When I visited Harvard's Natural History Museum's entomology collection, their curator showed me an ant collected and preserved in vodka at a dinner party hosted by Stalin. When I asked him if he had a favourite item in his collection, he said there was one creature he wished he still had – Gutenberg's bedbug. He told me how

[Johannes Gensfleisch zur Laden zum Gutenberg (1398–1468)] Gutenberg invented movable type and so introduced printing to Europe.

the phone had rung one day and it was the Boston Library, who said, 'We've found a creature in our Gutenberg Bible, can you check it out for us?' They sent the creature over so the curator could have a good look. He called them back later that day to say, 'You've got a bedbug belonging to Mr Gutenberg.' He gave the bug back to the library and never saw it again.

Even if Gutenberg did lose a lot of sleep while creating movable type and his Bibles, it was certainly worth it. He invented a new way of communicating, transformed the rate of literacy through-out the western world and started a revolution that remained unprec-edented in human culture until the arrival of the internet in our lifetime. Before Gutenberg, the only way to create a book was by hand. In the west, this was the job of monks, who worked in scriptoriums in chilly monas-teries. They probably had inky hands, sore backs and, by the end of each day, rather tired eyes. Yet they laboured on, spreading the good word. In the east, a Chinese blacksmith, Pi Sheng, had invented movable type four centuries earlier, but his invention hadn't been adapted for use by a machine. In China, type was imprinted on the page by hand rubbing, which made the process only slightly more efficient than the copying by a medieval scribe.

When Gutenberg put all the ingredients together, crucially, with the invention of his type mould, and began printing his Bibles, a lot of scribes soon found themselves out of a job. Now, a book could be created more quickly, by machine. This machine could, amazingly at the time, create as many identical copies of the same text as you needed. Suddenly, anyone lucky enough to own a Gutenberg Bible, no matter where they were in the world, could turn to page 20 and read from the same text.

Just imagine the work that went into this one book. For years, Gutenberg toiled in secret in a little hamlet downriver from Stras-bourg. He couldn't risk anyone finding out the techniques he was developing. He shaped each of the 200 or so letters he needed for a Bible out of metal, by hand. Then, using the type mould, he made copies of the letters. They were set into a form, covered with ink made in his workshop and pressed, using a machine he may well have adapted from a wine press, on to either vellum, as with this Bible, or paper. Vellum – calfskin – is more precious than paper, which itself was worth almost as much gold. Gutenberg wanted all his Bibles to be printed on vellum, but it was just too expensive.

The ink shimmers, because it contains metal compounds. It's set off beautifully by its decoration in rich golds, blues, greens and reds. As soon as a page of the Bible was printed, it was handed over to an illustrator in Gutenberg's home town who illustrated the initials, and then to another in Bruges who completed the intricate decoration of the Bible's columns and borders. When the book was complete, it was bound. It came out of the workshop and changed the world. In just 50 years, the number of books printed with movable type went from zero to 20 million.

When, nearly five centuries later, Morgan bought the manuscript of Pudd'nhead Wilson from Mark Twain, the author told Morgan, 'One of my highest ambitions is gratified – which was to have something of mine placed elbow to elbow with that august company which you have gathered together to remain indestructible in a perishable world.' This is why the Morgan Library and Museum is so special. The 'august company' really is wonderful and each precious work is safe in the quiet vaults below Manhattan. No wonder the muses love this place so much.

[**The Morgan Library's Gutenberg Bible on vellum**]
I had an afternoon alone with this world treasure, in the reading room of the Morgan Library and Museum.

[OBJECT 02]

Harrison Schmitt's
SPACESUIT

[Location]

**The SMITHSONIAN NATIONAL AIR and SPACE MUSEUM Storage Facility
Suitland, MA, USA**

VISITING APOLLO ASTRONAUTS
have been asked,
'WHEN YOU WERE
ON THE MOON,
did you happen to see my auntie?'

I ALMOST FORGOT TO LOOK at the moon today.

Those are the words on the first painting I ever chose for myself. I saw it in a little arty café in Cochin, Kerala, India. At the other end of the subcontinent, in Nepal, people think the dead live on the moon. Visiting Apollo astronauts have been asked, 'When you were on the moon, did you happen to see my auntie?'

Since my trip to the storage facility of the National Air and Space Museum, when I look at the moon I see hundreds of spacesuits, lying quietly in the cold, and two knees, thickly coated in moon dust.

When I visited the museum, the spacesuit storage facility was located, rather appropriately, in Suitland, Maryland. To get there, I took a Metro from central Washington DC and then walked along a highway, melting in the summer heatwave and being hooted at by people who were probably wondering what on earth I was doing there. Eventually, I arrived and was greeted by the museum collection conservator, Lisa Young, and curator, Cathleen Lewis. They opened a spacey, silver door, walked us into a middle room, like an airlock, and then into a room filled with spacesuits in stasis.

It's a cold (18°C/65°F), narrow room lined with hundreds of headless bodies on metal bunk beds. Each body is covered with a sheet, as if it

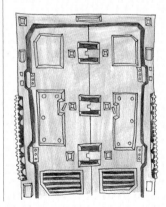

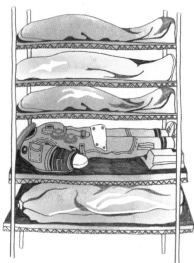

[Spacesuits]
The spacesuits are dressed on mannequins and are laid out flat on their backs on metal bunk beds five to six bunks high.

[Planet Earth]
'It suddenly struck me that that tiny pea, pretty and blue, was the Earth. I put up my thumb and shut one eye, and my thumb blotted out the planet Earth. I didn't feel like a giant. I felt very, very small.' (Neil Armstrong)

were a morgue for spacesuits (only these suits are not 'dead', they're being preserved for future generations). In total, there are 287 suits in the collection, but only a little more than half of these are in storage at any time. The others are on display or on loan to other museums around the world. Each one is referred to by the name of the astronaut who wore it, and each is displayed on a mannequin and laid out flat on its back on the metal bunk beds, five to six bunks high. We pulled back a sheet and uncovered a body.

It was the spacesuit of Harrison H. 'Jack' Schmitt of Apollo 17, the only scientist to walk on the moon. His spacesuit is covered in grey dust, especially the knees. It looks like ash, but it is moon dust. The moon dust is the reason why this suit is not on display.

Schmitt is a geologist. When the Apollo astronauts were in training, they went partying together. Schmitt would sit there among the pilots, talking about rocks. He was chosen for Apollo 17, the final manned mission to the moon, because scientists at NASA were going bananas. They couldn't believe that, of the 12 men who had walked on the moon, not one was a scientist.

There had been some lighthearted scientific experiments – playing golf, dropping a feather and hammer at the same time to see which would fall first (they fell at the same time), and some lunar samples had been brought back to Earth, but no one who could make snap scientific decisions on the moon had ever been up there. As a geologist, Schmitt could do, in another world, what he did all the time on the Earth – dig to find out more about what the planet was made of. The scientists at NASA insisted that Schmitt was given a seat.

Hours into the return trip, the crew of Apollo 17 took one of the most famous photographs of all time, a photograph of our planet called 'The Blue Marble', of the whole Earth lit up by the sun. Africa was in daylight, and Antarctica was lit by the December solstice. Although NASA credits the whole crew with taking the photograph, as they were all using the camera, passing it between them, it's acknowledged now that the iconic image was the work of Schmitt.

Much later, he and Gene Cernan left Ronald Evans behind in the command module and landed the lunar module in the Taurus-Littrow valley of the moon. It was December 1972. They stayed on the moon for three days, driving 16 kilometres across the light side. They saw lunar plains, took measurements of the gravitational field of the moon, passed steep mountains, drove around small craters and stood beside enormous boulders and glittering rocks.

Whenever they saw interesting things they jumped out to gather treasures to take home. They were ecstatic, especially Schmitt. He began singing, 'I was strolling on the moon one day,' skipping, bouncing and humming happily on his way. Gene Cernan, not a geologist, sung along too.

In total, they brought back 109 kilograms of rock. One of these samples is named Troctolite 76535. It formed when the moon was only 300 million years old and it has a faint magnetic field, suggesting that the moon itself may once have had one. Troctolite rock is found on Earth in several places, including Cornwall, the Isle of Rum in Scotland and western Australia. Schmitt also collected orange soil, which suggested the possibility of water, and maybe even life, at some point in the moon's history.

In his travels across the moon, a quarter of a million miles from Earth, Schmitt fell over or made contact with the moon more often than any other Apollo astronaut. His suit got very dirty as he crawled along collecting rocks, or from when he fell over and pushed himself upright again. Most of the Apollo spacesuits were dry-cleaned when they arrived back to Earth, but Schmitt's never was. NASA wanted to preserve the final Apollo mission spacesuits just as they were. So dust from the lunar surface remains embedded in the fibre. I peered at the knees of his spacesuit. They were thick with grey lunar soil. I really got to look at the moon that day.

Apollo 17 was the flight when the astronauts were on the surface of the moon for the longest period of time, travelled furthest across it and collected the most lunar samples. This suit is just as it was when Schmitt, one of the last two men on the moon, left its surface, splashed back into the Pacific Ocean, took the spacesuit off and put his Earth clothes back on. It's too precious to be displayed in the museum.

The people who have seen this spacesuit are the collections staff of the museum, scientists, researchers and the Apollo astronauts who come to see their suits, often with their grandchildren (Alan Bean, Apollo 12, is the astronaut who visits his suit most often), and NASA engineers. NASA's

[Schmitt on the moon]
Schmitt checks out a lunar boulder on the moon. You can see the lunar rover to the right of the photo.

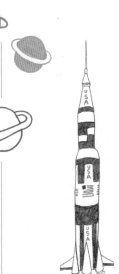

[Harrison Schmitt's Spacesuit]
Schmitt's suit is too precious
to put on display; it is covered
in grey moon dust. I also saw
Neil Armstrong's suit, gloves
and boots.

design team is working on suits for Mars. The Mars suits will need to last longer and be able to be taken on and off more than the Apollo suits, but they're a good place to start. Schmitt's suit is especially useful in aiding with their design, as he tested it to the max, bounding about with rocks in his hand. They've looked inside using x-radiography and studied in detail the lunar soil that clings to it.

After marvelling at Schmitt's suit, I looked around the room. On the bunk adjacent to it I saw a boot sticking out from beneath its sheet. It had a circular patch of Velcro on the sole. 'What's that?' I asked the curators, pointing at the boot. 'Oh, that's Neil Armstrong,' they said. This Velcro-soled boot was covered with an additional lunar boot when it stepped on to the moon but, still, it had covered the foot of Neil Armstrong when he took his 'one giant step for mankind'.

Only Schmitt and Cernan's lunar boots are back on Earth: they're here in the museum collection as two of the most complete flown suits that made it back. The boots Neil wore inside the spaceship had Velcro on the soles so that he could stand still. The interior of the ship had Velcro laid down like a carpet so that, whenever the astronauts needed to be rooted in one place, they could stick themselves on to the ship. Presumably, they walked around making loud, ripping noises.

Neil Armstrong's suit and under boots have been in storage for five years, having conservation work done on them. They won't always be behind the scenes and the same goes for a lot of the suits. They're here resting, between exhibitions, 'in shavasana position', as Lisa put it (that's the yoga position where you lie on your back, meditating). It may be years before these suits are put on display, but it is possible to display them.

Schmitt's will need to wait decades, at least, until it can come out of storage. Museums have not yet found a way to display it without damage to the suit and its precious moon dust.

Since I saw the suits, they have been on the move. They now live in their new storage facility, in Chantilly, Virginia. The new facility is part of the Air and Space museum's sister museum, built near the airport, so that new air and space exhibits can be flown straight into the museum collection. The suits were moved in trucks, a few each day, snuggled into crates to keep them safe. The collections staff considered moving them in coffins but decided against it. In their new home, the suits are stored according to mission.

Now that I have seen the suits they wore, how fragile they are, considering they kept men alive on the moon, and now that I have seen lunar soil, on dusty knees 2 centimetres from my nose, the moon landings feel much more immediate. I wasn't alive when mankind landed on the moon, so I missed the excitement that everyone who was must have felt listening to their radios, watching TV all over Earth and then gazing up at the white thing in the sky and imagining humans there in space. Now I know it wasn't a hoax (unless of course the sheets we didn't pull back actually covered Mickey Mouse suits …).

The moon landings also seem more surreal. The suits are made out of fibreglass fabric, a material that was first manufactured for household items. Cathy remembers that her 'parents had fibreglass curtains, the height of fashion in the sixties'. The suits seem far less robust than I had imagined. They have holes where the breathing apparatus was screwed on. They look so normal that they seem strange. They're very low-tech, very human.

Seeing the suits has made me feel that something greater than NASA and Nixon must have been at work to get those men up there, keep them safe and bring them home. I've read that there was only a ten per cent chance the astronauts would make it back alive. Now, when I look at the moon and think of those fragile suits lying in shavasana, it feels to me as if the moon wanted to meet mankind. Maybe Mars will be next.

[Apollo 17 moon landing]
Schmitt stands by the flag on the moon. You can see Earth in the black sky above.

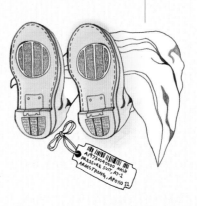

THREE PIECES
OF MARS

[Location]

The VATICAN OBSERVATORY
Castel Gandolfo, outside ROME, ITALY

'It's STRANGE to THINK that WE HUMANS

— *WHO ARE ALL MADE of STARDUST* —

LOOK UP at the SKY to STUDY GALAXIES,

WITHOUT OFTEN REFLECTING ON THE FACT

that WHAT we're actually STUDYING is LIGHT.

The things we're looking at

ARE NO LONGER REALLY THERE.'

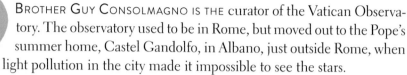

BROTHER GUY CONSOLMAGNO IS THE curator of the Vatican Observatory. The observatory used to be in Rome, but moved out to the Pope's summer home, Castel Gandolfo, in Albano, just outside Rome, when light pollution in the city made it impossible to see the stars.

I took a train from Rome to Albano. When I arrived, Brother Guy was waiting on the platform. I had thought he might be in monk's robes, but he was wearing a red waterproof jacket, jeans and trainers. That is because he is a Jesuit and his order don't wear robes, they prefer to blend in and work among lay people. He was immediately friendly, bright and charming and I knew it would be a fun day.

We walked up through the sleepy town until we reached the main square. It was quiet but for the sounds of birds and a few people chatting in restaurants. On one side of the square is a pink wall which divides the town from the papal grounds. Built into this wall is a door with a sign beside it carved into stone that reads 'Specola Vaticana'. We opened the door and entered the Papal Grounds and the observatory's museum. Guy explained that the Pope's house is 2 kilometres away from the museum, across orchards and fields.

The observatory isn't often open to the public. More often than not, the curators and astronomers have the place to themselves. However, the day I visited they were preparing for the arrival of 500 diplomats from around the world the following week and there were several people painting walls and polishing clocks in anticipation.

Guy showed me a film he was putting together for their visit. It tells the history of the observatory, one of the oldest astronomical institutions in the world. It was founded in 1582 when the Church replaced the Roman, or Julian, calendar with the Gregorian (which introduced the idea of having a leap year every four years to eliminate the discrepancies in time that had built up over the centuries). At first, the observatory's telescopes pointed out at the universe from inside the Vatican itself, from a room called the Tower of the Winds.

The telescopes were brought to Albano in 1935. Guy has worked here for years. 'It's much better out here, the security isn't so tight,' he jokes. He spends half of his year here, researching, writing and teaching astronomy students. The other half of the year Guy spends in the desert, at the second Vatican Observatory in Tucson, Arizona. This is the home of the

Vatican Advanced Technology Telescope, a very high-spec model with an internal mirror designed by a man called Roger Angel. 'Yes, the Pope's telescope was designed by an Angel,' said Guy. 'It is used for exploring new areas of the universe. I use it for looking at the colours of faint comet-like objects out beyond Neptune. These are the things that Pluto was part of before we realized that Pluto is not a planet but part of the vast band of Trans-Neptunian objects.' He works there with a team of 14 others.

Back in Albano, Brother Guy works with another team to look after the observatory. He ushered me into the vast library of 20,000 books and journals. His favourite book is by a fellow Jesuit brother, Father Angelo Secchi (1818–78) and is called *Sistema Solare*, written in 1859. 'It is the first book I've found that talks about the planets as real places you could walk around and have adventures on. Secchi takes facts and then uses his imagination to bring it all together. This book started planetary science. Before then, astronomers were far more interested in stars. Suddenly the planets became "places" rather than dots in the sky. They became things, not light.'

Guy showed me the Mars chapter of the book and pointed out where Secchi describes Mars as having *canali* (Italian for 'channels') on its surface. Some people thought, incorrectly, that Secchi was describing canals, like the ones on Earth, which did much to encourage the idea that there was life on Mars.

Outside the library is Brother Guy's domain: the museum and its collection of space-related artefacts. There are different meteorites that flew around in space for around 15 million years until landing on our planet. Brother Guy explained that '10,000 pieces of rock fall to the Earth each year, but we humans collect about five of them, if we're lucky. Most land in the ocean, or are lost because they look like ordinary rocks.'

There are also three pieces of Mars. Each piece of Mars rock is from a different part of the planet. How do we know they are from Mars? Firstly, because other meteorites contain metals and Mars rocks do not. Secondly, they are a billion years old, which is young, compared to the 4,568 billion-year ages of the other meteorites. And, thirdly, bubbles of gas trapped inside them have been tested using a mass spectrometer, and it turns out that they exactly match the atmosphere of Mars, as recorded by the Mars Rover.

[Mars canals]
Secchi drew some of the first colour illustrations of Mars and referred to the *canali*, the Italian word for channels, on the surface of the planet. Some nineteenth-century and early twentieth-century astronomers thought 'canali' meant 'canals' and used them as evidence that there was life on Mars.

[Three pieces of Mars]
The Vatican Observatory owns three pieces of Mars rock, each one from a different part of the planet.

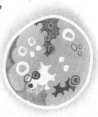
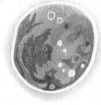

The Vatican also has a globe of Mars, showing the channels on the planet, and a globe of the moon, the first ever made by NASA, given to the Vatican as a gift.

I asked Brother Guy if he had a favourite treasure in the collection. He said that it changed all the time; he loves the Mars rocks, but his favourite meteorite that day was Allende. There are two tons of it in the world and it revolutionized science. 'It fell in 1969, just before the moon landing. NASA had been buying all sorts of toys with which to measure moon rocks, which they hoped the astronauts would bring back to Earth. So they were able to test their toys on Allende. They discovered that the little white bits inside the meteorite were dust from stars that existed even before the planets were formed. This changed the way NASA thought about the solar system; they had known it was about 4.6 billion years old but, thanks to Allende, they could measure the age more precisely, to 4.568 billion'.

Brother Guy got even more cosmic. 'It's strange to think that we humans – who are all made of stardust – look up at the sky to study galaxies, without often reflecting on the fact that what we're actually studying is light. The things we're looking at are no longer really there.' That is one reason why he likes working in the meteorite lab, among the 'real stuff', which he can pick up and measure.

We decided to visit his lab, but to have a drink first. Over a delicious coffee, which Brother Guy served in 'Specola Vaticana' cups, he told me how he had ended up as curator of meteorites at the Vatican. He grew up in Detroit. He loved space and saved up 16 books of stamps to swap for his first telescope. He joined the Jesuit order and it was they who decided that this was the job for him. He says he would have been just as happy serving soup, if that is what the Jesuits had decided, but he is surely the perfect man for the job here at the Vatican.

Inside his lab, one surface is covered with microscopes and one weird instrument that looks like a saucepan, used to suck water off meteorites. The rest of the room is full of cupboards filled with drawers containing slices of meteorite. Propped up on a cupboard is a painting of the planets, each one studded with jewels. No one really knows who made it or how it ended up in in the lab, but it's beautiful.

Brother Guy popped a 4.6-billion-year old meteorite into my hand. This was the oldest in the collection and was found in France in 1810.

Lots of locals saw it fall from the sky and then had to convince sceptical scientists that it was space rock. It has a handwritten label attached to it telling how it fell to earth in L'Aigle.

On the wall is a photograph of the current Pope looking into a microscope at a section of meteorite. Brother Guy showed him two; one found near his hometown in southern Germany; the other one in the Ukraine in 1866. Brother Guy showed me the second slice. He took it out of its drawer and slid it under a microscope that shone polarized light. 'It's like looking through a kaleidoscope,' I said. Brother Guy turned the slide in circles, and bright colours shifted into new patterns. It was bizarre that so many shapes could appear from something that looked so bland and tiny on the slide. 'All the meteorites do this under polarized light,' Brother Guy added, 'but this is the prettiest of them all.'

Brother Guy made a Christmas card out of an image of the meteorite I was looking at, because he thinks a pattern within it looks like Jesus in a manger. He gave me one of the cards. On the back, it says, 'The meteorite samples formed in the proto-solar nebula around our sun, 4.56 billion years ago.'

This card is not your average Christmas card, and not one you'd expect to get from the Vatican, at least, not unless you know about Brother Guy and the two Vatican observatories.

[Brother Guy J. Consolmagno] Brother Guy was assigned the job of astronomer at the Vatican Observatory when he became a Jesuit. He showed me around the Vatican meteorite collection at the Pope's summer residence.

[OBJECT 04]

a piece of
NEWTON's APPLE TREE

[Location]

THE ROYAL SOCIETY
London, England

He was SITTING UNDERNEATH an APPLE TREE *WHEN an APPLE FELL from the TREE* and **BOUNCED off his HEAD.** **NEWTON WONDERED WHY.** HIS ANSWER? *A THING HE CALLED GRAVITY.*

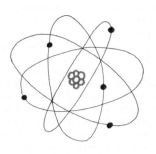

THE ROYAL SOCIETY IN LONDON began in 1660, when a group of scientists decided it would be valuable to meet once a week and discuss experiments. Today it is one of the oldest scientific academies in the world.

Their archive is split between a salt mine in Cheshire – to access anything down there you have to go in a miner's lift and put on a hard hat – and a basement in its HQ in London.

I headed downstairs into the basement, which is stuffed with a quarter of a million manuscripts made up of the musings, publications and letters written by some of the greatest scientific minds that have ever lived.

Mixed in among the books and writings are 200 objects, including slides of a goat with the bends (used when working out dive tables), a wonderful doodle on blotting paper by top scientists and the then prime minister gathered at a meeting about the Transit of Venus in 1882, and a wooden potato masher made by a young Ernest Rutherford for his grandma. I looked a bit confused. 'Rutherford,' said Keith Moore, curator of the Royal Society's library and archives, 'split the atom.' Rutherford is buried in Westminster Abbey, near Sir Isaac Newton.

[Sir Isaac Newton (1643–1727)]
Isaac Newton was born in Woolsthorpe, Lincolnshire. In the garden grew a Flower of Kent apple tree connected with the tale of Newton's discovery of the law of gravitation – a story which Newton himself started.

Pretty much everyone has heard the story about how Newton first described gravity. He was sitting underneath an apple tree when an apple fell from the tree and bounced off his head. Newton wondered why. His answer? A thing he called gravity. Anyone who has looked deeper into the tale comes up against people saying it wasn't true.

But Newton knew the value of a good anecdote and told it himself. In the Royal Society library there is a first-hand account of him describing the event to William Stukeley, author of *Memoirs of Newton's Life* (1752):

After dinner, the weather being warm, we went into the garden and drank thea [sic], under the shade of some apple trees; only he, and myself. Amidst other discourse, he told me, he was just in the same situation, as when formerly, the notion of gravitation came into his mind. Why should that apple always descend perpendicularly to the ground, thought he to himself; occasion'd by the fall of an apple, as he sat in a contemplative mood. Why should it not go sideways, or upwards? but constantly to the earths centre?

So the apple tree really did inspire Newton, even if the apple didn't fall on his head. The account is online on the Royal Society's website if you want to see it.

Just as Newton had never before considered why it was that apples fall to the ground, even though I had heard the story many times before I'd never wondered which actual apple tree had inspired him. That was, until I saw several pieces of it behind the scenes at the Royal Society.

Newton's fabled apple tree once stood in the garden of his childhood home, Woolsthorpe Manor in Lincolnshire. In 1800, the inspirational tree blew over. Luckily, it re-rooted itself, and a new tree, an offshoot from the original, is still flourishing there today.

The owner of Woolsthorpe Manor saved some pieces of Newton's original apple tree after it blew over. Some of them are in the Royal Society archives. On a shelf down in the cool basement are two fragments, as well as two rulers and a prism made from the wood. One of the fragments is in a little pink plastic bag, because it has just been on an adventure, up into orbit aboard the Space Shuttle *Atlantis* in 2010. It will remain in the pink bag, because the bag is now part of its history.

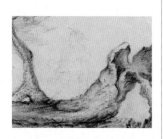

[*Newton's Apple Tree* by Thomas Howison]
If you look really closely you can see a ghostly figure of Sir Isaac Newton sitting on a branch of the fallen tree.

The apple wood was taken up into orbit so that it could experience zero gravity. The plan was also to drop a real apple on the space station and film whether it was subject to gravity or not. They weren't able to do the test because an astronaut who didn't know what they were up to – she will remain nameless – saw the apple lying around and ate it. They could hardly pop out to the shops, so they had to make do with a pear. You can watch a film of it floating.

Keith told me the pear is flying, not because it wasn't subject to gravity, but because the space station is falling, and the pear with it, in orbit. 'Just look at the astronauts' hair,' he said. It floats above their heads.

Also in the archives is a lock of Newton's hair – perhaps with high concentrations of mercury in it, as a result of his alchemical experiments – and his death mask. 'This is the closest you'll get to Isaac Newton,' said Keith.

We looked at a drawing of Newton's apple tree, sketched by Thomas Howison in the 1820s. It is of the original tree, which lies dead on the ground, and the re-rooted tree beside it. Keith had just been having a good look at it and discovered a new secret. We peered at it (have a look yourself) and could just make out the outline of Newton sitting underneath the tree. Keith had seen the picture countless times but had only just noticed the faintly drawn figure beneath it. 'The archives are still turning up secrets,' he said.

On a shelf beside the pieces of apple tree sits Newton's reflecting telescope (he donated it to the Royal Society; they lost it for a while but it turned up again in the 1730s in an instrument maker's workshop). It has two mirrors inside, and two tubes, which you slide to focus the mirrors.

Before Newton had the brainwave of using mirrors, looking at the stars meant holding two enormous and unwieldy lenses far apart, tied together by pieces of string. Newton mounted his old, big telescope on a maypole, which he'd bought on Charing Cross Road.

He invented this small, wood and leather reflecting telescope while he lived in Cambridge. Later, he came to London and worked from a laboratory at the Tower of London, where he was Master of the Royal Mint. Imagine him peering up into space from his rooms inside the Tower.

When he made his telescope he sent his idea to the Royal Society and included a drawing. I loved looking at Newton's sketch, complete with an eye looking down into the telescope. Then I was able to put my own eye

[Newton's reflecting telescope]
Newton sent a sketch of his invention to the Royal Society. I saw it in their library. He included a sketch of his eye, looking down into the telescope. I was able to put my own eye to the telescope, just as he would have done centuries ago.

[Newton's *Principia*]
The Royal Society has the original proof copy of Newton's masterpiece *Philosophiae Naturalis Principia Mathematica*, down in the basement.

to his telescope, just as he would have done. All I could see was the wall of the basement, but I got the idea. Amazingly, centuries later, the Hubble space telescope was built using essentially the same design.

The Royal Society owns many of the letters Newton sent over the years, explaining what he was up to. Some were expanded upon and turned into publications. The original manuscripts of these texts are here in the archive.

We looked at the original copy of the *Principia* (*Philosophiae Naturalis Principia Mathematica*) that Newton sent away to be published. This first copy was written up by his secretary and has marginalia in Newton's hand and in the writing of his friend Edmund Halley – of Halley's Comet fame – who paid for it to be published.

The Royal Society was planning to cover the costs, but the publication of *A History of Fishes*, by Francis Willughby and John Ray, had left them out of pocket. Samuel Pepys was the Society's president at the time and is named on the title pages of both the *Principia* and *A History of Fishes* (his diary wasn't published until 123 years after he died).

Willughby had been Ray's student and the two travelled together studying and collecting birds and fish. When Willughby suddenly died, Ray saw his three books – about birds, fish and games – through the press. The twosome's collection of birds and fish is stored at Willughby's family home, Wollaton Hall, which, incidentally, starred as Wayne Manor in the Batman film *The Dark Knight Rises*.

Back in 2010, Keith had the pleasure of showing Newton's *Principia* to some Apollo astronauts – Gene Cernan, Neil Armstrong and Jim Lovell – when they visited the Royal Society. He really enjoyed their visit. 'I am a child of the sixties; that is why I got into all of this,' he told me.

As they turned the pages of the tome, Gene Cernan talked about how he had experienced Newton's third law of motion – that every action has an equal and opposite reaction – first hand, in space. When he flew on Gemini 9, he had to assemble a backpack in zero gravity, with little light, outside the spacecraft. Nothing was holding him anywhere, so as he tightened a valve, his entire body span in the opposite direction. Everything he touched would touch him back and send him tumbling back out into space. When he touched the spacecraft, it repelled him. He had trouble getting back inside and when he finally made it his boots were filled with sweat.

From then on, NASA put hand and footholds on its space capsules so that the astronauts could anchor themselves in space. The astronauts were also trained in water so they could experience weightlessness. By the time Cernan flew to the moon with Harrison Schmitt, on Apollo 17, he knew how to get around without gravity.

When the Royal Society lent their fragment of Newton's apple tree to NASA astronaut Piers Sellers to take up to the space station, they also sent along a picture of Sir Isaac Newton. The crew put it in the window of the space station so that Newton could look out: they thought he would have liked the view. Imagine what Newton might have come up with, if he'd had the chance to spend time up there with them, quietly looking around at the universe getting on with what it does, and figuring out how things work.

[Two pieces of Newton's apple tree]
A piece of the apple tree that inspired Newton was taken onto the space station, along with a photograph of Newton, below.

Imagine what Newton might have come up with, if he'd had the chance to spend time aboard the space station.

the first
CULTIVATED PEARLS

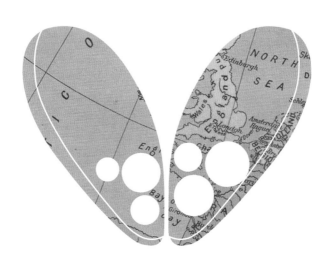

[Location]

The LINNEAN SOCIETY
London, England

'WHAT'S THE USE of THEIR HAVING NAMES,'

the Gnat said,

'IF THEY WON'T ANSWER to THEM?'

'NO USE TO THEM,' said Alice;

'BUT IT'S USEFUL TO THE PEOPLE

THAT NAME THEM, I SUPPOSE.'

Alice in Wonderland, Lewis Carroll

'YOU COULD SAY THIS ENTIRE room is a hidden treasure,' said the curator of the Linnean Society as the door swung open to their basement storage facility. She flicked the lights on to reveal a wood-panelled room lined with 1,600 books and drawers filled with 14,000 plants, 3,198 insects and 1,564 shells, which were the private collection of Carl Linnaeus, the man who named the natural world.

Carl von Linné (1707–78), who was born Carl Linnaeus, was a Swedish botanist. He standardized the system of scientifically naming plants with two Latin names, the genus (e.g. *Ginkgo*), followed by the species (e.g. *biloba*). This is called binomial nomenclature, and it is now used internationally for all plants and animals, even us humans. We are in the genus *Homo* and our species is *sapiens*, hence *Homo sapiens*, 'the wise man'. Linnaeus came up with our name.

It's a really clever system if you think about it, because anyone around the world can understand what plant or creature you are talking about.

[The world of Linnaeus]
I went to see thousands of specimens and books that belonged to Linnaeus. They were brought from his home in Sweden to London, and were used to found the Linnean Society.

It's essential for botanists, zoologists and museum curators caring for collections of specimens.

When a new species is discovered, scientists must explain to other scientists what it is and what it looks like. So the first thing they do is pick one member of the species as a holotype, or 'type', specimen. This is the example of the new species that will forever define it and is often the first example of the species found. Most of these 'types' are in museums around the world; thousands of them are in this room because Linnaeus gave them their scientific names.

There is not, as yet, a type for *Homo sapiens*. A palaeontologist named Edward Drinker Cope (1840–97) asked for the job in his will, but he turned out to have syphilis, so was struck off the list. Arnold Schwarzenegger has been proposed. Many say it ought to be Linnaeus, as he came up with the idea. His body is well preserved in the cathedral in Uppsala, Sweden, so there is a chance of this happening yet.

The specimens housed at the Linnean Society used to be in Uppsala, in Linnaeus's home, where he lived with his family. When Linnaeus died, Joseph Banks (1747–1820) – the director of Kew Gardens and a passionate botanist – tried to buy the collection, but in the end a young student of his, James Edward Smith, bought it with money he borrowed from his father, and shipped the whole lot to London, where he founded the Linnean Society.

This is the cave of riches that I went to see. It is just inside the entrance to the Royal Academy of Arts. I met the librarian, Lynda Brooks, in the library, and we ventured downstairs to the basement, where the collection lives. She turned a key that opened a door into Linnaeus's world.

The entire room smells like a lovely combination of old books and wood polish. The top shelves are filled with books Linnaeus wrote himself, and his reference books. The lower drawers and shelves are filled with thousands of insect, shell and plant specimens collected by him and by his 'apostles' – his students, who collected around the world for him. These men of science would also act as pastors, priests or doctors whilst on collecting expeditions.

We began with the plants. Linnaeus pressed each one carefully, described it and gave it a scientific name, and then stored it away. Later, these were parcelled up, so each plant is now a brown paper package tied up with green string, each one stacked upon another. We unwrapped one package and, inside, we found the type specimen for *Delphinium*. Two hundred and fifty years after Linnaeus named it *Delphinium* (after the Latin for 'dolphin', because of the shape its flower makes as it opens, like a dolphin leaping out of the waves), it is still a vivid blue colour because it has been kept in storage, out of the light. This is just one in his library of thousands of plants.

We also unwrapped what was for Linnaeus a very special flower, *Linnaea borealis*, which was named after him and became his signature flower. If ever you see a painting of him, look for the flower. He usually has it draped through his fingers. When alive, it is pink, and its delicate petals carpet the floor of woodland in Sweden. At night, the pink burns in the darkness. The type specimen in the archive has turned brown over the centuries, unlike the delphinium. Pink and red flowers lose their vibrancy more quickly than blue and yellow ones.

Scientific names aren't just for scientists. They tell stories. Buttercups are in the *Ranunculus* genus. They often grow near water and *ranunculus* is the Late Latin word for 'little frog', a species also found near the water. Water lilies are in the genus *Nymphaea*, after the water nymphs in Greek myths. The laurel *Kalmia* was named by Linnaeus for his Swedish student Pehr Kalm; the black mangrove *Avicennia* he named for the Persian physician Avicenna. He also reused classical names: *Acer* (maples), *Quercus* (oaks). The only plant Linnaeus named after a female body part is a blue vine popularly called a 'butterfly pea'; he gave it the genus *Clitoria*. If you look up your favourite plant, it is bound to have a good story hiding in its scientific name.

The same goes for animals. Some animals Linnaeus named descriptively, like the southern flying squirrel, *Glaucomys volans* ('the white mouse that flies'); in others, he added things that made him smile. He named the blue whale – the largest animal that has ever lived on earth – *Balaenoptera musculus*. In Latin, *musculus* means 'little mouse'. He named the house mouse at the same time: *Mus musculus*. There are no mammals in the basement room of the Linnean Society – though some do still survive in Sweden – but there are a lot of fish pressed on to paper, their skin flattened as if they were flowers, as well as corals, shells and insects.

[*Linnaea borealis*]
Linnaeus's signature flower, the twinflower or *Linnaea borealis*, named in his honour.

[Linnaeus's pearls]
Linnaeus was the first person to culture artificial pearls in a mollusc. Some of his pearls turned out better than others.

[Andromeda]
Linnaeus drew this sketch inside the journal that he wrote while in Lapland.

There is also, in among them, a little box that contains pearls made by Linnaeus. They are the first artificial pearls ever cultured in a mollusc. He made the pearls by jamming a piece of limestone into a freshwater mussel, *Unio pictorum* (the 'painter's mussel', so called because artists would use the shallow valves to mix their pigment), and holding it there so the mussel would create a pearl around it. Then he put the mussel back into the river for six years, giving the pearl time to grow.

The pearls are small and roundish, apart from one elongated brown one that looks like it went a bit wrong. One has been cut in half, so I could see the irritant he put inside it to make the mussel form the pearl. It looks like a seed in the middle of the pearl.

Linnaeus sold his secret in 1762 to a Swedish merchant called Peter Bagge who got a permit from the king to make pearls, but even though he paid 6,000 dalars (more than £93,000 today) for a monopoly on the right to make pearls, he never got around to making any. Linnaeus once said that he wished he'd become famous for creating these pearls rather than for classifying nature. After taking a good look, we put them back in their box, in their drawer, and closed it shut.

Next, we took down some books. The first was a green leatherbound book with 'LINNAEUS' embossed in gold letters on the front. It was his journal from a trip he made to Lapland. It is filled with his notes, in his slanting handwriting, on the people, flowers and creatures of Lapland, and wonderful – if not that competent – drawings of local life.

We turned the pages and saw his charming sketches of ploughs, fish, skis, insects, coral, local Laplanders, embroidery on Sami clothing and tents. There were drawings of how the Lapps slept, ate, dried fish and even the kinds of games they played (throwing balls and a game that looks like chess). There is a beautiful sketch of a crane fly, and an interesting one of Andromeda being threatened by a sea monster beside one of an *Andromeda* plant being threatened by a newt. I really liked his drawing of an owlet and one of a Sami baby wrapped up cosily.

He tells how to cure chilblains with roasted reindeer cheese, how to fix a broken pot by boiling it in milk and how to make thread from reindeer hooves. He described the singing in Lapland: 'No Laplander can sing, but instead of singing utters a noise resembling the barking of dogs.'

The journal was published as *Iter Laponicum* but it was brilliant to see the real thing, written in Lapland. Linnaeus brought it back to his home in Uppsala, along with a drum and a Lapp costume. There is a painting of him wearing it holding the drum and his *Linnaea borealis* plant, in the library upstairs at the Linnean Society.

I'd been told that Linnaeus was the first person to grow a banana in Europe, so I asked Lynda whether there was anything banana related in the collection. She opened up a book called *Musa Cliffortiana Florens Hartecampi*, all about that first banana. It was grown in the garden of Linnaeus's friend George Clifford, in Holland. *Musa* is the genus for banana; it was named from *musz*, which is the Arabic word for 'banana'; or perhaps for the nine Greek muses themselves. Inside the book is a fold-out drawing of the fruiting banana plant. It ends with a question: 'Will my banana grow for years?'

Lynda then showed me Linnaeus's most famous work, *Systema Naturae*. Published in 1735, it's a history of all the living things he knew about at the time, divided up according to his sexual system for classifying them. He caused a bit of a scandal at the time by suggesting plants had a sex life. There are so many names he adopted which we still use today; magnolia, clematis, digitalis, jasmine, fuchsia, salvia.

Animals are included in the *Systema*, written down in a table, according to the genus Linnaeus assigned to them. If there was an animal he wasn't sure about, he put it in 'Worms'. He put humans in the same box as apes, which he didn't want to do, but he couldn't see a way around it. Anything he wasn't sure actually existed he put in a box called 'Paradoxa', which contains the satyr, phoenix, dragon, unicorn and pelican. He wasn't sure he believed in pelicans, because they were supposed to feed their young on their own blood. He also named stones, fossils and minerals. This first edition copy was huge, the only one that was published in such a big format. Linnaeus used to fold it into four and carry it around with him.

There are two bookcases filled with copies of Linnaeus's work. He had many of his own publications bound with blank pages between printed ones so that he could make his own notes as he reread his books and update them as he found new species. His handwritten ideas are all over the blank pages, mostly in Latin. This room is the only place in the

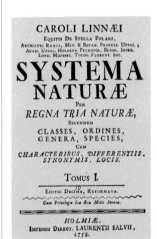

[Systema Naturae]

The first edition of *Systema Naturae* had only 11 pages but Linnaeus added to the book over the years, adding new species as he discovered them. The 13th edition appeared in 1770 and was 3,000 pages long. 'God created – Linnaeus organized.' That was how Linnaeus summed up his lifetime achievements.

world where there are so many copies of Linnaeus's books covered in his own annotations.

The day I visited the collection, thousands of *Homo sapiens* were rushing straight past the doors of the Linnean Society to see the David Hockney exhibition. I saw it too. Just think of all those flowers Hockney painted all over Yorkshire, some buried under snow, others popping up into the sunlight after the winter underground, each one with a scientific name, many of them coined by Linnaeus.

The entire collection has recently been digitized and is up on the Linnaean Society's website. Researchers around the world look things up regularly, leaving the centuries old collections undisturbed in their wood-panelled room. There is a postcard of Linnaeus in there, propped up against the books, watching over the lot.

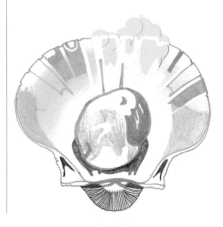

[OBJECT 06]

LAMOUROUXIA VISCOSA
Seed from Mexico

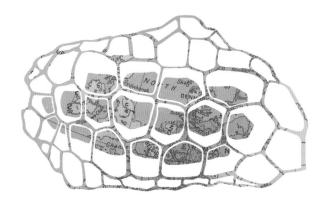

[Location]

Kew's MILLENNIUM SEED BANK
Sussex, England

THOUSANDS *of* TINY TIME TRAVELLERS
LIE FROZEN in THE EARTH in SUSSEX.

[A Mexican seed]
Lamourouxia viscosa is one of millions of seeds inside the seed bank. Its honeycomb design is a perfect adaptation for catching puffs of wind.

THEY ARE SEEDS, INSIDE KEW'S Millennium Seed Bank (MSB). This particular seed is *Lamourouxia viscosa* from Mexico and is one of millions stored there. It has a lovely honeycomb cage, so that it can float in the air and spread the range of its plant. I like the design of this seed but, really, I could have chosen any of the seeds preserved in the vaults of Kew's Millennium Seed Bank, because each is unique and precious.

Seeds first appeared on Earth some 360 million years ago, and since then they have spread across all environments. They are amazingly diverse, come in all kinds of shapes and range in size from the largest seed in the world, the coco de mer palm (*Lodoicea maldivica*) from the Seychelles, which looks like a big, curvaceous bottom (Linnaeus called it *Lodoicea callipyge, callipyge* meaning 'lovely-bummed') to orchid seeds the size of a speck of dust.

Some seeds can remain alive in the ground for hundreds of years if need be, until the conditions are just right for them to germinate. A date palm seed estimated to be 2,000 years old was discovered in 1963 when Herod the Great's fortress of Masada near the Dead Sea was excavated. It was planted in 2005, and now Methuselah, as the plant is called, stands over a metre high. The amazing ability that seeds have to pause in time was the inspiration behind the Millenium Seed Bank Partnership.

Wolfgang Stuppy, seed morphologist at the seed bank, showed me around. He explained that one in five species of plant on Earth is faced with extinction. In 2000, Kew began collecting seeds as life insurance for the future. They started by collecting thousands of seeds from every species of wild British flowering plant and freezing them so that, in the future, if any become extinct, we will have their seeds, here in Sussex. It will be possible to defrost them, grow them and reintroduce them to the countryside. There are about 1,400 native seed-bearing plants in the UK, and 90 per cent of them are protected here, carefully frozen for the future. Britain was the first country in the world to do this with their seeds.

The seed bank has a nursery in which it grows flowers that once adorned British meadows countrywide, such as the cuckoo flower, green field speedwell and the harebell. Slowly, the people who work there are trying to get Britain to remember its native wild beauty. Some plants that were once extinct, such as a starry aquatic herb, called starfruit, have already been reintroduced into the countryside.

The seed bank has also begun to stretch its green fingers across the world. Working with more than 50 countries worldwide, it has so far been collecting wild flowering plants that grow in the world's dry lands. When turned into food, clothing, medicine and building materials, these flowering plants help to support 1 billion people. To date, the seed bank has saved seeds from ten per cent of the world's wild plant species, and is adding to that number all the time. In the future, the range of seeds collected will hopefully expand to include those from the tropical rainforest, and then from all types of terrain found on the planet.

We began our trip around the seed bank in Stuppy's office, where he showed me the seeds he particularly likes. The most beautiful, for me, are the blue seeds from the Malagasy traveller's tree. The seeds are spread by lemurs, which are native to Madagascar. Lemurs can only see the colours blue and green, so Stuppy has a hunch that the seeds are this unique colour so that the animals can spot them and gobble them up.

We headed off down the corridor and entered a white-walled room filled with seeds. This is the drying room. When seeds first arrive at the seed bank, they are put in here. They are all still in the packing containers their countries have sent them in – plastic boxes and vials, glass jars, little freezer bags, cloth bags, paper bags, brown envelopes and packing crates. We didn't stay long as, Stuppy explained, 'your sinuses dry out before long', but all newly arrived seeds stay here for at least three months.

After they have dried out, the seeds are taken next door and sieved, and subsequently put into what Stuppy calls 'the zigzag blower', to get rid of any fruit so that just the seed remains; these are then cleaned and x-rayed.

[Entrance to the seed bank]
The grey door that leads into the seed bank is surrounded by a yellow panel, set into a wall of silver. You can see it from the floor above if you visit the public area of the seed bank.

[Freezer]
We couldn't go inside the freezers where the seeds are kept as it's too cold – the staff who work there wrap up warmly in thick fleeces or big jackets.

If most of the seeds in the batch are ripe, and have no insects living inside them, they are put into containers ready to be frozen.

The actual seed bank, and the freezers that contain the collection, are underground. The entrance is through a grey door surrounded by a yellow panel set into a wall of silver. If you ever visit the public area of the seed bank, you will see a metal staircase that leads down to this door, but you can't go down there, or through the door.

Stuppy buzzed us in. The doors reminded me a bit of the spacey ones that led into the room filled with space suits at the National Air and Space Museum's storage unit in Suitland, outside Washington D.C. On the other side of the doors there were no space suits; instead we found ourselves in another drying room. Every seed selected for freezing is dried a final time before going into its freezer, and each seed container is numbered so that the seeds can be catalogued and found later on.

As we looked about, Stuppy was yawning rather a lot. I thought maybe he was bored by showing me around, but it turned out that his wife had just had twin boys. 'I've started keeping a diary of how many times they wake me up in the night,' he told me, 'and last night it was eight.'

As we chatted about his twins, we looked into the freezers that lead off from this room. We couldn't go inside, as it's too cold in there – the staff who work there wear big jackets or fleeces. The seeds are stored at -20°C (-4°F), but a series of fans adds a wind chill factor, so it feels like -40°C (-40°F). We peered through the glass at the contents of the seed bank, stored in boxes on the grey metal shelves that line the freezers, or in drawers.

At the moment, only two freezers are filled with seeds. Freezer A contains the seeds that are taken out once a decade for testing. They are put into water and incubated to make sure that they are alive and will germinate. Freezer B's collection contains a replica of the seeds in Freezer A, but these seeds are never touched; they stay quietly frozen for the future.

A third freezer is being filled at the moment, and this is just the beginning: there is space for many more as the seed bank increases its collection. 'You could get 38 double decker buses in this underground vault,' says Stuppy. Already these freezers contain the greatest concentration of plant biodiversity on the planet: 10 per cent of the world's wild plant species. In years to come, this will diversify even more. The MSB is hoping to save 25 per cent by 2020. We went back upstairs for a look at the incubator rooms, where seeds from Freezer A are periodically grown into seedlings to make sure that the seeds being stored are still healthy. Each brightly lit incubator is kept at a different temperature: 5, 10, 15, 20 and 25°C (41, 50, 59, 68, 77°F), depending on the type of plant they are set up to incubate. We popped our heads inside one; it smelt damp and mouldy. Inside were the seeds of a plant called *Cousinia platylepis*, and they were germinating well.

I asked Stuppy what happens to the germinating seeds. 'They belong to the country of origin, so they are all destroyed. The only reason for growing them is to make sure the seeds in the freezer are still alive and healthy,' he answered. He explained that bio-piracy is a big problem, which countries want to guard against, so acquiring seeds from other countries involves lots of contracts and teams of lawyers, and part of the deal is that no germinating plants will be grown without permission having been given by the country that sent the seed.

Brazil won't let anyone keep seeds from its country, because it doesn't want anyone to own seeds from Brazil which might be valuable later – a wonder drug perhaps, as yet to be discovered, that grows in the Amazon. 'What about other countries?' I asked. 'America doesn't have a large national seed bank for wild species (they have many large crop seed banks, though). Svalbard, Norway, only has crops. The Germplasm Bank of Wild Species at the Kunming Institute of Botany, in China, and the MSB are the two biggest seed banks for wild species in the world', Stuppy explained.

In an ideal world, the MSB would not need to exist; instead, the plants contained in the frozen ark of seeds would be growing naturally in the wild. As it is, the MSB sees its project as a race against time. Who knows how many life-saving plants are growing on the Earth that are yet to be discovered? Imagine if one dies out before its unique properties are found? I wonder how many precious medicines are frozen in the vaults now.

We're facing a global emergency. By the end of this century, half the world's existing plants could be extinct. It is up to us to change. Our lives depend on plants for food, fuel, medicine, textiles, chemicals and for the oxygen we breathe. Without plants, we cannot survive, so why are we not doing more to grow what we can and to protect what we have? At least the seed bank is giving us options for the future while we sort things out. It's a start.

Scientists at Kew are looking into the effects of climate change on plants, and are studying wild species that have traits that will be needed in crops if the Earth heats up – for example, short stems and bigger leaves; wild flowers are a miracle of adaptive design. Mainly, however, the frozen seeds are here as a life insurance for plant species and for human beings of the future.

When I left the seeds behind, I went for a wander around the gardens that surround the seed bank – the grounds of Wakehurst Place. The gorgeous landscape is a showcase for some of the frozen seeds beneath the ground, a future generation of beautiful flowering plants.

[OBJECT 07]

Things beneath the
FLOORBOARDS

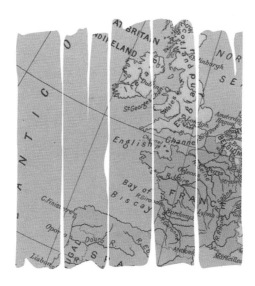

[Location]

MUSEUM of the HISTORY of SCIENCE
Oxford, England

THESE THINGS AREN'T on DISPLAY,

BECAUSE they're FRAGILE and UTTERLY UNIQUE.

They're THE ONLY PHYSICAL MEMORIES

of the FIRST MUSEUM in BRITAIN.

[**John Tradescant the elder (c.1570s–1638) and John Tradescant the younger (1608–62)**]
The two Tradescants, father and son, were gardeners with a shared passion for interesting plants and strange curiosities.

THE FIRST MUSEUM IN BRITAIN was The Ark, in Lambeth, London. Two gardeners, John and John Tradescant, opened it. They were father and son. The duo went on plant-hunting expeditions around the world to harvest the best of the new lands being discovered, and on their travels collected things they found interesting.

They were consumed by beauty, and gathered up bundles of flowers to fill English gardens: poppies and stocks from France; white jasmine from Catalonia; daffodils from Mount Carmel; tulip trees and a mimic passion flower from North America; as well as vegetables such as cos lettuce, plums, scarlet runner beans and possibly the first pineapple in England. In 1630, John Tradescant senior became Keeper of His Majesty's Gardens, Vines and Silkworms. When he died, his son took over the role.

The Tradescants' other great contribution to cultural life in England was their museum. They had amassed so many treasures while seeking out colourful plants that they decided, in 1626, to open up their home, Turret House, to the public. They called it The Ark and began charging people 6d to see the things that they had found in the New World and Europe. These treasures were things few people in England had ever seen before, and The Ark was described as a place 'where a Man might in one daye behold and collecte into one place more curiosities than hee should see if hee spent all his life in Travell'. The collection included plants, a chameleon, a pelican, cheese, an ape's head, shells, the hand of a mermaid, stones, coins, a toad-fish, birds from India – even a dodo, which at the time was not yet extinct.

My favourite thing in The Ark is Powhatan's mantle, a coat belonging to the chief of the Native American Indian tribe that lived in Virginia when the first settlers arrived. Powhatan's daughter was Pocahontas, and she married the leader of the English settlers, John Smith. Perhaps Tradescant senior collected it when he went there in 1637, almost certainly at the king's request. He made three trips to Virginia and brought back all kinds of flowers, plants, shells and treasures including *Tradescantia virginiania*, a plant that still grows in England today.

The Tradescants had a catalogue printed, *Musaeum Tradescantianum*, which was the first of its kind in Britain. It listed the objects in their collection, divided into sections like 'shell-Creatures, Insects, Mineralls, Outlandish-Fruit', 'Utensills, House-holdstuffe' and 'rare curiosities of Art'. Everything was given equal weight, even things that were made up, like mermaids and unicorns.

Powhatan's coat was catalogued in the 'Garments, Vestures, Habits and Ornaments' chapter, and described as 'Pohatan, King of Virginia's habit, all embroidered with shells, or Roanoke'. There were other things from Virginia too – a habit of bearskin and a match-coat made of raccoon skins. Just below these in the list were 'Henry the 8, his stirrups, hawkes hods and gloves' and, further down, 'Edward the Confessor's knit gloves'.

Both the Tradescants were buried in the churchyard at St Mary at Lambeth. Today the church is the Museum of Garden History, the first museum in the world dedicated to gardening. If you visit the collection you will see the tomb in the knot garden outside the museum. It is decorated with objects from the Tradescants' collection. Legend has it that if you dance around it 12 times as Big Ben strikes, a ghost will appear. On the tomb is a poem probably written by John Aubrey describing the Tradescants, who:

> … *Liv'd till they had travelled Orb and Nature through,*
> *As by their choice Collections may appear,*
> *Of what is rare in land, in sea, in air,*
> *Whilst they (as Homer's Iliad in a nut)*
> *A world of wonders in one closet shut* …

[Turret House, Lambeth, London]
The Tradescants filled their home with so many curious treasures that they decided to charge the public to come and have a look. They called the first public museum in Britain 'The Ark'.

[Powhatan's mantle]
A visitor to the Tradescant museum in 1638 recorded seeing 'the robe of the King of Virginia' and it was later catalogued as 'Pohatan, King of Virginia's habit, all embroidered with shells, or Roanoke'. The robe is now on display in the Ashmolean Museum in Oxford.

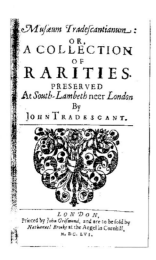

[*Musaeum Tradescantianum*]
John Tradescant junior wrote a
catalogue of the collection – the
first of its kind in Britain.

Their 'world of wonders' passed eventually, and controversially, into the hands of Elias Ashmole, who gave it to the University of Oxford. The Tradescant Ark was opened as the Ashmolean Museum, in Broad Street, Oxford, in 1683. It was the first purpose-built public museum in the world.

There were three floors in the museum. The Ark collection was on display on the top floor, along with other natural history artefacts. The ground floor was used for lectures and teaching, and the basement was a laboratory. All the original signs above the doorways on each floor are there, explaining what each room was used for.

Today, The Ark and the Ashmolean Museum have moved across the city of Oxford, and the original Ashmolean building has been taken over by the Museum of the History of Science. When they renovated the building in 1999, they lifted the floorboards on the first floor. Beneath them were all kinds of treasures from the original museum.

When the first discovery was made, the current museum curators joined the builders in digging up these secrets. They felt like 'floorboard archaeologists', sifting through dust rather than the earth. They pulled out all kinds of simple things, most of them dating from the eighteenth century, rather than from the very beginning of the museum in 1683.

The ephemera they pulled out of the dust includes: the label from the key that belonged to Dr Plot, keeper of the museum; a letter from J. Chapman, who worked there; labels from portraits; a lizard; a book cover; the remains of a posy of flowers; and an unopened letter –which they aren't going to open. I'm not sure how they can resist. I liked a small house, cut out of paper, made by someone daydreaming while at the museum, and a sketch of 'Edward', a keeper of the museum, with a little flower drawn beneath him.

There are things which whoever dropped them must have been upset to lose – a ring; a penknife and a child's tooth with a hole drilled through it which had probably been tied on to a string as a keepsake. Perhaps the child's father or mother wore it and crawled around on the floor of the museum looking for it when it fell off the string.

The most everyday things are the eighteenth-century pencil sharpenings and cherry stalks – very mundane at the time, but fascinating now. There are also lots of wax seals and coins. All of these tiny treasures that fell out of people's pockets or off the walls, or slipped off tables, have survived by chance. They weren't supposed to have made it into the twenty-first century, but that they did gives us a lovely feel for life in Britain's first museum. Everything suggests a human touch. These things aren't on display, because they're fragile and utterly unique. They're the only physical memories of the first museum in Britain.

Now, there are around 2,500 museums in Britain, and more than 55,000 museums in the world, each with unique collections; and most of the items in these collections are kept behind the scenes. More than 100 million people visit museums in Britain each year. I wonder what the Tradescants would have made of that? When they opened The Ark in their home in Lambeth, I bet they couldn't have imagined the trend they were starting.

[Found beneath the floorboards]
Museum curators felt like 'floorboard archaeologists' as they found pieces of history that had fallen beneath the floorboards of the original Ashmolean Museum.

[OBJECT 08]

a **BEJEWELLED** Cross

[Location]

MUSEU de ARTE SACRA
Salvador de Bahia, Brazil

The WORLD'S THIRD BIGGEST COLLECTION of SACRED ART

lives in a museum and former monastery

in SALVADOR, the CAPITAL of VIBRANT BAHIA, in BRAZIL.

I TOOK A TAXI TO the Museu de Arte Sacra to see the collection. When the taxi driver dropped me off, he said, 'The museum is down the hill – walk down that little street. When you come out, come straight back up to this main road. Don't hang around outside the museum, it can be dangerous.' So, nervously, I legged it down a side street into the pretty courtyard of the museum.

Once safely inside, I met Francisco Portugal, who has been the curator of the museum for 14 years. He wanted to show me the most precious treasure they have in the collection: a glittering bejewelled cross, which lay hidden under the floor of the building for centuries as buried treasure. It hasn't been exhibited for 40 years, as the museum is worried, now the area around the museum can be sketchy, that it might get stolen.

It is kept wrapped in a white cloth under lock and key inside a safe somewhere in the building. I didn't see where. The curator asked his assistant to fetch it and bring it into his office for me to see. We waited there, looking out at the beautiful views of the ocean until his assistant reappeared. We stood up, and she unwrapped the treasure. It was a golden cross, decorated with precious jewels. As she placed it on the table, the sunlight streaming across the ocean and in through the curator's office window bounced off the jewels and scattered around the room.

We gathered around to admire the cross. It's a processional one, so would have been carried from the base. It was made in Brazil, out of precious gold and jewels. At the top is a circle of golden rays bursting out of another central circle, which looks like a smoothed crystal. The circle opens up to be a cubbyhole for Communion bread. On top of the golden rays sits a small golden cross. The piece is decorated with diamond

droplets, amethysts, topaz, emeralds and rubies. Six cherubs float around its edges. You'll just have to imagine it because there are no published photographs of this most sacred cross.

Once upon a time, the room we stood in was a monk's bedroom. The whole museum has been shaped out of the former Convent of Saint Teresa de Avila, which was founded by the Order of Barefoot Carmelites in the mid-seventeenth century in the former capital of the colony. The monks who lived here were Portuguese. They arrived in Bahia in 1660 and built a little hospice by the sea; then, in 1685, they built a convent beside it, with a church modelled on the Church of Nossa Senhora dos Remédios (Our Lady of the Remedies), of Évora in Portugal, which dates from 1614.

The curator didn't know exactly when the cross was made but, once it was in the monastery, the monks protected, polished and proceeded to the altar carrying it. During Communion, they would open the central crystal to take out the Communion bread with which to feed the souls of their fellow monks.

At the end of the nineteenth century, Bahia fought for independence from Portugal. The convent was taken over by Portuguese troops trying to keep Bahia for their country. The monks were forced out of the monastery, but before they fled they buried this precious cross beneath the floorboards of their home. After the monks, and then the troops, had left the convent, it fell into ruin and was left derelict for many years.

In 1958, the University of Bahia restored the convent and church and turned it into the Museum of Sacred Art, exhibiting art belonging to the church, and 500 treasures belonging to Brazilian and Portuguese museums, churches, convents and brotherhoods in Brazil. During the restoration, the cross was found in the ground. The restorers were overcome with pleasure at finding the buried treasure and carefully cleaned and polished it until it shone like new. They put it on display in the museum. However, within ten years, the area around the monastery went downhill and became rough and dangerous, so the cross was taken out of the public galleries and hidden away for safekeeping.

There is still plenty to see in the museum itself: 1,500 pieces of sacred art from the seventeenth and eighteenth centuries are displayed in the rarefied atmosphere of the monks' quarters, with a view of the glittering sea. You can see the first fresco painted in Brazil: a lotus flower with a female figure emerging from it.

The curator also took me into the former monks' church so I could see how light the space was, with pews of dark wood and a silver altar upon which the cross may once have stood during a service, dazzling the monks as they prayed. I thought about the monks who worshipped here carrying the bejewelled cross, opening it up during Communion and lovingly polishing it after a service. They could never have imagined where it would end up: inside a safe, locked out of sight, just in case.

As I left the museum and crossed the courtyard that leads out into the street, I remembered why the cross was tucked away and decided to follow the taxi driver's advice. I flew up the hill to the main road and hailed a cab, made it safely into the car and was thankful to have seen the beautiful cross safe in its charming museum.

[The Museum of Sacred Art, Salvador de Bahia]
The museum is inside what was once the Convent of Saint Teresa de Avila, founded by the Order of Barefoot Carmelites in the mid-seventeenth century. It's in a beautiful location by the sea, and must have once been a peaceful place to live.

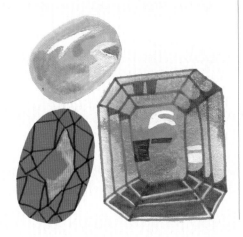

a **HAIDA SHAMAN's**
Rattle

[Location]

THE **WELLCOME COLLECTION**
London, England

One of the *GREATEST MEDICAL CURIOSITY CABINETS*
IN the WORLD
is in a FORMER POST OFFICE BUILDING
in *WEST LONDON.*

BLYTHE HOUSE IS A LISTED building, on Blythe Road, in Kensington. It began life in 1903 as the headquarters of the Post Office Savings Bank. The post office building was the first in London to have electricity and was split in half, with men and women working on different sides, each with their own entrance. Today, the Science Museum, the Victoria and Albert Museum and the British Museum use it as a store and archive. The Science Museum keeps its small objects here (its large objects are kept in a series of aircraft hangars, in an ex-RAF airbase in Wiltshire).

The Science Museum's treasure trove in Blythe House includes over 100,000 objects collected in the early nineteenth century by a pharmaceutical entrepreneur with a Midas touch, the devoted collector Sir Henry Wellcome (1853–1936).

Wellcome owned a pharmaceutical company. He made a fortune thanks to his invention of medicine in tablet form. He called them tabloids – as in a mixture of tablets and alkaloids in a small packet; this is where we get the word we use to describe small newspapers. He used his wealth to set up the Wellcome Trust, which today is one of the biggest medical charities in the world. He loved to collect medical curios and books, and had agents dotted around the globe buying up things they thought would interest him. They collected so much stuff he didn't get around to unpacking it all before he died. All of his books are stored in the Wellcome Library, on Euston Road, London. His objects were divided up between different museums around the world; some were put on display

[Louis Pasteur (1822–95)]
Pasteur was a French chemist and biologist who invented pasteurization. Some of the things he used in his research are in storage in Blythe House.

[A Haida shaman's rattle]
Of all the countless medical curiosities I saw in the Wellcome storage in Blythe House, I liked this rattle made out of cane and puffin beaks the most.

at the Wellcome Collection, on Euston Road, London (where the library is) and a tenth of his objects was brought over to Blythe House.

A team of archivists cataloguing the collection I came to see has been working for five years and has sorted over 230,000 items. It's likely to take them another seven years to go through the lot. No one curator has ever seen it all. I spent three hours walking in and out of rooms, pulling open drawers and looking through shelves of artefacts with Selina Hurley, assistant curator of medicine at the Science Museum.

The medical treasures are sorted into rooms by theme. Each room has its own smell: the oriental room smells like incense; and the dentistry room like the bright liquid you gargle when you sit up, at the dentist's. All of the rooms made me feel quite uneasy as they are filled with objects created to help people who were unwell.

We opened a door that led into a room filled with Roman votive offerings – models of injured parts of the body that were offered to a god to give thanks, or to ask for a cure; all over the walls are little clay feet, arms, legs, ears and even penises. Another room contains folk charms. Selina told me, 'Every time I come in here I stumble across something different.' Opening a drawer, she discovers a wizened object; 'I think that's a dried mole. Ah, here is a frog – he doesn't smell too bad – he was used to cure cramp and kept in a little bag. A lot of things like this work through transference. You hold something and transfer your pain into it.' Beside it is another example of this: a dog's tooth used as a teething charm for babies (the pain would be transferred from the baby's tooth to the dog's). Lots of objects are labelled 'curious object, use unknown'.

Another room is filled with piles of forceps to assist in birth; another with large glass storage bottles from pharmacies (one was for leeches). There was a cupboard with intricate Japanese *memento moris* (reminders that we all will die and to seize life with both hands), and a little ivory skeleton leaning on an alarm clock. I looked at a shelf lined with tiny ivory seventeenth-century anatomical figures. They were all lying flat, and I lifted their tummies off to reveal their insides. Particularly unsettling was a shelf crammed with prosthetic limbs, including a hand with a Bible on the end, and another with a scrubbing-brush attachment.

We came across the archives of Joseph Lister, the pioneer of antiseptic, and artefacts that belonged to Louis Pasteur, the French chemist and father of germ theory. There were items used by Pasteur in his study of anthrax, and some of his earliest preparations for quinine, dating back to 1820. Pretty much anything you could think of related to the history of medicine is in one of the rooms inside the Wellcome labyrinth. If you can't find it, maybe it is still waiting to be unpacked.

Of all the objects I saw, I liked a rattle made of cane and puffin beaks the most. It is unlike anything else in the collection, and stood out, even from its nest inside a drawer. It seemed to be filled with life and spirit. At first I had no idea what it was, so I asked Selina, and she told me it was a rattle made by the Haida people, and would have belonged to a shaman.

[Haida Gwaii]
The Haida are the indigenous people of Haida Gwaii (Islands of the People), an archipelago off the coast of Canada.

The Haida are the indigenous people of Haida Gwaii ('Islands of the People'), a group of islands off the coast of Canada, which, until 2010, were known as the Queen Charlotte Islands. Their name for a shaman is 'sGaaga'. The sGaaga is both a medical doctor and a faith healer. The Haida describe the sGaaga as people with a direct line to God. They turn to them in times of sickness and uncertainty or when they want to know the future or explain the past.

The sGaaga would have made this rattle (some time between 1890 and 1935) after collecting puffin beaks from the shore. Puffins shed their bright orange bills in winter and re-grow them come spring. Without its bill, a puffin looks funny, it has a little pointed beak instead of the rainbow splendour we're used to seeing. Usually, they hide out at sea at this time of year, so humans rarely see them in this state.

Puffins were symbolic for the sGaaga, because the birds dive into the water and disappear into another realm; shaking a rattle made from their beaks symbolized moving to another level of existence. The beaks were tied to circles of wood representing a cosmic doorway. The rattle would have been one of a pair and used only by a shaman.

Selina told me that, in 2009, 12 Haida people came to the Wellcome Collection to look at the puffin bill rattle, as well as two other items made by their people: a pipe and a comb for brushing cloth. Both are made of a rock called argillite, found only on Graham Island in Haida Gwaii. If you see something made of argillite, it was made by the Haida, because they are the only people who use it. The 12 Haida crammed into the tiny room I saw the rattle in, within Blythe House. Selina told me, 'Their reaction to the rattle was really mixed; the younger generation were quite happy to pick it up and play with it, but the older generation wouldn't go anywhere near it because it has such a spiritual significance.'

I checked in with Vince Collinson, a representative of the Haida people who visited the Wellcome archive. He explained, 'The rattle was originally used by sGaaga, which would explain our elders' hesitancy and some of our young people's lack of hesitancy, as there are no "old style" sGaaga left today, so they can't understand their powers. The last person in Skidegate (a Haida community on Haida Gwaii) who was operated on by a sGaaga passed away in 2007.'

Vince told me of another dimension to their visit to England. Some museums in England have other artefacts belonging to the Haida, including some of their ancestors' bones. The Haida Repatriation Committee is working to bring home these treasures so the souls of the ancestors can be laid to rest and the Haida nation healed. Vince explained, 'We have a very close attachment to the land of Haida Gwaii. The water, animals, birds, those are our identity, our business card. We believe the souls of the dead don't rest in peace if their bones are not left in their homeland.'

He told me that, following the visit in which they looked at this beautiful puffin rattle, a Haida ancestor held in the Pitt Rivers Museum for over a hundred years was repatriated and reburied in August 2010, a process initiated over ten years earlier by the Haida. 'It was truly a momentous, historic day of healing for both the Haida and the British.' This was not the first time ancestors had been given back to their people. Between 1992 and 2004, the remains of 460 of their ancestors were brought back to Haida Gwaii. An 'End of Mourning' ceremony was held on the islands in 2006, in which their souls were released to Gaahlandaay Tllgaay (Spirit Land). The Haida are hopeful that many of their belongings – and not just their ancestors' bones – will be returned to them. Nika Collinson of the Ts'aahl Eagle Clan explained how important is it that Haida treasures are restored to them. 'As Haida treasures return home, elders come to see them … as [the elders] remember, they begin to talk, bringing the history, use and stories of these treasures out of concealment and passing this knowledge on to the next generations to learn from. Without the return of these cultural materials, so much of this knowledge would not come to the surface and subsequently would not be passed on.'

There were once tens of thousands of Haida people. When Europeans arrived on the islands, this number quickly fell to fewer than 1,000, because of introduced diseases, including measles, typhoid and smallpox. Today, there are around 5,000 Haida, around 2,000 of whom live in Haida Gwaii, with others in Prince Rupert, the lower mainland of British Columbia, Seattle and Alaska.

The Haida are known for their tall totem poles, which they call 'monumental poles' – or 'gyaagang.Ngaay' in Haida. They say the first pole carvers were inspired by and learned from a pole they saw standing out in the ocean. The monumental poles are carved from red cedarwood, and it takes a year to create each one. The totem poles were used to tell stories, to mark important events, to show status and to mock people. This still goes on. In 2007, a shaming totem pole was put up in Alaska featuring the upside-down head of the ex-CEO of the oil company Exxon. The totem pole was made to express anger over the unpaid debt the company owes for the *Exxon Valdez* oil spillage of 1989. In England, in Windsor Great Park, near Windsor Castle, there is a 30-metre-high totem pole made in 1958 from a 600-year-old tree felled on Haida Gwaii. It was given to the Queen to commemorate the centenary of the founding of British Columbia.

The ancient Haida lived in houses made of cedar which slept 30 or more people. They ate mussels, oysters, oolichans (a fish) and oolichan grease (fish oil). High-ranking men and women tattooed their clan crests (depicting animals, the supernatural or clan histories) on to their skin. All the Haida had a deep respect for the environment. They travelled in cedarwood canoes. If you look on the back of a Canadian $20 note, you will see an artwork called *Spirit of Haida Gwaii*, by Haida artist Bill Reid, which depicts a Haida chief in a canoe with many other creatures of Haida Gwaii, including the raven, the frog, the eagle and the bear.

The Haida language has no relationship to other languages – rather like Basque and the Ainu language once spoken on the island of Hokkaido in northern Japan. There are fewer than 40 remaining speakers of the language, most of them over 70 years old.

I'd like to imagine the Haida rattle finding its way back to Haida Gwaii so its people can remember the days of the sGaagas. When it is returned, I am sure the Haida will say 'Háw'aa' –'thank you'.

[Totem poles]
The Haida are known for their totem poles, which they call monumental poles. They carve them from red cedarwood trees, and each one takes a year to make.

[OBJECT 10]

FRANCIS CRICK's
SKETCH of DNA

[Location]

the WELLCOME LIBRARY
London, England

IT MIGHT LOOK LIKE A STRAND OF PASTA,

the slide of a helter-skelter,

OR AN OCTOPUS'S TENTACLE,

BUT THIS SKETCH SHOWS *a* MOLECULE *of* DNA.

IT WAS DOODLED by SCIENTIST FRANCIS CRICK

– OR BY HIS WIFE –

when he was working out what he called

'THE SECRET OF LIFE':

THE SHAPE of DNA.

I saw the pencil sketch of DNA in the Wellcome Library, on Euston Road, London. The drawing belongs to the Francis Crick archive, which is made up of 2,000 paper files (or 200,000 sides of text/images) amassed by Crick during his career.

There I met Ross MacFarlane, research officer at the Wellcome Library, and he showed me a selection of its treasures.

We began with the oldest thing there, the Johnson Papyrus, a piece of a book, or scroll, from the fifth century AD. It was found in Egypt. It is the oldest surviving illustration of a herbal. What's a herbal? It is a book with names or drawings of plants, usually with information about the plant as well – including its culinary, aromatic, medicinal or hallucinatory powers, and sometimes legends associated with it. In this case, the ancient, precious drawing is of a bluey-green comfrey plant. Below it, in Greek, is an explanation of how the plant can be used for healing. This is how herbalism developed: by trying out plants and seeing how they made you feel. By trial and error the properties and medicinal uses of different plants were discovered and passed on to others.

We also looked through a diary belonging to Robert McCormick, ship's surgeon and natural history expert on HMS *Beagle*. There is no mention of Darwin in the entire diary. Ross suggested McCormick was probably rather cross that Darwin had turned out to be such a natural history know-it-all, as that wasn't the reason for him being brought on board the *Beagle*. Darwin joined the expedition late in the day when Fitzroy, the captain, decided he needed someone who knew about geology to come and keep him company, someone, most importantly, who would pay his own way. Darwin fitted the bill. Although I know he wasn't a real geology pro because I visited the Sedgwick Museum of Earth Sciences in Cambridge – who own Darwin's rock collection from the *Beagle* – and they showed me a diary of Sedgwick's, in which he mentions taking Darwin on a quick expedition to give him a crash course in geology just before he set sail.

I also looked through an early guide to swimming written by a Cambridge don in Elizabethan England, and a letter written by the antiquarian Sir Hans Sloane, who collected the countless treasures that became the basis for the British Museum collection. In the letter, he talks about a door that leads from his garden into a coffee shop designed as a cabinet of rarities, where he went to chat over coffee with other local pals who were interested in new ideas and discoveries. I wondered whether he would mention chocolate, for he introduced drinking chocolate to Britain in 1687. He didn't. But you've probably tasted something similar to his blend; 'Sloane's Milk Chocolate' recipe eventually passed into the hands of Cadbury's.

Then I came to a white file filled with photographs, scientific papers, personal letters and musings. Ross pulled out the sketch. I instantly recognized the spiralling ladder that carries the Earth's variety of life forms. The image was sketched in 1953, 84 years after Johann Friedrich Miescher discovered DNA in 1869.

Miescher found out about DNA – which he called nuclein – when, doing a grim-sounding experiment on cell-digesting, he extracted some enzymes from a pig he had bought at a butcher's and some cells from bandages used by a soldier during the Prussian War, which was going on at the time. He suggested that nuclein might be involved in heredity, but then discounted his own idea, saying it wasn't possible that one single molecule could account for all the variation seen within species. He thought that would be far too simple.

So Francis Crick and James Watson, helped by the work of Rosalind Franklin, didn't discover DNA, but they did work out what it looked like. They struggled to conceptualize the exact shape of the molecule for years, and were helped enormously by Rosalind Franklin's skill as an x-ray crystallographer.

Franklin had spent four years researching crystals in Paris before moving back to London to work on investigating the structure of DNA. She was given jam jars full of gooey DNA and began to take x-ray photographs of it.

Meanwhile in Cambridge, Crick and Watson made a homemade metal model of DNA as a way to represent, in reality, the ideas they were carrying around in their heads. They had several false starts. They made a triple helix in 1951 and invited Franklin to see it, and she pointed out the molecule as they had made it would never hold together. In 1953, after seeing a photograph taken by Franklin, their ideas fell into place. Finally, they got the model right, and made their physical double helix. This sketch was made around the same time: it was part of the process of

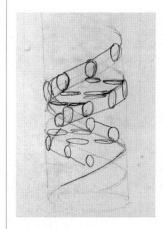

[Crick's doodle of a DNA molecule]
As we leafed through Crick's papers I instantly recognized the spiralling ladder that carries the Earth's variety of life forms.

[Watson and Crick with their model of DNA]

They made a model as a way to represent, in reality, the ideas they were carrying around in their heads.

grappling with exactly what the DNA molecule looks like. When finally the image became crystal clear in their minds, the scientists were ecstatic. Crick said, 'It is not easy to convey, unless one has experienced it, the dramatic feeling of sudden enlightenment that floods the mind when the right idea finally clinches into place.'

Crick and Watson published their realization in the 25 April 1953 edition of *Nature*. The order of the names on the paper (Watson and Crick) was decided by the flip of a coin. The pair went on to win the Nobel Prize for their discovery, along with Dr Maurice Wilkins; Franklin, who had been pivotal to the research, died before the prize was awarded. Hopefully she would also have been honoured with the prize, had she been alive to receive it, for it would not have happened in the same way without her.

Now we know that a DNA molecule looks like the image in the sketch: a double helix. Every living creature on earth is made up of right-handed spiral shapes like this. The sketch, according to experts at the Wellcome Collection shows a few key features of the molecule. It is right-handed, it has two strands running in opposite directions, and the building blocks of the strands (nucleotides) have one part that forms the backbone of the molecule and another (the base) that sticks out into the middle of the helix to join with a base on the opposite strand. This joining of two bases is essential in order for DNA to pass on genetic information from one generation to the next. That's quite a lot of information, crucial to our existence on Earth, in one pencil sketch, don't you think?

There are at least 50 million cells in your body, and each one contains nearly 2 metres of DNA. Extracting your own is quite easy. If you're the kind of geek who wants to try, follow these steps:

1. Swish salt-water around your cheeks.
2. Spit it into a glass containing water and washing-up liquid.
3. Mix for a minute or so.
4. Pour some ice-cold vodka, slowly, into the glass.
5. In a couple of minutes, you will see some white strands form. These are strands of DNA. If you were able to look closely at them, you'd see the double helix shape sketched in Crick's drawing.

After co-winning the Nobel Prize, Crick became a household name. He was invited to all sorts of events, but he preferred to concentrate on his work, and keep to himself. In the archive is a ready-made, multi-purpose reply card from the 1960s, which reads:

Dr Crick thanks you for your letter but regrets that he is unable to accept your kind invitation to
– send an autograph
– help you in your project
– provide a photograph or read your manuscript
– cure your disease
– deliver a lecture
– talk on the radio or act as chairman
– appear on TV or become an editor
Delete where appropriate.

[Crick wins a Nobel Prize]
Telegram to Crick announcing his Nobel Prize, 1962. He won the prize jointly with Watson and Dr Maurice Wilkins for their work on the molecular structure of DNA and 'its significance for information transfer in living material'.

Later in life, Crick moved from Cambridge to San Diego, and worked at the Salk Institute there. He lived in a house called the Golden Helix. There he began focusing on neurobiology. He wanted to look inside the human brain, to study the networks, connections and firing patterns of neurons, as he thought they held the key to understanding mental activity and consciousness.

The Wellcome Library bought Crick's papers in 2001, while he was still alive. They consist of his research papers, letters from people who were ill, a lovely letter from a young boy saying he'd enjoyed meeting Crick and letters from colleagues. They all give you a sense that Crick, like all scientists, was – of course – a real person. It makes science seem less removed from normal life.

Crick was keen for his work to become a part of this vast medical library, which anyone can access free of charge. On the day I visited, the library was packed with medical students cramming for exams. Perhaps one day, one of those students will make a breakthrough in healing and add their work to the collection, alongside the discoveries of herbalists in the fifth century and scientists like Crick.

[OBJECT 11]

TABLET K.143,

School Exercise Book of Ashurbanipal, King of Assyria

[Location]

THE BRITISH MUSEUM
London, England

THE FIRST THING I THOUGHT

when I met Irving Finkel,

KEEPER of ANCIENT MESOPOTAMIAN

LANGUAGES and CULTURE

at THE BRITISH MUSEUM,

was: WOW, what an AMAZING BEARD!

AS WE WALKED ACROSS THE great hall, we started chatting. Finkel is very friendly, kind, interesting and seriously clever. He is one of only a hundred or so people in the world who can read cuneiform, the oldest form of writing in the world.

He was first shown the basics of how to read the script, when he started at university and he knew 'within about 20 minutes this was what I wanted to do for the rest of my existence'. He learned cuneiform, and later applied to work with it at the British Museum. He got the job. 'In that moment, I achieved my life's ambition.'

Since that day in 1979, he has been working on the world's largest, most cosmic jigsaw puzzle, piecing together pieces of cuneiform writing. His domain has been the Arched Room, a three-tiered room where all 120,000 of the British Museum's behind the scenes cuneiform tablets are stored.

On the top two levels are books about cuneiform and the cultures that employed this form of writing. On the ground level is a long run of tables for cuneiform scholars to write at. The walls are lined with bookshelves that once stored the British Library's Mills and Boon collection. Now they are filled with trays, each one containing glass-topped boxes. Inside the boxes are clay tablets covered with ancient cuneiform writing. It looks like an alien script.

[Irving Finkel in the Arched Room]

Irving Finkel is assistant keeper for Ancient Mesopotamian script, languages and cultures at the British Museum in London. He showed me a selection of clay tablets covered in cuneiform writing, the world's oldest known script.

[A cut reed]
Cuneiform appeared in ancient Iraq in about 3000 BC, first as a simple pictographic system, but rapidly evolving into a fluent means of recording language. The lines of the script (called wedges) were pressed into the clay with a cut reed, used like a pen; 'It looked a bit like a chopstick,' explained Finkel.

[The library at Nineveh]
King Ashurbanipal built his capital in a city called Nineveh. At the heart of his palace he lovingly built up a library, filled with the clay tablets Finkel showed me in the British Museum.

Cuneiform script is made up of short, straight lines which go in different directions. The lines (called wedges) were imprinted in pieces of soft clay with a cut reed, used like a pen; 'It looked a bit like a chopstick,' explained Finkel. Cuneiform means 'wedge shaped', from the Latin *cuneus*, or wedge. The word doesn't rhyme with uniform: you pronounce it 'cu-neigh-i-form'.

A lot of the clay tablets in Finkel's domain come from the Royal Library of King Ashurbanipal, who lived in the sixth century BC. 'He was king of the world at the time,' Finkel told me, 'a proper *Arabian Nights* king – harems, exotic foods, hundreds of servants, chariots.' But he was also literate, and he loved clay books. He built his capital in a city called Nineveh (today called Kuyunjik, in Iraq) and, at the heart of his palace, in the citadel, he created his library.

The library contained spells, myths about gods and heroes, stories of wrestling with bulls, recipes, astrology, medicine, histories, books on fortune telling, poems, love letters – and multiple copies of the *Epic of Gilgamesh*. Until I visited Finkel's realm, I hadn't been aware that the story had come down through the generations to us written on pieces of baked clay.

The library also housed maps, plans, dictionaries, books of grammar and mundane tax forms, everyday 'to do' lists and legal records. There were a few 'weirdo' things, also, Finkel told me. 'Like what?' I asked. 'Well, you know, strange dramas: there is one about a relationship between a god and his mother-in-law that was probably performed as a play in Babylon.'

The king ordered every temple in Babylonia, in the south, to give him a copy of every piece of literature they owned. In some cases, pieces of writing had to be commandeered for the royal library.

Every piece of clay writing in the library is written in exactly the same style of cuneiform. The king employed a roomful of scribes to read every single thing that went into the library and copy it out into perfect Assyrian cuneiform writing, 'like BBC English,' Finkel suggests. Important things were baked to terracotta, so that they would survive for a long time, and less important things were simply laid out in the sun to dry.

The cuneiform on one particular clay tablet looks completely different to the rest. It has really big, childish writing on it and looks totally out of place. Finkel picked it up and began reading, tracing his finger across the clay tablet in his hands.

Turn your faces to the petition manifest in my raised hands.
May your fierce hearts rest,
May your reins be appeased, grant me reconciliation
That I may sing your praises without forgetting to the widespread people.

[Cuneiform on a clay tablet]
This clay tablet was King Ashurbanipal's school exercise book. He may have put it in his library as a keepsake from the days when, as a child, he learned to write.

It's an incantation, written in a child's hand, with letters a centimetre high which aren't joined up. It was written by King Ashurbanipal when he was a child and learning to write. This is his school exercise book. Just as you might still have a school exercise book or two at home, to remind you of when you were learning to write, the king must have decided to keep this clay tablet as a souvenir of his childhood, a marker of the days when his love of literature was formed.

The tablet begins, 'Ea, Shamash, and Marduk, what are my iniquities?' and continues with an incantation to the gods to forgive the writer and release him from sickness. The prayer is written to appease the wrath of a god who has stricken him down with illness.

In the young king's case, at the time, he was more than likely copying the incantation out as an exercise.

'How old do you think he was when he wrote this?' I asked Finkel.

'About 12?' he replied. 'We don't know for sure.' There is only one tablet in the world of which scholars feel sure about the age of the scribe. That is because the scribe bit his tablet. Thousands of years later, the American curator who looked after it saw the teeth marks, slipped the tablet in his pocket and took it to his dentist. The dentist said that the marks were made by the teeth of a seven-year-old boy who lived over two millennia ago.

The boy who copied out the incantation grew up, became king, ruled for 39 years and, over that time, built up an epic library. Two and a half thousand years ago, the clay tablets were stored upright on shelves, like we store books – except for a few things, such as love letters, which were kept in baskets.

The fact that the library has survived is something of a miracle. Towards the end of King Ashurbanipal's reign, the city of Nineveh was ransacked and destroyed by the Medes and the Babylonians. They set the king's precious library on fire. A whole upper floor came crashing down to the ground, and the tablets were smashed into pieces; the

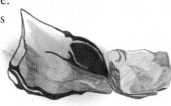

[The *Epic of Gilgamesh*]
Until I met Finkel I didn't know that the *Epic of Gilgamesh* came down to us written on a series of baked clay tablets.

city was left in ruins. Bizarrely, this devastation saved the library from destruction. The fire baked the library's clay tablets into terracotta, which survived for thousands of years inside the earth.

In the mid-nineteenth century, the world's first archaeologists started digging around what was once Nineveh and found these pieces of baked, smashed-up clay with strange writing upon them. Some pieces that had been caught in the fire were black; others, which the fire had missed, were damp after millennia inside the earth. Fortunately some of these were still intact. All the archaeologists had to do was lay them out in the sun to dry, just as the scribes had done when they were creating the library back in the sixth century BC.

Thanks to the archaeological permit, the pieces were brought to England to the British Museum. Over time, the meaning of the writing was worked out. The Babylonians unwittingly left a code for the nineteenth century scholars who had discovered them.

The cuneiform tablets in the library are written either in Sumerian, which is unlike any language we have today, or in Akkadian, which is related to modern Semitic languages and easier to make sense of. The Babylonians also wrote bilinguals, with a line of Sumerian translated into a line of Akkadian. 'The bilinguals are gold dust,' said Finkel. 'This was code-cracking with a crib from the codemaker.' In the nineteenth century, the decipherers of Akkadian began with words like 'mother', 'father' and 'tree', and with numbers, then began to recognize prefixes and suffixes and slowly worked out the shape of the language. Once they'd worked out how to read Akkadian, they used the bilinguals to work out Sumerian.

Ever since then, curators have been gluing fragments of the clay tablets back together. 'This is the greatest jigsaw of all time,' Finkel explained. Each time a piece of clay is matched to another piece found smashed in the ground, a spell, an ancient recipe or a story comes back into the light.

Over the last three decades, Finkel has been slowly bringing more and more of ancient Nineveh into the twenty-first century. He loves the thrill of it: 'There is nothing so satisfying as the moment when you rejoin two pieces of writing that have been separated for two and a half thousand years. Of course, the tablets are often broken at the most exciting moment, just when the hero finds the heroine, and says ...' Finding out the rest of the ancient story when you find the missing piece of clay tablet must be a sublime moment.

In many tablets that weren't part of Ashurbanipal's library, Finkel can recognize the work of different hands, just by looking at the shape of the calligraphy on different tablets; just as we all have different handwriting, each person who wrote on a clay tablet wrote in a slightly different way.

Almost all of the tablets, no matter what their size, are covered with writing, on the back and on the front. 'If you write a postcard home to your auntie, you usually fill all the space up, don't you?', Finkel asked me. The scribes of Nineveh of 600 BC were no different.

They put a little more effort into their writing in one sense, though, by inventing right-justified text. If they couldn't fill a line with text, they filled it with dots or drew a horizontal line. 'It looks more authoritative. We do it sometimes, now that we have computers, but we don't often make the effort, like they did, when we're writing by hand.' He pointed out the dots and lines on some clay tablets to me so I could see it for myself.

Finkel is a great host. He is able to make the Ancient Assyrian world come alive. When I left the Arched Room and walked into the public galleries of the British Museum, I found myself in Room 9, which is filled with reliefs from the king's palace in Nineveh. Suddenly, everything in that room was shimmering with life. I now know that beyond the reliefs showing images of battle and war is a library filled with love letters, stories, poems, spells, recipes and a school exercise book of the last great king of Assyria.

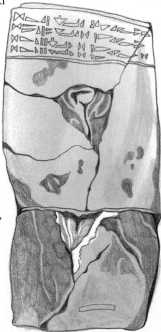

Anyone can go to the Arched Room to take a look: 'If you have the keys to treasure, as we do, it is unforgivable not to give people access to it. We're very proud that anyone can come in here and read and see things they would like to see,' Finkel explained. He often shows children the wonderful clay tablets and would love to persuade them to learn cuneiform and enjoy the rewards it brings. 'There is still so much to do. We need students to study cuneiform and keep the giant jigsaw going.'

I had a look at his actual keys, the huge bunch of them he carries around each day. The biggest, oldest one is the key to the collection: it opens the Arched Room in which the tablets are stored. On it are the words 'If lost, 20 shillings reward' – not a generous reward then, considering the treasures the key can unlock for you.

[OBJECT 12]

VLADIMIR NABOKOV's
Butterfly Genitalia Cabinet

[Location]

MUSEUM of COMPARATIVE ZOOLOGY
Harvard University, MA, USA

> '*I FOUND IT and I NAMED IT,*
>
> **BEING VERSED IN TAXONOMIC LATIN;**
>
> Thus became Godfather to an insect
>
> AND ITS FIRST DESCRIBER —
>
> *AND I WANT NO OTHER FAME.'*

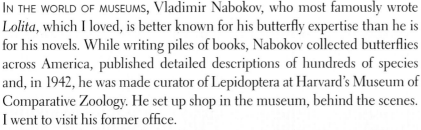

IN THE WORLD OF MUSEUMS, Vladimir Nabokov, who most famously wrote *Lolita*, which I loved, is better known for his butterfly expertise than he is for his novels. While writing piles of books, Nabokov collected butterflies across America, published detailed descriptions of hundreds of species and, in 1942, he was made curator of Lepidoptera at Harvard's Museum of Comparative Zoology. He set up shop in the museum, behind the scenes. I went to visit his former office.

The room is lined with metal drawers, each filled with rows of butter-flies. Lots of his butterflies are stored in the drawers, along with thousands of others collected by different curators over the years. There is a desk pushed up against a window that looks out over the university campus. Nabokov worked from here. It's a different desk that is now used by the current butterfly curator, but it is kept in the same place.

I stood by the desk and looked out of the window, and I saw students milling about chatting, eating lunch, reading and daydreaming. I imag-ined Nabokov doing the same, looking out, over butterflies, to watch the students at play. The only difference now is that today they're reading iPads rather than books and there are food trucks, not packed lunches. Otherwise, I'd imagine Nabokov would feel right at home.

[Nabokov at home, 1965]
Vladimir Nabokov loved everything to do with butterflies; he read about them, drew them, wrote about them and collected them throughout his life.

[Nabokov's butterfly cabinet]
Nabokov kept his butterfly penis
specimens inside little glass vials,
packed into cigar boxes.

There is a photograph of him framed and hung on the wall beside the window. The image shows him holding up a butterfly, one of the hundreds he prepared in this room.

In the corner, by another window, is a small, dusty, wooden cabinet. It's about a metre high, with two doors. Open the doors, and inside are hundreds of little glass vials, with corks for lids. Inside each one is a tiny butterfly penis. There are more butterfly bits on glass slides, stacked inside small boxes on shelves inside the cabinet.

There are also index cards that seem to be written in Nabokov's writing; they describe each of the genitalia. Like the specimens, they are just as he left them in the 1940s.

I took out a box, picked out a slide and held it to the light. I could just about make out a little black spike: the genitalia of a single male blue butterfly. The glass vials used to have preserving liquid inside them but the fluid has dried out since Nabokov prepared them, so each butterfly penis now rattles around inside its bottle. It is really quite a strange thing to do – to hold a glass bottle, containing a butterfly's penis, collected years ago by the famous author.

It might seem a bit of a weird thing for him to have done, that is, if you've read his novels but don't know much about butterfly curating. But a butterfly curator wouldn't find his collection strange at all. Studying male butterfly genitalia is one of the best ways of telling one species apart from another. It's a better way than looking at just their wings and their size, because many butterflies look so similar.

The cabinet isn't very important to the butterfly world – there is nothing of great scientific importance inside it – but I found it fascinating that Nabokov loved butterflies as much as books. His twin passions wove their way through his life from when he was young.

His father taught him as a child to chase, catch and collect butterflies while roaming around their family home of Vyra, in northwestern Russia, and a love of butterflies was something they shared together. His mother showed him how to really look and to remember. These skills would come in handy for both writing and butterfly curating.

When his father was imprisoned in Russia for his political activities, eight-year-old Vladimir brought a butterfly to his cell as a present.

Nabokov was forced into exile in Europe in 1919. There he visited vast museum halls to look closely at the shimmering rainbow of butterflies on display. He married in Berlin in 1925, and he and his wife Vera roamed the mountains at weekends, collecting hundreds of specimens.

By 1940, he was living in Paris and, when the German tanks rolled in, he and his wife and their son, Dimitri, fled to America. In his apartment he left behind a set of European butterflies.

It was in America that he took up his first professional appointment in the world of butterflies, as a research fellow at Harvard's Museum of Comparative Zoology. He was appointed in 1942 and stayed for six years. He had imagined being a curator as a child and collected all the time.

In his autobiography, *Speak, Memory*, he describes how his governess sat on a tray full of butterflies he had collected himself and squashed them: '… A precious gynandromorph, left side male, right side female, whose abdomen could not be traced and whose wings had come off, was lost for ever: one might re-attach the wings, but one could not prove that all four belong to that headless thorax on its bent pin.'

At Harvard he saw plenty of these gynandromorphs, part of the huge collection created by butterfly curators over the decades. I saw one for myself; it is kept in one of the metal drawers – one wing was iridescent blue, the other half blue–half black with white flecks. Other interesting butterflies I saw, lifeless on pins, were a now-extinct Xerxces Blue, which once flew in the San Francisco area, and a huge green and yellow butterfly whose collector had been eaten by cannibals in Papua New Guinea.

Over 20 butterflies have been named in Nabokov's honour, including 'Lolita' and 'Humbert', which are named after the two main characters in *Lolita*. He wrote the novel on index cards while on butterfly-collecting trips with Vera. After he'd finished writing, she'd type up his handwritten cards. When he tried to burn an early draft, she saved the pages from the flames.

The Nabokovs loved these long, butterfly-collecting adventures. They would set off from Harvard at weekends and during the holidays: Vera always at the wheel, because Nabokov never learned to drive. Once they drove a thousand miles across North America, taking on a blazing Kansas storm, just to spot a single species of butterfly.

Blue butterflies fascinated him, and he and Vera would pursue them all over the North American wilderness. Once he'd collected his specimens

[Butterfly hunting]
Nabokov and his wife Vera spent weekends butterfly hunting.

[Morpho butterfly]
Rare genetic mutations produce gynandromorphs like this morpho butterfly, which is male on the left side and female on the right. Nabokov wrote about finding a gynandromorph as a young boy and was pleased that Harvard had one in its collection.

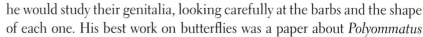

he would study their genitalia, looking carefully at the barbs and the shape of each one. His best work on butterflies was a paper about *Polyommatus* blue butterflies. He examined the genitalia of 120 of the creatures, which lived in the Neotropics, and found that different species had flown to the New World from Asia in a series of waves over millions of years. He said that 'a modern taxonomist straddling a Wellsian time machine' would have witnessed the colonization.

At the time, his findings weren't really given much credit, but recently, in 2011, researchers at Harvard University sequenced DNA from the blues and found that Nabokov's musings were correct. Blue butterflies flew in five waves from Asia to the New World – just as Nabokov had at one time emigrated with his family from Europe to America.

When asked in an interview for *The Paris Review* in 1967 whether he had felt at home during his time in America, Nabokov said he was 'as American as April in Arizona'. Asked if anything reminded him of the Russia of his youth, he replied, 'my butterfly hunting, in a loop of time, seemed at once to resume the butterfly chases of my vanished Vyra.' The 'fairly wild' landscapes of north-western America were, he pointed out, 'surprisingly similar to the Arctic expanses of northern Russia'.

Butterflies reminded him of home and, wherever life took him, he felt comfortable, butterfly net in hand, waiting to catch one of his precious, delicate creatures – rather like catching memories and ideas, and transforming them into characters at his writing desk. 'My loathings are simple: stupidity, oppression, crime, cruelty, soft music,' he once wrote. 'My pleasures are the most intense known to man: writing and butterfly hunting.'

In a letter to his sister (1945), Nabokov wrote that 'to know that no one before you has seen an organ you are examining, to trace relationships that have occurred to no one before, to immerse yourself in the wondrous crystalline world of the microscope, where silence reigns, circumscribed by its own horizon, a blindingly white arena — all this is so enticing that I cannot describe it.'

He became utterly hooked on collecting, pinching the delicate, colourful creatures at the thorax, then studying them carefully to find out everything he could about them. There was a price to pay – late in life, Nabokov's eyesight failed, ruined by all the hours he'd spent looking at tiny genitalia under a microscope in the back room of Harvard's museum.

[OBJECT 13]

Charles Dickens's
FELINE LETTER OPENER

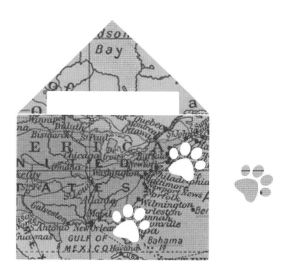

[Location]

The NEW YORK PUBLIC LIBRARY
New York City, USA

'WHAT GREATER GIFT
THAN the LOVE of a CAT?'

So asked Charles Dickens. He had at least three cats. One was named William, until Dickens realized she was a girl and renamed her Williamina. She had kittens, and he kept one, which became known as the Master's Cat. It used to snuff out his candle to get his attention. A third cat was called Bob. He helped Dickens open his letters.

Bob wasn't a spectacularly talented cat; the way he helped was rather odd. When dear Bob passed on in 1862, Georgina Hogarth, who was Dickens's sister-in-law, had his little paw – which once padded around on the author's lap, walking all over his writing or whatever he was trying to read, as cats seem to love to do – immortalized as the handle of a letter opener.

She had the strange feline and ivory piece engraved 'C. D. In Memory of Bob. 1862' and gave it to Dickens as a gift, to remind him of the love of his cat. He kept it in the library at Gad's Hill, so that it was at his side as he wrote. It is now in the Berg reading room on the third floor of the New York Public Library in Manhattan. It shares a space with Dickens's writing desk and chair – the ones he used when travelling – and 13 prompt copies the author had made to help him when doing public readings.

What's a prompt copy? I'll let Isaac Gewirtz, the Berg curator explain: 'Dickens wasn't only a great writer, he was a fantastic actor: he loved to perform his work, rather than simply read extracts from it. He filleted his novels, pulling out the most dramatic scenes. Then he had two or three copies printed and bound in case he lost one. His main copy he annotated, with stage directions and cues for himself. We have 13 annotated prompt copies here in the Berg.'

How brilliant to be able to see what Dickens's audiences couldn't.

[Charles Dickens's letter opener]
The handle is made out of his cat Bob's paw.

One of the most popular of his readings was *A Christmas Carol*. The library owns the prompt copy he used to perform the story at public readings. He made this particular copy in a unique way.

Over to Isaac: 'He had a binder remove the leaves from an 1849 copy of his novel and stick them to blank leaves which were then bound together as a new volume. Then he took this new book and read through his text, rewriting and simplifying tricky sentences. He got rid of evocative passages that set the scene in London and cut out descriptions of characters' emotional states because he could convey those in the tone of his voice.'

He covered the copy with annotations, like a stage manager might annotate a script for a performance. He added cues, such as 'Tone down to Pathos' and 'Up to cheerfulness', which would remind him of how to play scenes; and he also underlined bits, such as 'For it is good to be children sometimes, and never better than at Christmas, when its mighty Founder was a child himself.' He used postage stamps as Post-it notes, to mark the places he wanted to read from. The corners of the stamps that were stuck on to the page are still there, while the bits that stuck out have fallen off.

[Charles Dickens performing his work]
Dickens loved to give public readings and had prompt copies of his work made, which he could annotate and then use to read from on the nights of his performances.

His cat Bob, who was immortalized in the letter opener, was named after Bob Cratchit, Scrooge's assistant in *A Christmas Carol*. It's fitting then that Bob's paw shares a cabinet with the library's prompt copy of the tale the writer used for years at his wildly popular readings.

Several of these readings took place in America. He made two tours there: the first, in 1842, turned a bit ugly when he criticized American publishers for pirating his works, and when he travelled in the South, saw slavery at first hand for the first time and wrote angry articles against it. When he came back in 1867, all was forgiven. This time, he performed twice in New York, in the cavernous Steinway piano display hall on East 14th Street, and at the largest church in Brooklyn. People lined up in the snow for tickets – some even slept outside to be sure of a spot in the crowd: the queue, by opening time, was a mile long. The lucky people inside heard Dickens read from the book that is now in the library.

Reading it doesn't give you the perfect idea of what his audiences heard each night – no two performances were the same. Sometimes Dickens would make things up on the spur of the moment, or slam the

[Charles John Huffam Dickens
(1812–70)]

book shut with a flourish and perform from memory. He knew his stories by heart and could act them perfectly.

So how did the letter opener and prompt copies end up in New York? Well, when Dickens died, he bequeathed his estate to his sister-in-law, the lady who had given him the macabre letter opener. She wrote letters of authenticity for everything.

She sold some things, and passed others on to Dickens's son. The letter opener and other Dickensian treasures were bought by a publisher in New York called E. P. Dutton; they had a sale, and two brothers – physicians of Jewish Hungarian descent called Albert and Henry Berg – turned up and bought the lot, to add to their glittering collection of American and British literature.

In 1940, the surviving brother, Albert, gave everything to the New York Public Library, and built an Austrian oak-panelled room for researchers. The Berg reading room was the result.

The street that leads to the New York Public Library is lined with quotations. I read them on my way to visit the library, then I walked up the steps to the entrance, which are guarded by two lions, cats a lot bigger than Bob.

When you walk into the Berg reading room, you see, on the right-hand side, a portrait of Henry Berg, beside the works of his favourite writer, Thackeray; and on the left-hand side is Albert's portrait and all the writings of Albert's favourite author, Charles Dickens. Only the researchers, most of whom come by appointment to read items in the collection, see the prompt copies, while waiting for a book to be brought for them from the vaults.

Albert Berg left a handsome sum to pay for future curators, and to make sure their collection of the works of 104 authors continued to grow. The first curator, John Gordon, who would become a friend of Albert Berg, acquired Virginia Woolf's papers in 1958. He took them home with him and laid them out on the living room floor so that he and his family could have a good read through them all.

Isaac is in charge today, and he would never do such a thing. 'That was a different time,' he said. 'Today we have works, printed and manuscript, by over 400 authors, with manuscripts and letters by and to Trollope, Keats, Wordsworth, Conrad, Hardy and Yeats, and the largest collection of

Virginia Woolf and Auden papers in the world.' They even have Virginia Woolf's walking stick, which was found in the river after she had drowned herself.

The Berg Collection is still growing: 'We have the papers of Annie Proulx, Paul Auster and my favourite author, Vladimir Nabokov.' I told Isaac I'd seen Nabokov's butterfly cabinet at Harvard University, and he said, 'Oh yes, we have most of the journals he annotated and his scientific drawings of butterflies.'

I was interested to know what happens with modern authors, because surely so many first drafts are now on computer hard drives, and so many letters are sent by email. 'Paul Auster tends to type letters and fax them, and keep the faxed copy, so the library has his outgoing and incoming letters, which is unusual. For several authors we have some floppy disks containing emails, and sometimes we get printouts of emails as well'.

Everything is stored safely in the Berg vaults, except for material relating to the brothers' two favourite writers – Thackeray and Dickens – and of course the letter opener made from the paw of Dickens's beloved cat Bob.

I asked Isaac what his favourite things are? 'If the whole place were on fire and I could rescue only one item, I would probably save T. S. Eliot's typescript of *The Waste Land*, with his annotations on it, because of its monumental status in the history of English literature. I also love William Blake and if permitted a second object I'd save his *Songs of Innocence and Experience* with its beautiful watercolours – created using a technique of relief etching which he devised, he said, through instructions given to him in a vision of his dead brother. Or maybe works by Nabokov…'

[Prompt copy of *David Copperfield*]
This belonged to Charles Dickens. He used it when he gave readings of his novel. It belongs to the Berg reading room at the New York Public Library, so only researchers who come by appointment get to see it, while waiting for a book to be brought for them from the vaults.

[OBJECT 14]

the HEART TOKEN

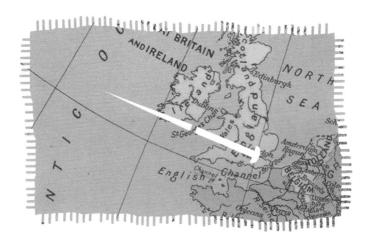

[Location]

The FOUNDLING MUSEUM
London, England

IT CONTAINED SO MUCH FEELING,

THIS PIECE of FABRIC CUT FROM THE DRESS

of the BABY being HANDED OVER

BY its MOTHER, for LIFE.

THE NIGHT THE FOUNDLING HOSPITAL opened its doors for the first time, on Wednesday, 25 March 1741 at eight o'clock, all the lamps and candles in the temporary building in Hatton Garden were blown out. The Foundling Hospital wanted the mothers who were unable to care for their babies to be able to slip unnoticed through the doors and deposit their tiny, warm bundles in secret.

By midnight the hospital was full. Many mothers were turned away. The Foundling Hospital committee minutes describe how 'on this Occasion the Expressions of Grief of the Women whose Children could Not be admitted were Scarcely more observable than those of some of the Women who parted with their Children, so that a more moving Scene can't well be imagined.' The Foundling Hospital had adopted 30 tiny foundlings; 18 baby boys and 12 tiny girls, all sleeping, feeding and squawking.

Two of the original foundlings died before they could be baptized. This was quite usual in London at a time when half of all babies born died in infancy. The first two foundlings who made it to baptism were named Thomas Coram and Eunice Coram, after the founder of the Foundling Hospital and his wife.

The Corams met in the American colonies. Thomas Coram cared for ex-soldiers and campaigned both for the rights of the Mohawk people and the rights of the daughters of colonists. When he returned to England he went to the City of London for business and saw children 'exposed, sometimes alive, sometimes dead, and sometimes dying' in the street.

[Mothers leaving their babies at the Foundling Hospital]

In the early eighteenth century, around a thousand babies a year were abandoned in the city and, sometimes, if a baby couldn't be taken care of, it would be quietly killed. Coram decided to do something about this. It took him 17 years to gather the support he needed to open the Foundling Hospital. Still running today, it is the oldest children's charity in England.

The Foundling Hospital was an instant success. Coram moved his foundlings out of Hatton Garden into a big building in Bloomsbury surrounded by rich pasture, full of green trees and fresh air.

The rich and well to do flocked to support the hospital, and artists, musicians and composers of the time lent a creative hand. Handel gave his first performance of the *Messiah* to a packed crowd in the Foundling Chapel, on an organ he had donated to it. It was such a hit he gave another performance two weeks later, and every year until he was too frail to conduct. Even then, he came and watched from a pew.

Hogarth donated paintings and encouraged other artists to do the same. The first indoor public exhibition was held at the Foundling Hospital, and it became clear that there was a public demand for art galleries. This led directly to the opening of the Royal Academy of Arts. Charity balls, charity concerts, charity albums, charity art shows – all these have their origins in the Foundling Hospital built by Thomas Coram.

Charles Dickens lived in Doughty Street, very near by. He was a fan, renting a pew in the chapel and several times referring to the hospital in his novels. In *Little Dorrit*, Tattycoram is a former foundling.

Soon, destitute mothers from across the country came to the hospital holding their own warm bundles in their arms. So many came that, before long, a lottery system was set up as a way to decide which babies could be admitted. Mothers had to draw a ball from a bag. If it was white, their baby became a foundling; if it was black, it returned home with its mother. If the mother drew a red ball, she could wait and take another turn if there was still a space for a baby at the end of the day.

When a mother left her baby she was asked to leave a token which would link her to her child, in case one day she was able to come back to claim him or her. Very often, the mother had nothing to leave so a piece of fabric was cut out of her dress, or the baby's (baby clothes were usually made from their mother's old clothes). The mother kept a fragment, and a matching fragment was attached to the registration billet that was kept for each child. The billets and tokens were stored in sealed envelopes at the Foundling Hospital. (They were found in drawers by a secretary of the hospital in the nineteenth century and bound into books, which became the archive that remains today.) It was heartbreaking to think that the children never knew of the existence of these tokens, had no idea that their mother's touch was there, hidden inside an envelope or book they would never see.

[**Foundling tokens**]
The tokens at the Foundling Hospital are said to have been a great influence on Charles Dickens when he came to write *Oliver Twist*. Unlike Oliver, the Foundling Hospital children were not given their tokens; they never knew their mother's touch was there, inside a sealed envelope or book.

The books are now in the London Metropolitan Archives, apart from one, which is in the museum itself. There are around 200 tokens on display in the Foundling Museum, mostly objects and trinkets left by mothers that would not fit inside the books, but the fabric tokens are fragile and all kept in storage.

When I visited the museum, I went behind the scenes into their archive. It is a small room on site, filled with paintings there isn't room to display and grey boxes full of things waiting to be catalogued. Few people come in here, but, the week I visited, a former foundling had been in and had unearthed a Foundling Hospital hymn book; the hospital's signature hymn was written by Handel. I was allowed to pick a grey cardboard box, lucky-dip style. Inside it I found tapestries made by girls at the Foundling Hospital, a bag belonging to Thomas Coram, and two tokens. One token was a bonnet with a heart-shaped card, the other was a handkerchief showing all the counties of England; both were carefully wrapped in tissue. These two tokens had once been on display but are now too fragile to show. The map is symbolic of the fact that the babies came from all over England and that the Foundling Hospital mission was unrestricted in access.

To see the rest of the fabric tokens, which have never been on display, I went to the London Metropolitan Archives, just behind the lively restaurant- and shop-filled Exmouth Market. I was handed several big leather-bound books containing tokens and certificates.

I put my hand on the cool leather front jacket of the first book and took a deep breath. I turned a page. I touched a piece of fabric. It contained

[Foundling No. 16515]
This is the token lovingly created
by Sarah Bender, for her son
Charles. Eight years later she
took her half of the fabric heart
and matched it to this half, in
the Foundling Hospital records,
and took her son home with her.
What a wonderful thing to see.

so much feeling, this piece of fabric cut from the dress of the baby being handed over by its mother, for life.

It was for Foundling No. 8959, a girl admitted on 19 June 1758. There is a note, which says, 'Florella Burney, born June the 19th 1758 In The Parish off St. Anns SoHo. Not Baptize'd, pray Let particulare Care be Taken'en off this Child, As it will be call'd for Again …' She was left with a linen token with black dots and red flowers on it.

I turned a page: 'Sarah Goodman, 4 months, please to deliver their child when called for …' A blue and white striped piece of fabric is pinned to the page.

I chanced upon Foundling No. 10455: 'I was born the 12th November 1758 … and baptized the 12th November 1758 by the name of Anne Irving, daughter of Thomas and Mary Beaumont.' Anne was left with a token made from a white and red patterned fabric. On the next page I saw the same fabric, belonging to Foundling No. 10456, and the same initial words: 'I was born the 12th November 1758 … and baptized on the 12th November 1758 by the name of Rebecca second Irving, daughter of Thomas and Mary Beaumont.' Twins, left together.

A baby girl was brought to the hospital on the same day as the twins. I looked at her navy blue ribbon token and turned over the piece of card on to which it was tied. It had a note written on it: 'Please to be carefull of this token as the child if living will be certainly owned, it is not christened and if it is not too great a favour beg it may be named Ann.' I hope she was both named Ann and called for again.

I had a look in the book of 1758 to see which babies had become foundlings on my birthday: Foundling No. 10670, 'a female not christened', was 'marked on the eye lids'; Foundling No. 10676, 'poor destitute infant being improvided for and having no friends it was born the 25th of this instant and is not yet baptized we request of you to name it Anne and register it in the name of Waller'. Little Anne had a note saying she had two conjoined toes on one of her feet.

There, among them all, was an unusual token, for Foundling No. 16515, a baby named Charles. His mother, Sarah Bender, made a patchwork needle case from seven pieces of fabric, and on it she stitched a heart. Above the heart, created in red thread, she stitched the initials C (for Charles) and S (for Sarah). She cut the heart in two on 11 February

1767 when she handed Charles over, with his broken-hearted token, to the Foundling Hospital. He was renamed Benjamin Twirl.

Eight years later, Benjamin was no longer a foundling. One summer's day on 10 June 1775, his mother took the cherished fabric she had held over the years when thinking about her son to the hospital, matched it to its other half and reclaimed her little boy. What a wonderful thing to see and touch, this fabric that tells the tale of how a mother got her son back and he his family.

But Benjamin/Charles was lucky. He was one of only 152 children of the 16,282 admitted between 1741 and 1760 to be reclaimed by their mothers. Disease and malnutrition meant that more than two thirds of the children admitted during those years died before their mothers were able to return.

Item
RDMSC RD 1/1/1

[Location]

ROALD DAHL MUSEUM
Great Missenden, Buckinghamshire, England

'NOBODY EVER GOES IN, NOBODY EVER COMES OUT'

Charlie and the Chocolate Factory

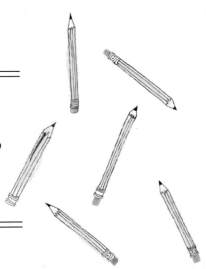

GOING BEHIND THE SCENES AT the museum devoted to the genius of Roald Dahl, I felt a little like Charlie Bucket must have felt, clutching his golden ticket as he walked through the wrought-iron gates of the factory belonging to confectionary wizard Willy Wonka.

Famously, Roald Dahl wrote in a writing hut, which he called his 'nest' or 'womb', in the garden of his home, Gypsy House, in Great Missenden, a pretty village in Buckinghamshire. Every morning, Dahl would wander out of his house, across the garden, and go through a yellow door into his hut. Inside, he had everything just the way he liked it. He sat in a wingback chair, which had been his mother's and placed a specially made writing table covered in a green billiard-table cover over his knees, just so.

He had a heater taped to the ceiling in the winter and covered the windows throughout the year – one with a shower curtain, the other with curtains in a fabric covered in blackbirds. On the walls he taped letters from his family and other things he loved. On a low table to his right he kept curious objects – a metallic ball made up of crushed silver chocolate-wrapping paper, a cuneiform tablet and his own invention, the 'Wade-Dahl-Till' (or WDT) valve.

When Dahl was living in New York, his son, Theo, was out in his pram, being pushed along by his nanny, when a taxi hit him. 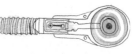 His skull was shattered and he started to go blind because of fluid on his brain. Dahl contacted Stanley Wade, a hydraulic engineer and Kenneth Till, a neurosurgeon. Dahl loved knowing what made things tick, had experienced brain injury first hand, and he imagined that, as a

threesome, they could come up with something truly brilliant. The trio invented the WDT valve to help Dahl's son recover. Three thousand children around the world were helped by their invention.

Also on the table, right beside his chair, he kept a mug containing six trusty yellow HB pencils and, above them, stuck to the wall, an electric pencil sharpener. He wrote with the pencils each day, on yellow A4 paper imported from America. As he wrote, Dahl stored everything – letters, notebooks, first, second and third drafts – in order, neatly tucked away inside his hut.

When the Roald Dahl Museum opened in the village just down the road from Dahl's house, all of these letters, notebooks and drafts of stories were moved to the museum. They are kept under lock and key in a small room, next to the museum archivist's desk. I went to have a look.

To get to the archive I went up some stairs leading off the courtyard of the museum. As the archivist unlocked the door, I looked out of the window of her office, down into a room of the museum below. It was filled with giggling children, and images of Dahl's creations.

We stepped inside the room, filled with row upon row of grey boxes. Inside each box are piles of letters, photographs and drafts of stories, in which each of these creations was brought to life, with HB pencil, on that imported yellow paper.

The seeds of some ideas live in the pages of Dahl's notebooks, two of which I saw. Each one is red, with the word 'Masterpiece' embossed on the cover. The books are filled with one- or two-line pencil scribbles: 'a pale grey face like a bowl of porridge', 'a woman with one large muscular calf. What does this denote?' and 'man in bathtub using kite to channel electricity'. Each thought shimmers with potential.

Some stayed in the notebook, while others were developed into stories, for instance, *The BFG*. I saw the moment Dahl thought of the character: he wrote the letters of the giant's name in one of the notebooks and circled them. Indeed *Matilda* had been in his ideas book for 20 years before he began to write about her.

Each story took a while to get right. In an early draft of *Charlie and the Chocolate Factory*, the Oompa Loompas were called Whipple-scrumpets. At first the BFG befriends a boy named Jody, rather than a tiny girl named Sophie who saw the giant at her window, catching dreams.

I pulled down the *Matilda* box because I was curious to see how that tale had evolved. I read through Draft 1. The story was called 'The Miracle Child', and Chapter 1 was called 'Wickedness'. In this first version, handwritten by Dahl in 1986, 'Matilda was born wicked and she stayed wicked no matter how hard her parents tried to make her good. She was just about the most wicked child in the world.'

Matilda plays the same tricks on her parents as she does in the published version, but her motivation is different: in the final draft she is trying to get her own back on her parents, who couldn't give a stuff about her, whereas in the original draft she did these things simply because she was 'wicked'.

The first draft is pretty short. There is hardly any mention of Miss Trunchball; Miss Honey is called Miss Hayes; and, at the end, Matilda dies. She discovers her magical powers – being able to move things with her eyes – in a class at school, and goes over to Miss Hayes's house to investigate her new skills. On the way home to Matilda's, she and her teacher see a car accident. Some children are trapped in a mini-bus, underneath a truck. With no time to lose Matilda lifts the truck off the mini-bus, using only the power of her eyes, and frees the trapped children. And then, exhausted from the effort, she dies.

It's not the story of the unloved, imaginative girl rescued by an understanding adult that everyone loves today, and has a totally different ending. It took Roald Dahl ages to get the story he wanted to tell to come out right. He handed each draft of yellow papers to his secretary, Wendy. Then he'd annotate her typed pages and carry on. It wasn't until Draft 6 that he was satisfied with *Matilda*. Perfection was a long process.

I wanted to know what the first item in the archive was, so I had a look and found a letter marked by the archivist as RDMSC RD 1/1/1. The letter is the first item in Dahl's 'Personal' file. It was written by a New York literary agent, named Harold Matson, to Miss Katherine Swan, who was the writer C. S. Forester's secretary. The letter tells an interesting story: the story of how Dahl became a writer.

The first story Roald Dahl ever wrote was a true one – which he embellished, with his nascent storytelling skills – about his time in the RAF in the 1940s. He was sent on a mission from Egypt to Libya. He hadn't had much training, and on the final leg of the trip he crash-

[*Matilda*, the musical]
The first draft of Matilda, which I read at the museum, is a totally different story to the one everyone knows and loves today.

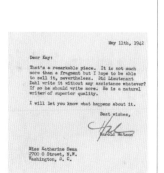

landed in the desert because he couldn't see a runway, and was running out of fuel. He fractured his skull and nose and was unable to see. Luckily, a pilot called Peter had seen the plane coming down into the desert and rushed to the wreck to pull Dahl's body out. Dahl carried on flying, but after severe headaches, a blackout and some time recovering in England he was transferred to an office job in Washington as an assistant air attaché. On the first day of his new job, he was sitting at his desk wondering what on earth he was supposed to be doing when the writer C. S. Forester came in and asked him if he had any good stories about the war. America had just joined the Allies and the public was hungry to hear stories of heroic deeds.

Dahl and he got chatting, and Forester invited him out for lunch. They were so busy talking and eating that Forester forgot to take notes and so he asked Dahl if he would mind sending over some anecdotes about his crash in Libya, which Forester could then shape into a story. Dahl did so, but he wrote the story out in full. Forester thought the tale was brilliantly written and replied to Dahl with the life-changing question: 'Did you know you were a writer?'

Forester sent the piece to his agent, Harold Matson, who then wrote this letter to Katherine Swan asking: 'Did Lt. Dahl write it without any assistance whatever? If so, he should write more. He is a natural writer of superior quality.' No wonder the letter is stored first in Dahl's archives. I imagine it changed his life.

The second letter in the archives is Dahl's reply to Matson, asking whether he'd like a piece about Greece. He asked to remain anonymous if his first story was published, as members of the RAF were not allowed to publish tales of the war. He also requested that if his writing was going to be illustrated, that the drawings of his plane be accurate. The next letter in the file is a reply from Matson saying that there was no problem about either anonymity or illustrations, and he had some good news: he'd sold the piece for £300.

It was published verbatim in August 1942 in the *Saturday Evening Post*. Dahl had called the story 'A Piece of Cake', but it was changed to 'Shot Down over Libya' to sound more dramatic. Dahl had changed details of the original story: being shot down made a better story than running out

[Item 1/1/1]
I held it in my hand: the very letter that set Dahl on the path to being one of the world's best-loved writers.

of fuel. Already Dahl's love of exaggeration for the sake of a good story shone through. He continued to write, and Matson became his agent. Dahl told the whole story himself in 'Lucky Break'.

Over his career Dahl wrote two novels, 19 short story collections, six film scripts, some television shows and a play. However, it was not until he moved to Buckinghamshire, asked a man named Wally Saunders (said to be the inspiration for the BFG) to build his hut and began writing fantastical children's stories that his career really took off. How lucky that Forester popped in to meet Dahl, and Matson wrote this letter, number 1 in the archives, that set the wheel of stories, letters and ideas in motion.

His children's stories are still loved by children of all ages. On my way from London to Buckinghamshire to visit the museum, I stopped for petrol. The Indian man at the till asked me:

'Going anywhere nice today?'
I told him, 'I'm going to the Roald Dahl Museum.'
'Oh,' he said, perking up. 'I love that guy! I love his stories.'
'So do I,' I said. 'Which is your favourite?'
'Oh, the one with the boy who puts white powder in the drink.'
'*George's Marvellous Medicine?*'
'That's the one,' he said, lifting his hands to the heavens and laughing. 'That one could have me giggling all day.'

Auguste Piccard's
BALLOON GONDOLA

[Location]

**The Science Museum's Large Object Store
Wroughton, Wiltshire, England**

ONE THING STICKS OUT
LIKE a BIG WHITE THUMB

in the SCIENCE MUSEUM'S LARGE OBJECT STORE.

IT'S a HUGE METAL BALL with a TRAPDOOR:

PICCARD'S GONDOLA.

AUGUSTE PICCARD (1884–1962) WAS AN eccentric Belgian scientist. He was fascinated by the stratosphere – the layer of the atmosphere that begins 16 kilometres above where you are sitting now – and made this gondola to take him there. Using it like the basket of a hot air balloon, he attached it to a balloon filled with hydrogen and floated up miles into the sky. It's amazing to stand in front of it and imagine Piccard climbing inside, shutting the door over his head and taking off.

Like many of the Science Museum's large objects, Piccard's gondola is stored in one of several aircraft hangars on an ex-RAF airfield in Wroughton, Wiltshire. It shares its berth with planes, including a Lockheed Constellation aircraft used to transport roadies and equipment on a Rolling Stones concert tour, and a very sleek plane designed by Burt Rutan (who also designed *Voyager* – the first plane to fly around the world without stopping for refuelling – as well as a hybrid flying car and space craft for Virgin Galactic). But the gondola has been higher than any of the aircraft in the hangars in Wroughton.

Piccard made his first trip to the stratosphere in 1931. He broke a world record for the highest any man had ever been and then crash-landed in Obergurgl, a little alpine town of 14 farms which, after a lifetime of sleepy obscurity, became known internationally when Piccard

[Auguste Piccard (1884–1962)]
The classic eccentric 'man of science', Piccard was the inspiration for Professor Cuthbert Calculus, who appears in many of the *Tintin* stories.

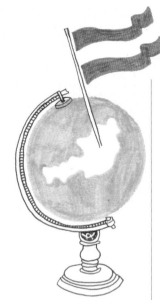

[Lift off]
Piccard sets off in his gondola
for his daring and romantic
scientific adventure.

accidentally arrived. This gondola in the Science Museum's behind-the-scenes collection was used for Piccard's second journey to the strato-sphere, when he reached 16,201 metres. He and his assistant took off one summer's day in 1932, from just outside Zurich. The launch was filmed by a news team from Pathé and released under the title '10½ Miles Above the Earth! Professor Piccard and Dr Cosyns, safe & sound after world's most daring & romantic scientific adventure'. In those days, science and adventure were still deemed to be 'romantic'.

The newsreader says, in his old-fashioned broadcasting style, 'The start was made at dawn from Dübendorf aerodrome near Zurich. The prepara-tions for the flight began at midnight. And thousands of people had made the journey from Zurich in special trains, whilst a battalion of Swiss troops held down the guy ropes.' He continues: 'When all was ready he clambered inside the gondola, which contained a mass of scientific instru-ments, and gave the signal to let go. The balloon rose quickly and even-tually climbed to over 10½ miles above earth. Just imagine – whilst we were sweltering in a heatwave, he was nearly frozen to death in 15 degrees Centigrade below zero.' He ends: 'From the practical point of view, Pro-fessor Piccard's experiment is of the highest scientific importance. One of the things it will definitely do will be to enable better weather forecasts to be made, and won't that be a boon when we are picking out our holidays!'

Watch the film online if you'd like to see Piccard leaning out of the gondola, waving goodbye with his hat in his hand. 'Off we go into ze stratosphere,' he seems to be saying (moustache blowing in ze wind).

Piccard was a funny-looking man. He had a bald head, with tufts of hair on each side, wore round glasses and, usually, a lab coat. When Hergé, the creator of *Tintin*, saw Piccard on the street, he recognized him as the classic eccentric 'man of science' and was inspired to create Professor Cuthbert Calculus, who appears in many of the *Tintin* stories: 'Calculus is a reduced-scale Piccard, as the real chap was very tall. He had an interminable neck that sprouted from a collar that was much too large ... I made Calculus a mini-Piccard, otherwise I would have had to enlarge the frames of the cartoon strip.'

Piccard loved adventure and believed that 'exploration is the sport of the scientist.' He practised this sport all his life and made 27 stratospheric ascents in total, reaching a top height of 21,946 metres. His balloon trips were useful as well as daring. He brought back information about the stratosphere, where no one had ever been, provided data that helped lead up to the first space flights and proved that it was possible for a human to survive at such an altitude (there had been several fatal attempts before). He researched cosmic rays about which nothing was known at the time. His gondola design and his balloon innovations (he used just a little hydrogen in the balloon on the ground, which expanded as he ascended) helped balloonists cross the Atlantic and Pacific oceans. He also contributed significantly to weather forecasting. Every day, balloons are sent into high altitudes to monitor atmospheric conditions and help predict the weather. Nowadays, they go unmanned, without a zany scientist inside.

[Piccard's gondola]
Piccard and his assistant tied this white gondola onto a balloon, climbed inside, shut the door, and headed upwards, towards the stratosphere.

It was not only heights that Piccard soared to: he helped set the world record for the deepest anyone has ever been down into the ocean. Jacques Piccard, his son (with his father's help), adapted the gondola design so it worked in the water. He called it a bathyscaphe, which means 'deep ship' in Ancient Greek. Inside one named the *Trieste*, Jacques travelled with Don Walsh to the deepest spot known on Earth, the bottom of the Challenger Deep in the Mariana Trench. This was in 1960. It took them 4 hours and 48 minutes to get down there. They ate chocolate as they descended through the still, clear water until they reached the bottom, where they measured the depth as 10,916 metres. They all but landed on a fish. Piccard said, 'Our fish was the instantaneous reply (after years of work!) to a question that thousands of oceanographers had been asking themselves for decades.' Later on, they saw a shrimp.

Until March 2012, they were the only humans ever to have made it so far down into the ocean. Then James Cameron made world headlines when he followed in the twosome's bubbles – Don Walsh was there to see him off – and dropped down, alone, into the abyss.

National Geographic streamed live news online, news stations covered the story, and he and his wife tweeted. She tweeted his last words to her: 'Bye, baby … See you in the sunshine,' and how a rainbow appeared over the spot where her husband had descended. Everyone wondered, will he make it? He wrote a list of things that could go wrong that was posted on the *National Geographic* website; it included being 'smashed into jam' should his pilot sphere implode. On the same webpage, it says that Don

Walsh had pointed out the risks of 'flying a research sub too close to a hydrothermal vent' where the water temperature is around 400°C (752°F) and would melt the sub's viewpoint.

As we know, James Cameron made it there and back with no problems, and described it as 'a very lunar, very desolate place', a 'completely alien world'. The next evening, he was at the London première of the 3D version of *Titanic*. 'Oh yeah! I am also that guy that does the red carpet stuff,' he said to the BBC's reporter. He filmed the deep-sea dive for a 3D movie release and broke a record for it being the deepest solo dive ever. He went far further than his earlier dives down to the sunken *Titanic*, but I don't think he got further down than Piccard.

Cameron talked to Don Walsh, who was there when he resurfaced, about the record: 'There's no way of measuring it super-accurately. You can bounce a laser off the moon and know within a couple of centimetres how far away the moon is, but you'll never know how deep the ocean is, because you're measuring waves, the sound through seawater, the changes in temperature and salinity. The error margin is tens of metres. I said, "Let's just share it." We shook on that.'

There is a younger Piccard who is carrying on the adventuring tradition. Auguste's grandson Bertrand Piccard has been around the earth in a balloon (1999) and is currently planning to circumnavigate the globe using only solar power to demonstrate the potential of renewable energy. The main challenge is gathering enough sunlight as he flies by day to last him through the night.

As well as the gondola, the behind-the-scenes warehouses contain thousands of scientific treasures, including one of the earliest UK cash machines; a submarine, like the one in *For Your Eyes Only*; the Channel Tunnel tunnelling machine; the world's first full-size hovercraft; an electric taxi from 1897; a hundred-year-old lump of reinforced concrete; and a Soviet supercomputer called the BESM-6 that was cutting-edge technology during the Cold War but now looks like a collection of blue wardrobes. The objects are spread out between aircraft hangars.

Peter Turvey, the curator of Wroughton's store, took me to see them all. We zipped around between hangars in his jeep, driving along the runway. The heaviest item we saw was the Wood Press. It weighs 127 kilograms and is part of the last printing press used in Fleet Street. It spewed out 50,000 newspapers an hour until 1987. In 1999, industrial archaeologists spent four months taking it apart and five more rebuilding it on site. Beside it, some of the things that were found inside the machine are on display, such as empty beans tins and shoes.

Piccard's gondola shares a hangar with Peter Turvey's favourite object: a tandem where the two riders sit side by side and cycle at the same time. Unsurprisingly – and unlike Piccard's – this is one prototype that didn't take off.

[Tandem bicycle]
The curator of Wroughton's collection has a favourite item: a tandem where the two riders sit side by side and cycle at the same time. It never really took off as an idea.

JASON JUNIOR

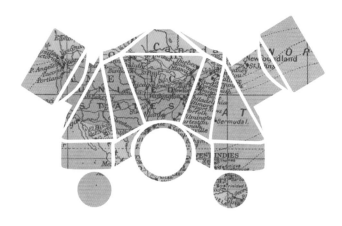

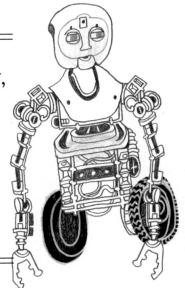

MUCH OF THE TECHNOLOGY WE USE EACH DAY,
WITHOUT THINKING ABOUT IT,
is powered by oil, a lot of which comes from
DEPOSITS FOUND BELOW THE SEABED,
WITH THE HELP OF ROBOTS.

THE FIRST THING TO SET 'eyes' on the *Titanic*, 74 years after it crashed into an iceberg in 1921 and sank to the bottom of the ocean, was a blue robot the size of a lawnmower. Its name was Jason Junior, or JJ.

JJ is a small Remotely Operated Vehicle (ROV), also known as a flying eyeball. Attached to a submersible called Alvin by an umbilical cord which transmits data, Jason Junior was dropped to 3,660 metres below sea level. It moved into the wreck and descended four levels down the grand staircase into the interior of the ship, sending back haunting images of the promenade deck and a room with a chandelier, still intact after years underwater. Robert Ballard, the leader of the undersea mission, said it 'was like landing on the moon'.

Ballard's dream of exploring the *Titanic* was made possible by investment from the US Navy. They wanted to investigate the location and state of two sunken naval submarines, USS *Thresher* and *Scorpion*. Ballard was the man for the job, and he agreed to do it in return for permission to use the same technology to look around the *Titanic*.

Jason Junior now lives at the MIT Museum. But it's also underneath 2,745 metres of water off the South American coast. When engineers at Woods Hole Oceanographic Institution (WHOI) constructed it, they made several copies of each part so that JJ could be reconfigured for its different missions. After looking around the *Titanic* and the sunken submarines,

[Jason Junior]
JJ is a small Remotely Operated Vehicle (ROV), also known as a flying eyeball. Attached to a submersible called Alvin by an umbilical cord that transmits data, JJ was dropped to 3,660 metres below sea level.

[JJ exploring the *Titanic*]
Jason was the first to set 'eyes' on the *Titanic*, which had sunk 73 years before. The ROV sent images of the ship back up to the surface.

JJ was adapted for other expeditions and taken on a mission by WHOI. While out at sea, the barge carrying it sank and JJ disappeared.

I spoke to Kurt Hasselbalch, curator of the Hart Nautical Collections at the MIT Museum, who knows all about JJ. The Jason Junior kept in the museum's stores is made from the only surviving parts of the JJ left above the ocean. 'We had WHOI recreate a display version of Jason Junior out of the original frame and body, and a few original parts,' explained Kurt. It sits, inactive, on a shelf, among all kinds of inventions and innovations. It's not on display, because there are 400,000 objects in the nautical section of the museum alone and there really isn't room to display everything at one time. Most objects are kept as a 3D reference library of ideas and inventions.

As for the sunken version of JJ, it may yet be recovered. 'We're waiting for someone to say "Hey! Let's go get it." It'll probably be James Cameron …'

I imagine the director of the blockbuster film *Titanic* would be a good person for the job. He has sent remote cameras into the *Titanic* to get footage of the interior, and used footage of an ROV exploring the wreck for the opening sequence of his film. More recently, in 2012, he went down into the Mariana Trench, on the day before *Titanic* 3D premiered in London.

Kurt explained that the tale of Jason Junior is part of a bigger story about naval technology. The navies of the world have state-of-the-art equipment: 'We don't even know exactly what they do have,' he said, but their ideas, and their investment in new technologies, filter into the world of science and industry and all come massively to affect our world.

Undersea exploration is crucial to so much of modern life but, because it's invisible, we who live on the surface of the Earth tend not to think about it too much. The ocean is used all the time for transportation of goods (this book, for example, was printed in China then shipped to bookshops) and that is the most obvious and visible trading that goes on in the maritime world. Yet the things you can't see have just as much impact on our daily life.

If you're reading these words digitally, the files will have been sent though undersea fibre optic cables. Every time you make a phone call or send an email, the information probably passed under the sea. Much of the technology we use each day is powered by oil, a lot of which comes from deposits found below the seabed, with the help of robots.

[Submarine fibre optic cables]
Every time you make a phone call or send an email, the information probably passes under the sea.

These robots are also doing vital work collecting data. The ocean is still the least known environmental region on earth, but there are countless robots exploring it under the sea right now. Kurt explained, 'Space gets all the attention, but there is a huge robotic presence in the ocean.' This presence is likely to increase. 'Twenty-five years from now you may well be able to rent time on a system to go down and take a look at the ocean depths. Personal submarines will be cheaper to buy than a private jet.'

I thought it might be a little weird if the ocean were full of people bobbing about in private subs, but Kurt reminded me: 'The ocean takes up 75 per cent of the surface of Earth. Essentially, when you're in a sub, you're flying in a vast, open space. Even if we had as many subs in the ocean as we do cars on the surface of the Earth, the chances of meeting anyone else on your underwater travels would be less than running into someone in the Sahara.'

Undersea navigation is a big technological challenge. You can't use GPS underwater, only acoustic signals – most marine mammals use acoustics for navigation and communication, but we're not as skilful as marine mammals yet; we have a lot to learn. Acoustic signals are used to find oil, to locate long-lost shipwrecks, to image the ocean bottom and to help find lost objects.

'So far, we can only use a really small bandwidth,' Kurt explained, 'so we can only send a small amount of information. It's not yet possible to send high-definition video; we still need fibre optics for robots like ROVs to achieve high-quality imaging of the deep ocean – sometimes robots go down with 80 kilometres of cable attached to them, along which they send back photographs and videos.' It's still done in the same way that JJ sent images of the *Titanic* back to Alvin. Imagine if the ROVs currently roaming around photographing Mars needed a cable to send images back to Earth. That would be one long, long cable.

Jason Junior was made with the help of lots of MIT graduates. The same goes for a lot of other things inside the museum archive. I went to check out MIT's Media Lab, where lots of zany people are working on exciting, cutting-edge ideas. I peered into a room containing a huge 3D printer, which is used to print out objects, and upstairs I saw two robots, called Leonardo and Nexi.

[Nexi]
I met Nexi, a big-blue-eyed
robot, in the Media Lab at MIT.

Leonardo was made by MIT in collaboration with Stan Winston Studios, which made movies such as *The Terminator, Aliens, Predator, Edward Scissorhands* and *Jurassic Park*. Leonardo has huge brown eyes and big rabbit-like ears. He's super-expressive. When the MIT designers introduced him to a puppet of the Cookie Monster, they told him the monster was bad, and Leonardo put up his hands in defence. He has retired now, and will probably end up in the museum in the future.

Even more personable is Nexi, a white robot with huge blue eyes. She raises her eyebrows in surprise, slants them in anger and can hear through her ears (they're microphones). She looks like a robot you could really chat to and people who see her for the first time react to her as if she were human. As with the far less human JJ, the Navy funded Nexi's development, via a research award. She is still being worked on in the Media Lab but, some day, technology will supersede her, and she may end up in the museum collection with Jason Junior.

I listened to a TED (Technology, Education, Design) lecture by Cynthia Breazeal who is director of the Personal Robots Lab at MIT. She talked about new kinds of applications for robots. She thinks they can be used for communication. 'Imagine this …' she said. 'What about a robot accessory for your cell phone? You call your friend, she puts her hand into a robot and bam! You're a mebot. You can make eye contact, you can talk to your friend, you can gesture … maybe the next best thing to really being there.' She continued by pointing out that families who are living far apart often talk on Skype. In her experience that way of interacting doesn't work well for children, because they want to play rather than talk. She said she could imagine a day when her mum could become a 'grandmabot' and play with her grandson, even though they live thousands of miles away from one another. She and her team at the MIT have also trialled robotic personal trainers, in the MIT lab and in the Boston area. Most people who tried the robots rated the quality of the robot's advice highly and said they trusted them. Many people dressed, named and talked to their robot.

I loved seeing the robots, but I wasn't so sure I'd want one in my house. When I left MIT, I went next door, to Toscanini Ice Cream, which is famous in Cambridge, Massachusetts. There, I ate the most delicious ice cream. One day, perhaps, expressive robots with big blue eyes will be able to make ice cream like this. I'd be so impressed.

[OBJECT 18]

UNDERWATER PAINTING
by Zarh Pritchard

[Location]

MUSÉE OCÉANOGRAPHIQUE de MONACO
Monaco

At the time, **VERY FEW PEOPLE HAD SEEN**
the COLOURS and CORALS
BENEATH the OCEAN FIRST HAND.
THIS WAS the BLUE PLANET
FOOTAGE OF ITS TIME.

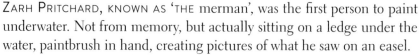

ZARH PRITCHARD, KNOWN AS 'THE merman', was the first person to paint underwater. Not from memory, but actually sitting on a ledge under the water, paintbrush in hand, creating pictures of what he saw on an easel.

He was born in 1866 in Madras, India, and was named Walter. In 1909, he changed his named to Zarh. He said this was because there were other men called Walter Pritchard and he kept getting their letters: 'One was a drunkard, another was a man who never paid his bills, and a third was constantly running away from his wife. It was this last Pritchard who determined me to change my name. I received a letter from his wife. She begged me to return to her, saying that the daughter, Mary, had grown into a fine, tall, good-looking woman. So I changed my name to Zarh, which is Persian for light.'

Which makes it all the more fitting that Zarh made a niche for himself painting a special, dancing light; the magical, shimmering light of the underwater world.

He began in the Firth of Forth, Scotland. He put on homemade swimming goggles, dived into the water and took a 'photograph' in his mind, observing the new colours and tints beneath the waves, and then ran ashore to paint the memory in his sketchbook. Each drawing took 30 or 40 dives to complete. He must have got pretty cold running back and forth, in and out of the water, to swim, then out again to paint, shivering away in his towel.

For the next 14 years he worked making costumes – for Sarah Bernhardt, among others – and spent a stint in New Zealand on a sheep run at Hawkes Bay, painting landscapes. Here, a local chief taught him how to paint underwater: the secret is to make a canvas from leather soaked in linseed, then it will hold the paint.

Then, he came down with pneumonia. His doctor prescribed a trip to Egypt, for the sunshine. Zarh decided to go instead to California, and then Tahiti. It was on this magical island that he found his true calling.

It was all the result of a drunken bet. At a dinner party, he met the brother of the last Queen of Tahiti, Narii Salmon. After many drinks, Salmon bet Pritchard that he wouldn't be able to paint a canvas while underwater. Pritchard bet him $500 that he could, so long as Narii would lend him his boat and his so-called 'diving suit', the only one on the island.

The two set off to see who would win the bet. Pritchard dropped into the ocean wearing the diving suit (essentially a diving helmet attached to a sou'wester, waterproofed with the sap of a breadfruit tree). Narii had his crew play a trick on Zarh, and they took him to the top of a 180-metre deep wall in the coral reef. He drifted at 23 metres until he found a shelf at 9 metres on which he could perch and paint. When he was ready, he tugged on a cord, signalling for the crew to send down his painting materials.

As Zarh painted in the silence of the underwater realm, watching out for shark and octopus, he created the first painting ever made underwater. His canvas was soaked in linseed and he stored his paints in a belt, each tube marked with a daub of its own colour, because he realized that the water would soon wash away their labels. Narii Salmon swam down to check on him at one point, wearing only a loincloth. He was grinning and didn't mind losing his bet. Zarh's painting was beautiful, capturing the twirling light of the sea.

Narii insisted on taking Zarh on as many trips as he wanted, showing him the reefs of Tahiti, lending the artistic merman his diving suit. Zarh was thrilled by the silence beneath the surface, watching creatures that

[Zarh at work]
He would paint on the floor of the ocean for half an hour and then come up to the surface to thaw out in the sunshine.

[Jacques Cousteau (1910–97)]
Cousteau was curator of the
museum in Monaco for years.
He co-developed the aqua-lung
(scuba diving kit) and pioneered
marine conservation.

had never seen a human before and bringing them back to the surface for all to see. He would paint for half an hour, then come up to get warm in the sunshine. He could leave his easel on the seafloor overnight if he wanted to, as there are few currents in the coral reef of Tahiti.

Once each painting was complete, Zarh carried it to the surface and added a powder to mimic the veil that covered everything he saw beneath the waves. He said, 'It is a dream world in which everything is enveloped in soft sheen. On reaching the bottom, it is as if one were temporarily resting on a dissolving fragment of some far planet.'

When Zarh had completed a set of around 50 canvases, he held an exhibition in San Francisco. They were all destroyed in a fire during the San Francisco earthquake of 1906. Zarh painted more, and sold his work to royalty and ocean lovers all over the world.

One admirer was Albert I of Monaco, who founded the Oceano-graphic Museum which sits, like a temple to the sea, on the edge of a cliff, above the glittering Mediterranean. Albert loved the ocean. He built the museum to celebrate the sea and encourage marine exploration. He went on trips with scientists to the Azores and Svalbard to collect species for his beloved museum, he drew up maps and he explored. In its heyday, the museum was the place to be if you were a marine scientist. Jacques Cousteau was director here for many years. It was he who took down Zarh Pritchard's paintings and put them in storage, when he modernized the museum in the 1960s.

There they remain, above the office of the curator of art. She took me to see them. We climbed up a staircase into a small attic room lined with paintings and pulled out the five Pritchards. Each one had been created underwater, some in Tahiti, some in the depths of a loch in Scotland.

The paintings have a smooth, dreamy, otherworldly feel to them. Like most people, I've marvelled over the amazing BBC series *Blue Planet*, and I've also been lucky enough to scuba dive with sharks, turtles and shimmering fish. Now we can all buy goggles and masks in seaside shops and look for our-selves at the ocean. But during Zarh's lifetime, this was all still to come. When he started painting, what lay beneath the surface of the ocean was a mystery. Prince Albert I collected his pictures

because they were pioneering studies of the world beneath the waves. At the time, very few people had seen the colours and corals beneath the ocean first hand. This was the *Blue Planet* footage of its time.

The first black and white photographs of the ocean were being taken, and the first films created, but Zarh's paintings were the first of their kind – paintings created under the sea. They brought secret images from the ocean floor up above the waves. Moreover, he painted them for art's sake, not for any other reason, just for the pleasure of creation.

No wonder then that Albert, Prince of Monaco, snapped up some of Zarh's paintings for his museum. He bought two of the paintings now in storage from an exhibition in Paris. The *Illustrated London News* wrote about the show in an article printed on 21 January 1922. The piece has an illustration of Zarh 'painting a picture 50 feet underwater' and it tells how Prince Albert of Monaco, 'whose interest in oceanography is well known', bought some paintings.

The article shows two of the paintings in black and white. It was a far richer experience seeing them in the archive in full, dreamy colour. In both, orange fish swim across the image. Zarh said he never painted if there were no small fishes around, for 'that is a sure sign of danger': sharks must be nearby.

The painting I like best is of coral statues in the lagoon of Maraa, in Tahiti. Zarh painted it while submerged in the lagoon, watching out for jellyfish. On 4 July 1925, after Prince Albert's death, Zarh was in Rio de Janeiro and decided to donate the painting to his patron. He wrote on the back of the painting that it was a gift to Albert I, from 'a sincere admirer of his great character and work'. I like this one because it was a gift to the museum and to its patron, and because it was created in Tahiti, where Zarh won the life-changing bet.

In 1950, when Zarh was 85 years old, he lived in Austin, Texas, the neighbour of Peggy Sparks and her two-year-old son. He would invite the two of them over for tea and homemade cookies and show them his underwater paintings. Peggy recalls he was particularly happy that his work had appeared in *National Geographic* and he told her he had painted a scene for the Emperor of Japan's aquarium.

[*Pillars of Basalt*, west coast of Scotland]
Zarh wrote a description of this painting – which I saw in storage at the museum – on the back: 'The rays of sunlight pass between columns of basalt into the dimly-lit undersea world'.

The elderly artist had a great impact on Peggy, who later painted por-traits, restored paintings and took up underwater synchronized swimming.
    Zarh even taught his neighbours how best to look at his paintings. Close one of your eyes and with the other look through a hole made by your fist. If you do it right, this will make it look as if the water in the undersea painting is moving. It worked for Peggy. See if it works for you. I asked the art curator and she said, 'It might … after a couple of drinks!'

[*Massif de coraux dans le lagon de Maraa*]
My favourite painting by Zarh Pritchard.

[OBJECT 19]

ANGLERFISH COUPLE

[Location]

THE SPIRIT BUILDING at the **NATURAL HISTORY MUSEUM,**
London, England

THE MALE DIDN'T HAVE MUCH of a LIFE.

HE HATCHED FROM
a SHEET of EGGS.

He used his superb smelling abilities to sniff out

THIS FEMALE and CHOMP into HER BOTTOM.

THEN HIS LIFE'S MISSION WAS ACCOMPLISHED.

[The happy couple]
How many fish can you see in this photo? The female is the big one, and her boyfriend, the worst boyfriend in nature, is hanging onto her bottom. You can see him if you trace a line from her jaw, downwards, to her backside.

HOW MANY FISH CAN YOU see in the photo on this page? Believe it or not, there are two, one of each sex. The female is the big one, and her boyfriend, the little one, is hanging on to her bottom. Trace a line from the female's jaw downwards to her backside, and there he is.

This happy couple lives in a glass jar on the third floor of part of the Darwin Centre known as the Spirit Building, behind the main Natural History Museum in London. They're rarely on display because they are one of only three complete anglerfish couples the museum owns and they need to be easily available to research scientists. If they were out on display in the main museum it would be difficult to access them when they were required.

This specimen (*Linophryne brevibarbata*) was collected in 1973 in the eastern central Atlantic. It came to the museum in 1995 and since then has been examined many times by researchers. This couple came out of hiding for the Sexual Nature exhibition in 2011, but now they are back in storage.

The male didn't have much of a life. He hatched from a sheet of eggs. He used his superb smelling abilities to sniff out this female and chomp into her bottom. Then his life's mission was accomplished. All he did,

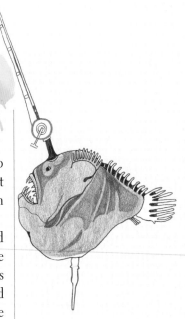

from that point onwards, was squirt sperm whenever it was needed. He spent the rest of his existence as a tiny parasite, living off the nutrients in the female's bloodstream, incapable of independent life.

He is not quite as stupid as he sounds: this is clever evolution. When the female is ready to spawn, she has a mate right there ready to do his job; hormones in her bloodstream tell him when it's time. Without this bizarre arrangement, the female might not be able to find a mate in the vastness of the sea.

There are 322 known species of anglerfish, living in both deep and shallow water. The male of one species (*Photocorynus spiniceps*) is the smallest vertebrate in the world (6.2 millimetres in length; the females average around 50 millimetres). Interestingly, some females get lumbered with more than one tiny male. The record number of males on a single female is eight, found on a specimen collected in 2000 off Japan.

This female has tentacles on her underside called barbels, but it's not clear what they are for. They do light up, so perhaps they could be used for attracting prey, or maybe they are landing lights for the laziest male in nature. The fish curators at the museum, Ollie Crimmen and James Maclaine, who showed me the star-crossed lovers in their glass jar, still don't know.

They held the jar up to the light so that I could peer in and have a good look at the tiny male. They pointed out the esca (from the Latin for 'food'), the fleshy growth on the female's head. This is where the anglerfish gets its name. The esca is attached to the end of a finray, which is used like a fishing rod and, in deep-sea species of anglerfish, it lights up, as a lure to attract prey. When this female was alive, if something edible approached her esca, then she would suck it in by opening her huge mouth, which is lined with needle-like teeth, and swallow it.

A lot of deep-sea anglerfish prey is bioluminescent, so the anglerfish have black-lined stomachs to stop their insides from glowing after lunch and distracting their next victim. Often the stomach is elasticated, so they can ingest animals bigger than themselves.

[The tank room]
There are countless treasures in the fish collection. Ollie and James add fish to the collection all the time.

This particular anglerfish pair is one of 22 million specimens looked after by the Natural History Museum. What about the two other pairs of anglerfish in amongst all those? One couple are a species called

[**Archie the giant squid**]
Archie, shortly after she arrived at the Natural History Museum. Now she is in a specially made tank that was built by the same people who made the tanks for artist Damien Hirst's shark.

Ceratias holboelli; they sound horrible, and they look it. They live in the tank room beside another, smaller female specimen which was found inside the stomach of a sperm whale. The second couple are of a species called *Malanocetus johnsonii*, otherwise known as the black sea devil. The female is a little monster, the size of a baked potato, with super-sharp teeth; her male is clamped on to her underside.

As well as the anglerfish James and Ollie care for are around 800,000 other fish. The collection is used like a reference library, so scientists can keep tabs on what we already know, and use that as a basis for new discoveries. Some fish are being wiped out before they've been scientifically described. Most of the specimens are in Victorian glass jars filled with alcohol for preservation (the spirit collection), stuffed, or skeletons (the dry collection). They're kept on miles of shelves heaving with specimens, from microbes to the colossal squid (*Mesonychoteuthis hamiltoni*). The largest ones are in tanks in the tank room, in the basement. James and Ollie took me down there in the lift and pushed open the heavy grey doors that seal the room off from the rest of the museum.

Archie, the giant squid (short for the scientific name *Architeuthis dux*), caught off the coast of the Falkland Islands, dominates the tank room. She arrived at the museum as a folded, frozen, pink blob, and was kept in a freezer while Jon Ablett and his co-mollusc curators decided how to proceed. Since this species is so rare in museum collections, it was decided to keep her complete and undissected, preserved in formal saline. She was defrosted – carefully, so that the mantle, head and tentacles defrosted at the same time – her tentacles were unravelled, and she was injected with 15 litres of preservative before finally being placed in her home. Her tank is on a stand, so I could look at the squid at any angle.

She is 8.62 metres long and her enormous tentacles spread the length of her 9.45 metre long acrylic tank (built in California by Casco Ltd, the same team that made Damien Hirst's shark tank). There is another set of tentacles beside her. These belong to the colossal squid, which shares her tank. It's an incomplete specimen of a species which, when fully grown, may be even bigger than a giant squid. (The museum does not have a complete specimen yet.)

Archie and the tentacles of the colossal squid are stored in the basement because it is the only floor in the archive that can support the enormous specimen (plus one). Another reason for keeping her here is the formal saline (a mixture of formalin and salt water) in which she is preserved, is more toxic than alcohol; the air around her needs to be monitored and vented in case of a leak. She's not a fish, of course – she's a mollusc – but this is the room of the museum that is best suited to be her home. You can visit her on a Spirit Collection tour.

Archie may hog the limelight, but there are countless treasures in the fish collection. I peered in at a small catfish called a candiru; in the Amazon, a naked man might be shocked to feel it swimming up his penis. I saw fish collected by Darwin on the *Beagle*, most of which were new to science when he collected them and are still being used for research today.

[Denticles]
Shark skin is composed of placoid scales (also called dermal denticles), tiny tooth-like structures which give it a rough, sandpaper-like texture.

Charmingly, I was shown an old UK record grayling specimen donated by a fisherman proud of his catch. His grandchildren have been to visit it. Less charming were several specimens of nature gone wrong, including a kitten with no face and a chicken with two heads; these were on display when the museum first opened and are now only used when children come in on school trips.

Next, we ventured towards the sharks, lifting the lid of a metal tank to reveal several rare species. These sharks helped Olympic swimmers to win gold medals. Fiona Fairhurst, a biomimetician – someone who incorporates good designs from nature into technology – was working on swimsuit ideas for Speedo. She set up shop among the tanks to study the sharks and their skin.

I stroked the skin of one of the dead sharks she worked with, and it was really rough, like sandpaper. That's because it is covered in razor sharp scales called 'denticles', like little teeth. They help the sharks swim effortlessly by controlling the turbulence of the water next to the skin of the swimming shark. Speedo incorporated the denticle design to make Fastskin®, their fastest swimwear ever. It was thought the streamlined, sharky swimsuit reduced friction on a swimmer's skin, and contributed to the winning of 47 medals in the 2004 Athens Olympics, including the six gold medal haul won by Michael Phelps. In 2008, 105 world records were broken, 79 of them by swimmers wearing the suit. Before the suits were banned by FINA (Fédération Internationale de Natation, the body responsible for administering competition in aquatic sports) in

2010 (they were not to be seen at the London Olympics), only two of the existing world records pre-dated their invention.

However, an ichthyologist – a fish expert – at Harvard said that, while the swimsuits may help a swimmer to go faster, this is because the suit changes the human body's posture, making it more hydrodynamic, rather than because the fabric itself decreases the drag. He says the denticle design works for sharks but doesn't have the same benefits for humans as our bodies are less flexible. There is more to be learnt if we want to catch up with nature.

James and Ollie add fish to the collection all the time. The public donate some, and the curators acquire others – they'd just returned from fishing in Burma when I met them. Ollie has tasted a lot of bizarre fish but his favourite is fresh mackerel, straight out of the sea: 'Whip it into a pan, flash fry and there you go.' Some fish come into the museum via unusual routes. When Archie came into the collection, she had fish trapped inside her mantle from when she was caught in the fishing net, and those fish were added to the collection, too.

Each time a new fish arrives, the curators take a small amount of tissue for a DNA sample. Ollie explained: 'We'd never have dreamt 20 years ago we would be looking through museum collections for DNA, but it's important now, and in the future we don't know what will be useful.' The fish is injected with a preservative called formalin (formaldehyde solution), which after a few days is replaced by a solution of 70 per cent alcohol, then the specimen is bottled, databased, labelled and added to the collection. This has been going on since the museum began, the first 'database' consisting of handwritten ledgers.

Every natural history museum in the world has a scientific collection, and only a tiny fraction of their collections is ever on display. The natural history museums in London, Paris and Washington have the largest collections overall. If a researcher needs to study a species over several centuries, or across a wide geographic area, they can come here, to the library of species at the museum. It's a lot cheaper than flying to every area of the world in which a species lives, and a lot safer than heading off to research a fish that lives in a war zone.

[OBJECT 20]

THE FIRST GIRAFFE
in France

[Location]

MUSÉUM NATIONAL d'HISTOIRE NATURELLE
Paris, France

SUCH a LONG NECK!

SUCH BIZARRE MARKINGS! a BLUE TONGUE!

The FRENCH were OBSESSED with HER,

and women began wearing their hair 'à la giraffe'

(a bit like Marge Simpson's)

AND POTTERS PAINTED CERAMICS GALORE

with the IMAGE of the PRETTY LADY GIRAFFE.

IN THE ARCHIVES OF THE Natural History Museum in France are 70 million objects of high scientific or heritage value belonging to the French nation. Mustachioed Monsieur Michel Guiraud has been curator of natural history at the museum for 20 years. He and Madame Michelle Lenoir, a lovely lady who is in charge of the collection of books, showed me around.

We began in the library. Michelle flipped the window blinds shut to protect her precious books, then began to pull out curious volumes. The books she is most proud of are those in the 'Vellum Collection', which is made up of 7,000 drawings on vellum, bound up into one hundred red leatherbound volumes which now live in the cool, dark library and are rarely visited.

The red volumes contain three centuries' worth of drawings of plants, animals and birds by the best artists in France. A few pages are missing, taken in the nineteenth century by naughty curators, perhaps to hang at home. We looked through them, marvelling at the detailed drawings of plants and animals collected over the decades since the museum began. The vellums were used as study material before photography took over as the best medium in which to collect images of natural life.

Many of the animals in the drawings once lived in the museum's Jardin des Plantes, France's most important botanical garden, which also has a zoo. I liked a sweet picture of a camel born in the Jardin des Plantes, drawn when she was only 28 hours old. I also love a beautiful drawing of a long, fluttering-eyelashed giraffe. Michelle explained to me that this baby giraffe was the first to come from Africa to France, and 'everyone went crazy for her.'

She arrived in 1827, as a gift from the King of Egypt. Born in the Sudan, the gangly giraffe was packed onto a boat and sent across the water from Africa to Europe; the boat had a hole cut on deck for her head and long neck to peer out of. Three cows were taken on the trip so she would have milk to drink. She was held in quarantine on the island of If, the former residence of the Count of Monte Cristo. Then, when she arrived in France, she walked for 41 days, from Marseille to Paris, to meet the King of France, Charles X. The procession across France was led by Geoffroy Saint-Hilaire, a top scientist and one of the founders of the Natural History Museum in Paris.

All the way along her route, the people of France poured out of their homes to watch her walk past: never had they seen such a mysterious creature. Such a long neck! Such bizarre markings! A blue tongue! The French were obsessed with her, and women began wearing their hair 'à la giraffe' (a bit like Marge Simpson's) and potters painted ceramics galore with the image of the pretty lady giraffe. In Lyon, 30,000 people turned out to see her cross the city.

When she arrived in Paris, she was installed in her own enclosure in the Jardin des Plantes. She lived there for 20 years, with a man from Sudan named Atir, who had travelled with her from Africa. Each night, he climbed a ladder to the mezzanine to sleep. From there, he could reach out to scratch the pretty giraffe's head.

The zoo in the Jardin des Plantes was founded in the 1790s by Saint-Hilaire. He started it with animals saved from the mobs of the French Revolution who attacked the royal menagerie in Versailles. The Jardin des Plantes was once royal property – le Jardin du Roi – a royal garden filled with medicinal plants, and the museum buildings once housed the royal natural history collection. The Revolution changed all that and the whole thing was opened to the public. The best natural history professors in France were hired to research and expand the collections, now brought together under the renamed Natural History Museum.

[The first giraffe in France]
She arrived in 1827, as a gift from the King of Egypt. A man from Sudan, where she was born, came with her. His name was Atir.

[*Head of a Giraffe*, by Nicholas Huet, 1827]
I love this drawing of the baby giraffe, painted when it first arrived in Paris. The drawing lives inside a red book in the library of the Natural History Museum in Paris.

The giraffe – like the other animals and plants in the Jardin des Plantes – was drawn by the best artists of the day. The beautiful drawing on this page of the giraffe's head and neck was created in the year the giraffe arrived in Paris. It was drawn by Nicholas Huet, something of a celebrity in the world of nineteenth-century natural history painting. The drawing has never been on show. It is too fragile. It was created for scientists, and for posterity. There are no copies and it is so old and precious it's best for it to remain within its leatherbound volume in the library, away from the light. We put the book back in its place and opened the blinds. The body of the giraffe is now in a museum in La Rochelle. We looked at a little model of her that sits on the window ledge of the library. Then we headed underground.

Beneath the museum are three floors of stuffed creatures and animals stored in jars. Few people know that this archive is here and the museum never does tours. It's very odd, once you know it's there, to walk across the courtyard and through the museum building and imagine the long corridors and dungeon-like rooms filled with thousands of dead animals, from tiny mice to huge lions, just beneath your feet. I imagined what would happen if they all came back to life.

The specimens are kept at a steady temperature of 15.5°C (59.9°F) so that the alcohol in the spirit collection doesn't vaporize and explode. (That would be a really bizarre explosion – bits of long-gone creatures from around the world flying everywhere.) It's one of the best natural history collections in the world. Michel believes seventy per cent of the world's 'type' specimens are here. It's a living collection and the museum keeps it all, because you never know what will be needed for research in the future.

A lot of the taxonomic specimens kept here are skins, taken from the skeletons displayed above ground in the Museum of Comparative Anatomy. Artists love to visit the museum to draw and learn about the inner workings of all sorts of bodies. I don't suppose too many of them have ever wondered what happened to the outer layer of the animals they are drawing. They might be surprised to know that they are standing on top of them. The skins have been stuffed, so there is a whole row of ten fierce lions, whose skeletons are upstairs in the museum, beside a row of shrews, teeth comically bared.

Michel said they have enough stories down in the dark archive to fill two or three books. He showed me a selection of the most iconic specimens. First, we met a black emu from an island just south of Australia that once belonged to Joséphine de Beauharnais, wife of Napoleon. She commissioned the French explorer Baudin to bring her animals to put in her menagerie. Baudin obliged with this small black emu which, when it died, came into the museum collection. It is the only specimen of this species known in the world and so is the 'type' for the species. Curators have gone back to the island where it was collected to look for more black emu, but haven't managed to find any. Scientists who have studied the creature in the archives don't know whether it is an elusive species of its own, or a form of the mainland species that evolved on the island to be very small.

Next, I saw an albino quail. It was shot by King Louis XV, and kept because it was an albino. It is one of the oldest specimens in the collection. Taxidermy was an embryonic art at the time, so arsenic soap was used to protect its skin from bugs. Michel told me, 'It also killed the taxidermists, but there were plenty of them at the time. We also have a white thrush shot by King Louis XVI. Maybe shooting albino birds was a French king's privilege …'

Finally, I saw a chimp that belonged to the Comte de Buffon (1707–66), who was the director of the Jardin du Roi which became the Jardin des Plantes. Luckily, Buffon himself isn't down in the archive … Or is he? I wouldn't be surprised if he were. Descartes' skull is there, but not his body. That, according to Michel, is in Sweden.

I went for a walk around the Jardin des Plantes, with a friend who was writing a poem about an orangutan and wanted to see the one that lives there. She'd seen a photograph – a friend texted it to her from the zoo – but she'd not seen him in the flesh. When we spotted him he was sitting up on a ledge, with a handkerchief over his head to keep the sun off. When he saw people watching him he swung about a bit, waving his handkerchief.

Afterwards, we walked out on to rue Geoffroy St-Hilaire, named after the man who led the gentle giraffe across France to Paris, and to the museum gardens. On this road there is an ornate mosque (and a tasty Moroccan restaurant with birds flying around inside it, and a hammam). It's a shame it was built a century after the giraffe lived in Paris because the sound of a call to prayer from the mosque might have made the giraffe from Sudan, via Egypt, feel more at home.

[Orangutan]
I went for a walk in the Jardin des Plantes with a friend who was writing a poem about an orangutan. We saw the one that lives in the zoo, sitting on a ledge, with a handkerchief over his head.

[OBJECT 21]

a GREAT AUK EGG

[Location]

THE NATURAL HISTORY MUSEUM at Tring
Hertfordshire, England

IT'S IMPOSSIBLE TO PUT A VALUE ON THEM.

IN a WAY, THEY'RE PRICELESS, as THERE

are so few of them in existence

(ONLY 75 IN THE WORLD)

and THEY VERY RARELY COME UP FOR AUCTION.

THIS GREAT AUK EGG IS one of the oldest and most valuable eggs in the Natural History Museum, which holds the largest egg collection in the world. No egg like it will ever be laid again because, around 1844, the last great auk (*Pinguinus impennis*) in the world was killed. There are five other great auk eggs in the collection, and all six eggs are kept in the back rooms of the Natural History Museum at Tring, where the museum stores its eggs, birds and nests. I know where they are kept, but I'm not allowed to tell you.

Very few people at the museum have ever seen them, let alone members of the public. They are very fragile, and the colour on the eggs can fade in daylight, so it's best not to display them. 'Sometimes people come to do research on them and I have to stand over them with a stick,' the curator of eggs joked. His predecessor at the museum was too nervous to touch them but, recently, they have been re-boxed and re-examined.

I was lucky enough to be allowed to see them. The egg curator laid the eggs out on the floor. Each one is wrapped in cotton wool in its own box and labelled with its history. The eggs are quite large: if you cup your hands in front of you they'd just about fit inside. They're smooth and oval shaped and come in shades of white, green, blue and brown. This particular creamy white egg is covered in wiggly lines that make it look like a toddler has been scribbling with a felt tip. No two eggs ever have the same pattern.

[A great auk egg]
This egg is one of the most valuable and the oldest in the Natural History Museum's behind-the-scenes egg collection. An oologist called Robert Champley found it in the Museum of Anatomy in Pavia, Italy. It was covered in dirt and stored in a wooden cup. It's covered in wiggly lines that make it look like a toddler has attacked it with a felt tip.

It's impossible to put a value on them. In a way, they're priceless, as there are so few of them in existence (only 75 in the world) and they very rarely come up for auction.

Seventy-five eggs in the world is actually quite a few. There are far rarer eggs in the back rooms of the museum in Tring. The curator showed me a tiny egg that belonged to the Samoan wood rail (*Gallinula pacifica*) collected on the island of Savai'i, Samoa, in October 1873. The birds nested on the ground and were gobbled up by greedy rats and pouncing cats which Europeans had introduced to the island. This mini egg, the only one in the world, is cracked. There is a handwritten label with it, dated 1971, which says, 'This egg was already broken,' from a previous curator to the present one, as if to say, 'It wasn't me!' He wanted future generations of curators to know that it wasn't broken on his watch, when the egg collection was moved from the Natural History Museum in London to Tring in the 1970s.

The great auk eggs are not only precious because they are rare. Much of the reason they so valuable is because they are iconic. In the Victorian era, it was quite a fashion to collect interesting things from around the world and display them at home in a 'cabinet of curiosities'. The idea was that it was possible to create a microcosm of the world in one room, which could be used to amaze and impress visitors.

This had been going on since the Renaissance in Europe, where 'cabinets' were entire rooms (rather than a piece of furniture), and would be stuffed full of paintings, sculptures, curiosities from overseas and unusual animal specimens. Royals and aristocrats created the cabinets as a sign of their good taste, and as an obvious display of the reach of their power.

Across Europe, many museum collections began life as the private collections of wealthy individuals. In England, the British Museum was founded with books belonging to George II and a variety of books, prints, drawings, medals, coins and other treasures belonging to Sir Hans Sloane (1660–1753), the Irish physician who introduced hot chocolate into England from Jamaica – you can still buy the chocolates named after him in the British Museum shop. Later, the natural history part of his collection became the foundation for the Natural History Museum.

[Sir Hans Sloane 1660–1753]
Sloane was an avid collector and lots of people came to his house to see what he had. Handel supposedly visited and annoyed Sloane by placing a buttered muffin on one of his rare books. Sloane's collection became the foundation of the British Museum.

The great auk egg became a must-have curiosity because of its beautiful patterns; any serious collector wanted an egg, or more than one if they could find them, and they changed hands for vast amounts of money. Captain Vivian Hewitt, the first person to fly across the Irish Sea, once owned 13 eggs, the most anyone has ever owned. He liked creatures that can fly, set up a bird sanctuary on Anglesey and at one time travelled with a pet parrot.

Robert Champley, an oologist, or egg collector (from the Greek for 'egg'), from Scarborough, was a keen collector and had nine by the late 1800s. This particular egg was one of them. Champley found it in the Museum of Anatomy in Pavia, Italy. It was covered in dirt and pushed into a wooden cup so it looked like an acorn. He bought it for five Napoleons (the old name for lire), which was probably less than it was worth at the time: 'I borrowed the amount from my Russian friend, and, after packing the egg carefully, left the museum, they seeming sorry that they had no more specimens and considered that they had got a good bargain … I had a box made for the egg the next day. The egg is perfect and thickly pencilled at the thick end.'

Lazzaro Spallanzani (1729–99), an Italian priest, had donated the egg to the University of Pavia. As a priest, he had ample leisure time and used it to work out why things that interested him occurred. He began the study of echolocation in bats, described animal reproduction, was the first to perform IVF (with frogs) and showed that newts can regenerate parts of their body if injured. He also worked out why stones skip on water when you skim them. His greatest work was on digestion, showing that gastric juices in the stomach do a lot of the work. He died of a bladder infection and asked that the bladder be put on public display in the Museum of Natural History at the University of Pavia.

The great auk was a brilliant bird. They were 75–85 centimetres tall and, like humans, stood upright on two feet. They were one of very few flightless birds that were native to the northern hemisphere in recent times. There were others, like the spectacled cormorant, which was bad at flying and reluctant to do so; the Syrian ostrich, which couldn't fly at all; and several flightless rails and grebes, all of which are now extinct. Now, the only flightless birds in the northern hemisphere are the North African ostrich and the Okinawa, Guam and Zapata rails.

IVF

75-85 cm

[Monument to one of the last great auks]

On the northern tip and highest point of the island of Papa Westray – one of the Orkney Islands of Scotland – there is a statue of a great auk. It was one of the last places in the world where the great auk was found before the last one was killed in 1813.

Great auks had black wings, a white tummy and a white head and went by many names, including geirfugl, gearbhul, aponar, binocle, moyack, 'The Wobble', garfugel (from *gar*, the Old English word for 'spear', because of the great auk's prominent and impressive beak, and *fugel*, for 'bird', from which we get the word 'fowl'). It was also known as a 'penguin', which meant 'white head' in Welsh.

Great auks were the original penguins. English and Spanish mariners who sailed the South Seas saw the birds we now call penguins and named them after the great auk. *Pingouin* is still the French word for the great auk and its relative the razorbill. The original French name for the southern birds is *manchot*, which means 'armless', because of how they look when they waddle.

There used to be millions of great auks around the shores of Canada, Greenland, Iceland and Great Britain, foraging in shallow waters eating fish, crabs and plankton. Once a year, they'd land on rocky offshore islands and lay an egg. Then they would incubate it in an upright position in a nest made from droppings until it hatched. The parents would then take turns feeding the chick, for up to two weeks, until the chick was ready to take to the sea alone.

The species was so abundant, it is almost like us trying to imagine that in the future there will be no seagulls, except for stuffed ones buried in museum archives. Unfortunately, being flightless, great auks were also terribly easy to catch and delicious to eat. The last great auk recorded in Britain wasn't even eaten. It was caught in the summer of 1840 on the remote Atlantic island of St Kilda. Imprisoned for three days in a bothy, blamed for a storm, tried as a witch and sentenced to death, the poor bird was beaten for an hour with two large stones before it died.

Thankfully, there are still some stuffed great auks at Tring for us to see, including one in a case that is sometimes loaned to other museums. The eggs curator once took it to Madrid for an exhibition; he flew with easyJet and kept it in a metal suitcase, which he thought about handcuffing to his arm for safekeeping.

[OBJECT 22]

A GLASS
JELLYFISH

[Location]

MUSEUM of COMPARATIVE ZOOLOGY
Harvard University, MA, USA

IT is in SUCH PERFECT CONDITION
IT SEEMS ALMOST ALIVE.

[Glass models of marine creatures]
430 intricate glass models of sea slugs, sea cucumbers, jellyfish and squid are kept in storage in drawers and on shelves labelled 'Blaschka glass invertebrates, please do not disturb'.

[Leopold Blaschka (1822–95) and Rudolph Blaschka (1857–1939)]
Father and son glass artists in their studio in Dresden.

THE MUSEUM OF COMPARATIVE ZOOLOGY was founded in 1859, making it one of the oldest museums in America. Its storage rooms are filled with 21 million specimens that will rarely, if ever, be displayed. Among these are the 430 fantastic glass models of beautiful marine creatures painstakingly made between 1886 and 1936 by the father and son glass artists Leopold and Rudolph Blaschka in their studio in Dresden.

The museum displays 3,200 glass models of flowering plants lovingly created by the German duo; they are visited by over 100,000 people a year. However, not many visitors to the museum know that there are glass creations not on display: the marine creatures, which are behind the scenes.

When the curator and I walked through the room in which they live, hundreds of tiny jellyfish and marine mammal tentacles and spines shivered in time with our steps. The sea slugs, sea cucumbers, jellyfish and squid are kept in drawers and storage cupboards, on shelves labelled 'Blaschka glass invertebrates, please do not disturb'.

If they were in a public area of the museum, all the human traffic would be too much for the delicate creatures and they might break apart. Also, the colours are at risk of fading from exposure to light. So, in storage they remain. But how did they get there?

The intricate pieces look contemporary, but in fact they were made over a century ago. They were used for teaching students and were, at first, on public display. The Blaschkas made hundreds of glass creatures for museums and universities all over Europe. They copied drawings in books, created things they saw with their own eyes out at sea, and kept specimens for reference in an aquarium in their workshop. They also made glass eyes, beakers and test tubes.

That was until George Goodale, the first director of Harvard's Botanical Museum, hired them on an exclusive contract to make more than

4,000 models of plants. It was too big a commission to refuse, and they never made zoological models again.

The twosome grew American plants in their own garden, which they rendered in glass, and made trips to the Caribbean for more samples. They worked on the plants together until Leopold's death, after which Rudolph carried on alone, heating and shaping glass into plants, until he died, 40 years later. The plants collection they created is called the 'Ware Collection of Blaschka Glass Models of Plants', and even today they are the most popular exhibits in the museum. When 25 were taken to New York City for an exhibition, they were driven in a hearse, as this was the smoothest ride the curators could find for them.

The Blaschkas' marine creations, which pre-date the flowers, still amaze scientists with their anatomical accuracy, and they last longer than real specimens that are stored in spirit, like the anglerfish and his fishy pals.

I saw a cannonball jellyfish (*Stomolophus meleagris*), stored in spirit. It was collected in 1862 by Harvard professor Louis Agassiz (1807–73) as a new genus, and a new species. Agassiz sent a description and illustration of the creature to the Blaschkas' studio in Germany, where they crafted this exact glass model of the specimen. I compared the two, real and glass, both kept in storage, and, while the creature stored in spirit had clearly seen better days and looked like nothing so much as a large white blob, the glass reproduction's features are still as clear as can be. It is in such perfect condition it seems almost alive.

Beside it is a miniature glass replica of a Portuguese man of war, with long blue tentacles. These creatures aren't jellyfish, they are sinophores, made up of a colony of creatures called zooids. They can't swim properly and rely on currents and winds to push them along.

Sadly, there isn't a 'fried egg jellyfish' (*Phacellophora camtschatica*). They look exactly like their name suggests. Their sting is so weak, you can't feel it, and neither can the little crustaceans that hitch rides on their bells and eat the plankton that gets trapped in their arms and tentacles.

Although the glass marine creatures can't be displayed, they will be kept for future generations in the museum collection, along with thousands of other behind-the-scenes specimens. These include the elephant skeletons in the attic, which can't be taken downstairs because the lift

[**Portuguese man of war**]
A Portuguese man of war isn't actually a jellyfish – each one is made up of a colony of creatures called zooids.

[Cannonball jellyfish]
The Blaschka's glass model
looked far more realistic than
the real specimen the museum
stores in spirit.

that was used to take things up is no longer there, and magic mushrooms collected by ethnobotanist Richard Evans Schultes, that kicked off a psychedelic revolution.

New things are discovered in the collection all the time. When reorganizing the worm collection several years ago, the curators came across a lot of parasites arranged by street names in Boston. It turned out that the parasites were collected by a local doctor who was recording the health of high society in Boston. Poor Miss Lottie Fowler, from Hayward Place, could never have imagined she would be best remembered for a tapeworm, 14 metres long, that once lived inside her and now forms part of the museum's back-room collection.

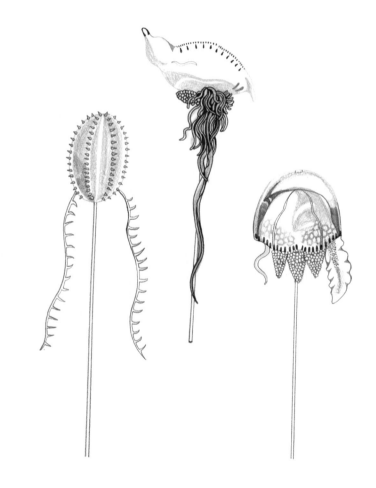

[OBJECT 23]

The interior of
VASA

[Location]

VASA MUSEUM
Stockholm, Sweden

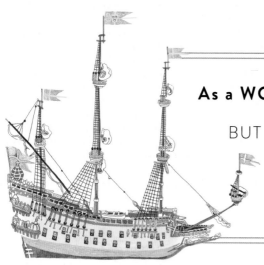

As a WORK of ART it is A MASTERPIECE

BUT as a WARSHIP it was A DISASTER.

You can see the entire distance it ever sailed

FROM THE ROOF OF THE MUSEUM.

IT'S IMPOSSIBLE TO MISS THE Vasa Museum in Stockholm. If you go down to the beautiful waterfront of the city, you'll see the masts of the only surviving seventeenth-century wooden warship in the world, sticking out of the top of the museum built especially to house it. That is *Vasa*. I'm not very into boats, and definitely not in any way into war, but I like the museum because, stripped of all its colours and beautifully lit, *Vasa* looks majestic, more like a piece of art than a warship.

The ship is lavishly carved, decorated with all kinds of images to impress the enemy and to appease the weather gods. There are lions holding the Swedish coat of arms, fruit to symbolize plenty, the figure of Hercules and the heraldic symbol of the Vasa dynasty of Swedish kings. 'Vasa' is the Swedish word for fasces, which means 'bundle of sticks'. Mussolini's Fascists took their name from the same word, and as a symbol used a bundle of sticks and an axe. An image of King Gustav II Adolf of Sweden with his arms outstretched, who reigned at the time and commissioned *Vasa*, is carved into the stern of the ship.

As a work of art it is a masterpiece but as a warship it was a disaster. You can see the entire distance it ever sailed from the roof of the museum. The day *Vasa* left Stockholm's harbour, bound for the navy's summer fleet base out in the Swedish archipelago, it sank in full view of the city just 1,200 metres into its maiden voyage. The top of the mast was visible above the water, just as it is now visible poking out of the roof of its current home. British and Danish spies who had come to investigate the warship

[Vasa]
Vasa looks majestic, more like a piece of art than a warship.

reported back that it now lay stuck in the mud of the harbour. Several people on board were killed – 15 skeletons were recovered from the wreck. Ten of these are on display, which I thought was weird, but, apparently, kids love to see them.

Vasa remained in the mud for 333 years. Then, in 1961, the ship was raised, with the assistance of the navy and a commercial salvage firm. The water inside the wood of the ship was replaced with a waxy chemical – now commonly added to cheap milkshakes, chocolate and cosmetics – which stabilized the wood so that the boat didn't turn to dust as it dried out. If you look closely at the ship, you can see the white wax dripping along its sides. When I touched it, it felt as though it had been dipped into melted candle wax.

A lot of Swedes think that, when they were kids, they climbed on board the ship. Fred Hocker, director of research at the museum, who showed me around, said, 'I've lost count of the number of people who've told me they've been on board, but really, they haven't, it's just that when Vasa was in its first museum building, the platforms were arranged so it felt as though you were on board. You can't really trust people's memories, to tell the truth. They remember what they think they saw.'

The reality is that very few people have ever been allowed on board. The museum is in a part of Stockholm that is still owned by the king: if he wants to bring anyone on board, he can, of course. He usually brings visiting heads of state. A trip below decks is also offered to Nobel Prize-winners, as a bonus, if they'd like to have a look. At the Vasa Museum, it is the inside of the ship that is the great secret, the hidden treasure.

I was allowed to climb aboard Vasa to see what lies beneath the deck. A flight of steps leads down on to the ship from the sixth floor of the museum. Fred Hocker tapped a code into an alarm system, swung open a gate at the top of the steps and we walked down on to the main deck. At the foot of the stairs was a row of smooth-soled bowling shoes – a pair for every curator, to keep their feet from marking the decks. I put a pair of blue plastic covers over my shoes and we set off to explore the ship's seven storeys.

We began with the admiral's view, high up on the sterncastle, looking down on to the deck. The deck was curved upwards, and I felt all at sea looking down over the deck and beyond to where people wandered around the museum floor gazing up at the sides of the ship. The admiral of *Vasa* nearly died, below deck, as the ship sank. If he had ever known what would happen to his ship, that one day, others would stand in his place, inside a museum, it would have surprised him, I'm sure.

Next, it was down some steps to the upper gundeck. From the museum floor, it looks as if there were lots of windows in the ship but, when the ship sailed, out of each one poked a cannon. The 64 cannons – on this deck and on the one below – divided the spaces into rooms, each one for eight people. They had no hammocks, so everyone ate and slept directly on the gundeck.

We walked to the forward end of the gundeck and looked out over the beak-head of the boat. I saw two square boxes that once had lids on – the ship's bathroom. I poked my head through a window and saw to my right, carved into the ship, a caricature of a Polish nobleman with the tail of a fish under a table, being squashed by the cathead (a crane for lifting the anchors). This was a joke, for the enjoyment of the 450 crew on-board heading into battle with Poland. A punishment in Poland for behaving badly was being made to sit under a table and bark like a dog. When *Vasa* was designed this little feature was added in so that the Swedish sailors would see the humiliated face of their enemy when they were sitting on the loo. The carving was propaganda for the crew, invisible from the out-side of the ship.

We headed towards the stern. I felt quite disorientated as the floor swoops down in the centre, and up at the bow and stern. There is more headroom than on similar warships, such as HMS *Victory* – that was one of the reasons why *Vasa* sank: it sat too high above the water – but the ceilings still aren't that high: as we were walking, I bashed my head on a light. Luckily, it wasn't a bolt. Most of the curators have scars on their heads as painful souvenirs from walking into these bolts in the ceiling.

As I bent over holding my head, Fred told me, '*Vasa* used to be a hard hat zone. But when we showed Queen Elizabeth around the ship, she refused to wear a hard hat.' After that, none of the curators wanted to wear one either, and so the hats were scrapped. Prince Charles and Camilla came aboard in the spring of 2012, and Prince Charles asked why hard hats were not worn. 'Sounds like my mother,' he said, on hear-ing the story.

We carried on towards the stern, me rubbing my head, until we reached the whipstaff, which sailors used to steer before the ship's wheel was invented. The helmsman stood holding it, watching a small compass, keeping *Vasa* on course for its short trip. He died at his post, and his skeleton was found beside his steering staff.

Behind the whipstaff was the Great Cabin, once richly decorated by the palace carpenters with fancy panelling and sculptures. A bench all around the cabin had fold-out beds. This was the admiral's bedroom – unless the king should come aboard, in which case the admiral had to move out (though, ultimately, of course, that never happened, as Gustav Adolf was fighting in Poland on the day the ship sank). Few people on board would have known it, but a hidden staircase leads from this cabin to the captain's cabin on the deck above.

We checked out the lower gundeck, which is similar to the one above it: a curved floor and highish headroom for a warship of the time. Most of the original crew would have been okay – the average sailor was 5 foot 5½, and the tallest skeleton they've found was 5 foot 11. All along the deck were ports cut for guns to poke out of.

Now we were three storeys down into the boat. Sometimes people don't want to go any further but I decided to take the plunge and descended a long wooden ladder, passing through another deck – the orlop – into the hold. Here was where the ship's provisions of ammunition, beer and meat – mostly beef and pork, but also moose, reindeer, chicken and more – were stored. It feels cool down here, as pipes send cold air into the hull, to keep the ship at 18°C (64.4°F) with 53 per cent relative humidity. Ideally, the museum would keep *Vasa* even colder, just a little above freezing, but that would scare away all the visitors to the museum, who I could hear there now, outside the ship. It felt strange knowing that nobody standing in the museum, level with where I stood, would have known I was there.

Inside the hull, down in the bottom of the ship, Fred pointed out where the guest captain and another sailor were found when the ship was dredged up. The guest captain was missing a toe and limped, and was unable to escape as the ship sank. Of all the sailors on board, his is the only name that is known: he was a friend of the king, and the king was notified in a letter of his death aboard *Vasa*. It was a bit creepy down in the hull, so I was happy to climb the ladder and scamper up the stairs to

[Sculpture of a crouching Pole]
Vasa was built for the war against Poland, and among the sculptures are several that belittle the enemy, like this one of a Polish nobleman, with the tail of a fish under the table. When the crew used the toilet on the beak-head they had a clear view of the crouching Poles.

the top deck and then to the 'dry land' of the museum gallery to join the crowds marvelling at the ship. The Swedish seem to like the irony that *Vasa*, which was once a disaster and a bit of an embarrassment, is now a national treasure.

When I left the Vasa Museum I walked around the harbour of Stockholm to see what was in store at the city's Modern Art Museum (Moderna Museet). Lars Byström, chief conservator, led me into the light, airy museum stores, which burst with ideas and creations. Everywhere I looked, there were great pieces of art. I saw a hand, sculpted by Picasso, and another oddly shaped figure by de Kooning. Hanging from sliding racks were an early portrait by Edward Munch of the Swedish writer Strindberg, and an early Picasso. *Fresh Window* – a blue window, with leather instead of glass – by Duchamp, had just been returned to the museum by Tate Britain, London and so was in the stores, propped up against *L'Énigme de Guillaume Tell* by Salvador Dalí, which was on its way to a show in Malmö.

In the conservation studio Lars showed me a small painting by Mondrian, called *The Rocky Coast of England*. It's a very straightforward painting of the coastline, and is so unlike his later work that the museum has never exhibited it, as it doesn't fit in with the vibe of the modern art on display in the galleries.

There are stacks of paintings in the studio, but one in particular stood out. It is called *The Acrobat* (1925), and it's a collage by Francis Picabia (1879–1953), a poet and painter born in Paris. It's of a man doing a handstand, on a wire. On both sides, Picabia has made a shadow out of painted cellophane. In the blue sky fly two white doves, and tiny blue birds, swooping among pencil stars. The curators at the museum love the painting, and I can see why, but they can't display it, as the cellophane will degrade in the light.

Exploring the colourful treasure box of ideas that is the backstage area of the Moderna Museet was a lovely contrast to climbing down into the hull of the salvaged, dark warship *Vasa*. As I left the vibrant storage behind and came out into the dazzling sunshine of Stockholm I could see its mast poking out of its building, a hint of the secrets inside, dredged up from the deep.

Flag from the
BATTLE of TRAFALGAR

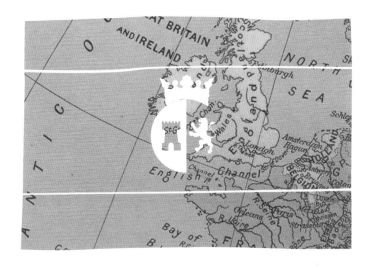

[Location]

The NATIONAL MARITIME MUSEUM
Greenwich, London

THIS FLAG HAS FLOWN AT TWO

HUGELY SIGNIFICANT MOMENTS in HISTORY.

THE FIRST was FLYING FROM THE BACK of a

SPANISH WARSHIP, SAN ILDEFONSO,

as it fought against the British fleet

LED BY NELSON

at the BATTLE of TRAFALGAR.

Its SECOND BIG MOMENT CAME when it was HUNG

from the ROOF of ST PAUL'S CATHEDRAL

during NELSON'S FUNERAL SERVICE on 9 JANUARY 1806.

In St Paul's it hung alongside a French flag also captured at Trafalgar, to symbolize the great victory Nelson had won with his bravery, his superior strategy and, finally, with his life.

After Nelson's funeral, it stayed in St Paul's for a century. Now, it belongs to the National Maritime Museum in Greenwich. They keep it in storage, because it's very fragile and they simply don't have the space to hang it. It is 10 metres long and 14.5 metres high and is the biggest flag in their collection.

'It's a whopper,' said Barbara Tomlinson, curator of antiquities since 1979. 'We haven't ever displayed it officially, but in the 1960s the museum was very naughty and hung it for one day from the front of the Queen's House,' one of the main, large, buildings that make up the National Maritime Museum. 'It trailed on the floor as it was too big for the building; we wouldn't get away with that now.'

'We wanted to exhibit the flag during a Nelson and Napoleon exhibition we had at the museum in 2005, but we just didn't have the space. Instead, we decided to photograph it and put the pictures online, so at least people can find out that it exists.'

The iconic flag from Trafalgar was slowly unravelled on the floor by a team of curators as a photographer hovered above, snapping away from a cherry picker – a platform on a hydraulic lift.

Lots of journalists turned up to watch, but then Prince Charles and Camilla announced their engagement on the same day, and the press, as Barbara put it, 'took off like scalded cats'. Since then, no one has set eyes upon it. It's unlikely it will ever go on display, and only a handful of people have been lucky enough to see it since it was removed from St Paul's over a century ago.

I visited the flag in its current home, inside one of the museum's storage units in Greenwich. There are lots of flags kept in storage, besides this one. They are kept on rollers – much the best way to store a flag, as you can unroll it when you like, and it doesn't get creased.

The museum hasn't found a roller big enough for Nelson's trophy flag yet, so it is folded up, wrapped in tissue paper and stored in a long cardboard box on the bottom shelf of a cabinet. We heaved the box out from its shelf and lifted the tissue paper.

The flag is made of wool and feels very coarse. It is red and yellow striped, with the arms of Castile and Leon in the middle. The name

[Photographing the flag from Trafalgar]
The Spanish flag, flown at the Battle of Trafalgar is the biggest flag in the National Maritime Museum's collection. Curators unfurled the flag on the floor of the museum and a photographer hovered above taking snaps from a cherry picker. Look how small the curators at the top are compared to the flag.

[HMS Victory]
Nelson led the British fleet into battle at Trafalgar onboard HMS Victory.

[**The Spanish surrender**]
Nelson destroyed the Spanish
and French fleet and stopped
France from invading his country.

of the ship is written on the hoist in ink: SAN ILDEFONSO. It has holes in it from where it was shot at during the Battle of Trafalgar, and it is frayed on the edges from when it flapped in the winds upon the stormy seas.

It's amazing to think of the flag being hoisted up from the Spanish ship off Cape Trafalgar as Nelson's fleet sailed towards it at noon on 21 October 1805.

That morning, the British fleet of 27 ships had prepared to attack a line of 33 French and Spanish ships in a daring move called 'crossing the T'.

As the enemy lined up across the bay from Cape Roche in the north to Cape Trafalgar in the south, Nelson decided the British would form two lines and charge right at the middle of the enemy line.

If you had been in the air above it, like the photographer in the cherry picker high above the flag, you would have seen the T – the enemy all across the top, the British heading towards it, up into the top of the T. This daring move, he called the 'Nelson Touch'.

Nelson, aboard his ship, HMS *Victory*, led one line, and Cuthbert Collingwood, aboard the *Royal Sovereign*, led the other. Collingwood had his dog, Bounce, on board. Bounce was tied up in the hold for safety. Collingwood is supposed to have said, on the day of the battle, 'I wish Nelson would stop signalling. We all know well enough what to do.'

As they headed towards the Spanish and French ships, the British sailors would have seen this flag flying from *San Ildefonso*. The ship was positioned near the right side of the top of the T, four from the end. As the British got closer, the French and Spanish opened fire and a bloody battle waged for four hours. This is when the flag got the holes you can see in it today – they were made by musket balls. Much later, perhaps when the flag was hanging in St Paul's, souvenir hunters armed with a knife or a pair of scissors cut out the larger holes on the left-hand side. Moths probably had a go at it too, before it was brought to the museum and properly conserved.

Just over an hour into the battle, Nelson was shot down by a sniper hiding on a French ship, *Redoutable*. A deadly musket ball went through his body, shattering two ribs, puncturing his lung and his pulmonary artery. He fell and was taken below deck, wrapped in a sailcloth and propped up against the side of the *Victory*.

The sound of battle raged on as Nelson lay dying, swayed by the ocean swell, murmuring 'Drink, drink; fan, fan; rub, rub,' as his stewards fed him lemonade and watery wine, fanned him, and the ship's captain rubbed his chest to ease the pain. By the time he died, at 4.30 p.m., his fleet had won the greatest victory, destroying or capturing 18 ships without losing a single ship of their own.

One of those captured ships was the *San Ildefonso*, and it was taken, with its flag, back to Britain. The ship that had been four down from *San Ildefonso* was *San Juan Nepomuceno*, also a Spanish ship. Its ensign flag still exists as well. The British handed it back to Spain, and it is looked after in a museum in Madrid. The two Spanish flags are the only surviving ensign flags from Trafalgar.

Nelson's body was brought home in a barrel of brandy on HMS *Victory* and was laid in state in the Painted Hall at Greenwich, opposite where the National Maritime Museum is today. From there, he was taken down the Thames by boat, to St Paul's Cathedral, for his funeral.

Nelson had destroyed the Spanish and French fleet and prevented France from invading his country. As this flag moved in the breeze inside the cathedral, the whole nation was in mourning.

His wife was at the funeral, but his bereft mistress, Emma Hamilton, was not. Nelson's requests in his will and on his deathbed to 'Look after Lady Hamilton' and to allow her to sing at his funeral were ignored. She wasn't even invited to the ceremony.

He and Emma had a daughter, Horatia Nelson. When she was born, they gave her an extra surname, Thompson, the nom de plume Nelson sometimes signed off with when writing in secret to Emma. Some famous writers are connected to Nelson – the Brontës. Their father was born Patrick Brunty but changed his name quietly to Brontë, perhaps in admiration of Lord Nelson, who was given the title Duke of Bronte by the King of Naples. Bronte is an estate in Sicily, and is the Greek goddess of thunder.

One of the lucky survivors from the Battle of Trafalgar was a man named John Franklin. He later died in the Arctic, while looking for the Northwest Passage. Opposite Nelson's flag in the storage unit is a message balloon made from paper that was used by a search party looking for Franklin

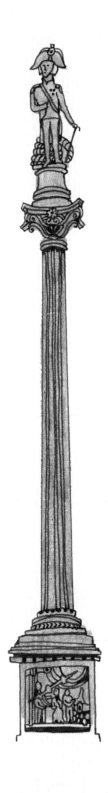

and his team out on the ice. They hoped the men were still alive and would see the balloons in the sky, or find their messages once the balloons fell and realize they were going to be rescued. Sadly, this was not to be.

On a cheerier note, the tiniest thing in the collection that is not on display is the world's smallest cannon. It can only be seen with a microscope. I had a look at it, and it's perfectly formed and tiny, but can't actually fire cannonballs.

A Mr Towson made it for a bet in 1828. While he was creating it, his maid opened the door, creating a blast of wind, which blew one of the cannon's tiny wheels on to the floor. Neither of them ever found it, so he had to make another. The cannon was shown at the Great Exhibition, and then Queen Victoria took it for her collection at Windsor Castle so she could look at it whenever she liked.

Eventually, it made its way to Greenwich, where it used to be on display. However, being a military cannon, it didn't fit the naval theme of the museum, so it was finally put into storage.

Lots of people visiting the museum used to ask Barbara where it was. This hasn't happened much recently, as people have forgotten about it, but when it first went into storage, Barbara said, 'It had to be nearby so we could whip it out whenever anyone wanted to see it.'

Unfortunately, the museum can't do that with the huge and fragile flag. The iconic treasure from Trafalgar will remain unseen.

They see where fell the Thunder bolt of war,
On the storm swollen waves of Trafalgar.
They see the spot where fell a star of glory,
The Finis to one page of England's story.
They read a tale to wake their pain and pride,
In that brass plate engraved 'HERE NELSON DIED'.

Branwell Brontë

A Blue Whale

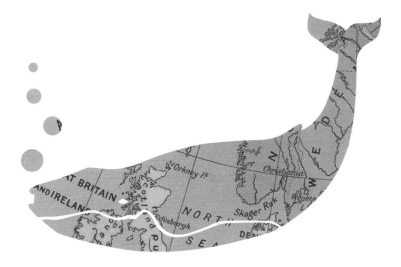

**National Museum of Scotland
Edinburgh, Scotland**

BESIDE THE SEA, on the OUTSKIRTS OF EDINBURGH

is a vast store filled with artefacts of all shapes and sizes;

a model of Lara Croft, an old water pipe from Edinburgh Castle,

the entire archival wardrobe of the clothing designer Jean Muir

AND A SKELETON OF THE BIGGEST ANIMAL

EVER to LIVE on EARTH: a BLUE WHALE.

THESE MAGNIFICENT CREATURES ARE SO big that even as newborns they weigh the same as an elephant.

This mighty blue whale beached up in Dunbar, on the coast of Scotland, on 5 October 1831. Locals thought it was a shipwreck. Some fishermen went for a good look, realized what it was and towed it to North Berwick harbour where they secured it in place with an anchor. When the tide went out the whale was left dry on the sandy beach.

A local doctor, Frederick John Knox, bought the whale to study it and learn about blue whales. His older brother, Robert Knox, was a fellow of the Royal College of Surgeons in Edinburgh. He got into trouble for buying bodies sold by Burke and Hare because it turned out they were the bodies of people who had been murdered. This scandal was in 1827–28, when Frederick John Knox was curator of his brother's anatomical museum but nobody was convicted so they carried on with their careers. Eventually Dr Frederick John Knox emigrated to New Zealand. But not before he fell in love with the blue whale.

The gigantic animal that now belonged to Knox weighed 200 tons. He couldn't study it on the beach, and he couldn't move it so what on Earth could he do with it? He began by offering the blubber to locals as manure. People arrived with carts and horses to help themselves to sup-

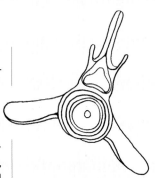

plies every day for a week until Knox was left with just the bones (weighing 28 tons), the tongue (the size of half an Asian male elephant), and whalebone, or baleen (whales have no teeth but have evolved baleen to filter out small animals from sea water).

Knox was amazed by the baleen, having not seen anything like it before. It is quite strange stuff: whales eat by diving down to around 200 metres, then 'lunge' several times, dropping their jaw, and swimming at around 11 kilometres per hour. The whales take a gulp of water, including any animals, like small fish, or krill, that are swimming around in the water. Then they partly close their mouth, and push out their tongue, so that the baleen sieves out the small fish, leaving them with clear water to swallow. The krill slips through the baleen though, and blue whales eat three tons of it a day during summer. They eat very little the rest of the year.

They can swallow nothing larger than a grapefruit. Knox described how disappointed the people on the beach were by the size of the giant creatures 'gullet', for it could only admit 'a man's closed hand'. This 'seemed to give universal dissatisfaction, and lowered the whale in the estimation of the mob at least fifty per cent'. The aorta however was over 90 centimetres in circumference, big enough for a toddler to crawl along.

[Blue whale skeleton]
The National Museum of Scotland keeps an entire blue whale skeleton in storage on a long, long shelf.

Baleen is made from keratin (the same protein that hair, horn and nails are made of) and was used to make whalebone corsets. You might think that corsets were made from whale's bones, but no. Thousands of Victorian ladies enveloped their bodies in what whales have instead of teeth.

Knox needed to get the baleen, the head and the skeleton to Edinburgh. He began with its head, which weighed 7 or 8 tons. On the first attempt the carriage that was carrying it collapsed and everything was taken back to North Berwick.

Again, they tried to move the head. Knox describes what happened:

'Eight, ten, twelve horses were put to the carriage. These horses were known to be the best in East Lothian; the word was given, the eyes of the horses flashed, their breath was in their nostrils, every muscle was in violent action, and a simultaneous effort made, and nearly every horse freed himself by snapping the chains which attached him to the carriage. The cranium of the whale stood unmoved, and seemed to laugh at the vain attempt'.

With the help of double-strength chains and thanks to the extraordinary effort of the horses, the whale head-lifting team finally managed to get the skull to Edinburgh. From then on Knox spent three years and three months preparing and preserving the skeleton that now lives back beside the sea, outside of Edinburgh.

Knox went on to write many papers detailing the whale's anatomy and behaviour. 'These animals are said to be most frolicsome when the storm rages most,' wrote Knox. When he was finished it was displayed in the Royal Institution, on Princes Street, Edinburgh where visitors gawped at its majestic size. It was one of the few blue whale skeletons on display in Europe. The model on display in the Natural History Museum is just a model, but this is real. For centuries it took pride of place in the museum in Edinburgh, where it was suspended above visitor's heads.

Blue whales are popular with everyone – perhaps because they are so astonishingly big – so why is this prize specimen no longer on display? In 2011 the museum reopened as the National Museum of Scotland after a £47.4 million transformation of its Victorian galleries and the whole building in which the blue whale flew was redesigned.

The blue whale was moved out to make room for a new display. I went to see what had replaced it in the new museum that sits on a hill, just over the road from a statue of Greyfriars Bobby and the cafe where J. K. Rowling wrote *Harry Potter* overlooking Edinburgh Castle.

I could see the spot where the enormous skeleton once hung. Now, suspended from the ceiling, there is an array of swimming and flying mammals and animals from across the globe, including a great white shark, a false killer whale and a hippo. The jawbone from the blue whale in storage is hanging up there too, but not the rest of its skeleton.

That doesn't stop people asking for it. Visitors who knew the old museum always wonder where the blue whale has got to, and every day museum attendants are asked whether they know where it is.

I found it in the National Museum Collections Centre, in Granton, a 20-minute car ride from the museum building in Edinburgh. The Centre is made up of about 15 buildings, that store around 8 million artefacts and specimens that don't fit into the various big museums in Edinburgh.

[The blue whale]
Before the museum was renovated the blue whale was on show. Now it is in storage and people who visit the museum often ask where it is.

The blue whale lives inside one of the biggest warehouses. The bones are painted grey and they lie, in order, along the length of a shelf that runs across the inside of the warehouse.

It was interesting that it has become such an intrinsic part of the museum that the curators had forgotten its history. They thought Knox had something to do with it, and thought maybe that he prepared the skeleton on The Meadows, the big park in the centre of Edinburgh, and the taxidermist I met on site wondered whether Jawbone Walk in The Meadows was named after the scene. But when I asked to write about the whale they kindly dug up its story from a nearly two-century-old tome, in the library, written by Knox. This is the story I have told here. It turns out that Jawbone Walk in The Meadows has nothing to do with the blue whale. There are two pairs of jaws on the Meadows today; one of them once decorated a stand of the Faroe Islands at an International Exhibition held in 1886.

The blue whale bones will stay here for the foreseeable future, kept company by a hippo on the floor beside it, lots of whale skeletons and two sperm whale skeletons. One sperm whale skull used to be on show. In those days children threw coins inside it, so there are coins in the collection now that came from the sperm whale.

Most whales that come into the collection nowadays have been found stranded on a Scottish beach. The museum preparators use biological washing powder to clean the bones ready for storage or display. This is what happened to the bones of the Thames whale. Do you remember the sight of that poor whale, on the news, and in the papers – a big bottlenose whale stranded in the heart of London, just outside the Houses of Parliament in 2006? Damon Albarn, the lead singer of Gorillaz and Blur wrote a song about her called 'Northern Whale'. He said it 'started off as a love song for someone I love and then a whale came up the Thames … and it turned into a song about a whale'. It's a sad song, for a sad tale of a poor whale. After attempts to rescue it came to nothing, its skeleton was preserved and cleaned up in the National Museums Collections Centre.

Sometimes natural history museums use tiny employees – thousands of beetles – to clean new specimens. They place new arrivals into an incubator full of beetles that crawl all over the body of the specimen and eat and

eat until all that is left are bones, but the National Museum of Scotland don't keep the beetles as they're too high maintenance. If one escaped it would gobble up lots of the collection and they don't want to have to deal with that.

Further into the warehouse I saw a bubble wrapped Indian elephant – the African one wouldn't fit through the door of the museum when it was renovated, and so it is still part of the displays. I also saw a new aardvark being prepared for display by the museum's taxidermist and looked at dinosaur footprints in crates, lots of armour, some Turkish kettles, pre-Columbian artefacts, things from Skara Brae, thousands of bikes and motorbikes, an old diving suit and a steam traction engine from 1907 being cleaned up for display.

The most beautiful thing I saw was a fifteenth-century triptych belonging to the National Gallery of Scotland being x-rayed before being sent to Los Angeles to be displayed by the Getty Museum.

The blue whale's skeleton wasn't beautiful, but it was quite amazing. I certainly didn't expect to find the biggest animal on Earth in the archives of a museum. Now I wish I could see a living, breathing blue whale, maybe one that is frolicking in a storm.

[OBJECT 26]

Logbook of the
KON-TIKI EXPEDITION

[Location]

The KON-TIKI MUSEUM
Oslo, Norway

HEYERDAHL AND HIS CREW,

plus a parrot named Lorita and a stowaway crab from Peru,

spent 101 DAYS at SEA, DRIFTING 8,000 KILOMETRES

on their raft ACROSS THE PACIFIC,

carried by the HUMBOLDT CURRENT, until THEY WASHED UP

on RAROIA ATOLL in POLYNESIA.

[Thor Heyerdahl (1914 –2002)]
Heyerdahl led the *Kon-Tiki* expedition, in which he and his crew, plus a parrot and a stowaway crab, sailed 8,000 kilometres across the Pacific Ocean, on a balsawood raft in 1947.

A SCUFFED-UP BLACK EXERCISE BOOK filled with tales of whales, storms and adventure on the high seas written by a handsome Norwegian scientist, Thor Heyerdahl, lives in the archives of the Kon-Tiki Museum. It is the logbook of the *Kon-Tiki* expedition, when Heyerdahl and five crew members crossed the Pacific – from Peru to the Polynesian islands – in a raft made out of nine balsawood tree trunks tied together with rope. They had a little bamboo hut built on top of the raft.

Kon-Tiki was named after a pre-Incan hero called Con-Tiki Viracocha, a sun-king who once ruled the land of the Incas. According to their history, when the Incas arrived, the sun-king moved to the Easter Islands. So Heyerdahl followed in his wake, to test out a theory he had that South Americans may have settled the Polynesian islands. He set sail in the *Kon-Tiki* to prove that it was possible then, and is now, to cross our world's biggest ocean on a prehistoric Peruvian raft. He built a perfect replica of an indigenous raft by referring to sixteenth-century manuscripts that described the boats and watching the rafts that local Peruvians still sailed off their coastline.

Once the boat was ready, Heyerdahl and his crew, plus a parrot named Lorita and a stowaway crab from Peru, spent 101 days at sea, drifting

8,000 kilometres on their raft across the Pacific, carried by the Humboldt Current, until they washed up on Raroia atoll in Polynesia.

While the raft that carried them safely across the Pacific is on display in the Kon-Tiki Museum in Oslo, the logbook in which Heyerdahl wrote daily tales of their life in the Pacific is kept out of sight. I slipped through a door, just behind *Ra*, another of Heyerdahl's expedition rafts, and headed upstairs to see the diary. The curator of the museum and I lifted it out of its archival box. It was bigger than I had imagined.

As I turned its crisp, weathered pages, I noticed that Heyerdahl's writing was of a normal size at the beginning. As the trip goes on, his writing becomes tinier and tinier, as he tries to squeeze in every last detail. He wrote in English, even though his Norwegian was, of course, a lot more fluent. Maybe he thought that if his words were written in English more people would easily understand them, should anything happen to the raft. It's also the language logbooks are generally written in. I thought it was testament to how amazing the Scandinavians are at English.

On page one, on 27 April 1947, Heyerdahl describes how the ship was christened *Kon-Tiki* by the expedition secretary, Miss Gerd Vold, 'who broke a coco nut against its bow'. Next, Heyerdahl describes the flags onboard his home for the next three months: 'Astern waved the Norwegian flag, in the top mast waved the Peruvian flag and the flag of The Explorers Club, and at its side the flags of the USA, Great Britain, Sweden and France.' Then he describes lots of press and diplomats from many countries checking out the raft: '60 visitors, totalling roughly 3½ tons, went on board at a time without affecting buoyancy of the raft noticeably.' The next day, the *Kon-Tiki* set sail. Heyerdahl wrote:

On board Kon-Tiki remained only the expedition members, which are:
Thor Heyerdahl, leader
Herman Watzinger, technical leader, 2nd command
Erik Bryn Hesselberg, navigator
Knut Magne Haugland, radio operator
Torstein Raaby, radio operator
Bengt Emmerik Danielsson, Steward
As a ships-pet a green parrot was presented to the crew
at the time of departure.

[*Kon-Tiki*]
As the raft swished into the Humboldt Current the crew found themselves in water that was teeming with life – they had visits from whales and saw thousands of fish.

The first day and night passed without incident: 'Quiet night, passed light starboard at 01.30.' For the next hundred days Heyerdahl jotted down the things that happened to them. I turned the pages and read what he had got up to. It sounds like they had a wonderful time.

As they moved into the Humboldt Current, they found it was teeming with life. They had visits from whales – once, they counted 120 splashing around the raft at the same time. One day, they were followed by a whale-shark.

On 24 July 1947, the crew saw a double rainbow, 'enormous shoals of dolphins swam around,' and they were all happy onboard. 'We are all able to enjoy a marvellous sun-set or a huge sea, and jokes are never wanting.'

On another day, they nearly had company when some natives on the island of Angatau paddled out in canoes to get a good look at them, but the *Kon-Tiki* swished past the island, so the Scandinavians didn't have time to get too acquainted with the locals.

Heyerdahl explained that they spent most of their time in the bamboo hut they had built on their raft. When I looked inside it at the museum, I thought how cosy it looked, their little cabin, with the small beds inside.

The trip was mostly free from danger, although Heyerdahl does describe two storms with 9-metre waves. The well-designed raft surfed the perilous waves.

Heyerdahl drew only one picture in the logbook. He wrote how, on Norwegian National Day, 17 May, in the very early morning, a huge fish, 94 centimetres long, leapt out of the ocean and on to the raft, waking everyone up. 'Bengt woke up too, sat up in his sleeping-bag and said quietly: "*Nå sådana fiskar fines inte!* (No, such fishes do not exist)," whereupon he fell asleep again.' Herman 'grasped firm around the belly of the twisting [fish], it vomited, and out came another fish, 8 inches long with big eyes and built much like a flying fish'. The fish that jumped onto the raft was a snake mackerel, and this was the first time any human had ever seen one. So Heyerdahl drew the fish as a souvenir of the day it leapt aboard to say hello. As day dawned, the crew raised the Norwegian flag, and that night they 'celebrated with toasting and singing on edge of raft while great waves chased by us in the dark'. They nearly lost their compass.

Near the end of the logbook, on the day they crash-landed ashore, he wrote: 'WE HAVE MADE IT. THANKS, GOD.' He must have been over the

[The Kon-Tiki crew]
After they crashed on the Raroia reef in Polynesia the crew stayed for a while, celebrating with the locals.

moon as he wrote these words in this book. Some days later, people on a neighbouring atoll saw their campfire and came over to have a look: they got a shock to find six blond, blue-eyed men and a wooden raft. The blonds stayed for a week, enjoying their atoll, before a boat came to collect them and rowed the raft to Tahiti.

A lot of the stories in the logbook were rewritten into a book, *The Kon-Tiki Expedition: By Raft across the South Seas*, which has sold 60 million copies and is one of the best-selling non-fiction books in the world. People fell in love with the story, perhaps because the Second World War had just finished and Heyerdahl's madcap experiment was light relief.

The museum keeps the handwritten and the typed manuscripts of this book in archival boxes, just beside the original logbook. Heyerdahl began writing the book on board, alongside his logbook, but I preferred reading through the logbook written in the intrepid adventurer's hand.

The diary has never been on display, and probably never will be. This is because it is fragile, of course, and has already got soaking wet, out in the ocean. However, it is also because, although Heyerdahl wrote everything in it, the stories belong to every man on board the raft, and they all went on to do different things after the expedition, so it wasn't easy to get permission from everyone to publish it.

Added to that, there are a few things in the diary which weren't really for public consumption. One of the stories Heyerdahl talks about in the diary but left out of the book was that one of the crew was dating Gerd Vold, the expedition secretary, and the two of them exchanged love messages via the raft's radio.

In the published book Heyerdahl also glossed over the day when they got drunk and nearly lost their compass, and the moment Heyerdahl needed to take down the sail in an emergency: he got so nervous untying it, he couldn't do it – he just froze with fear. Heyerdahl could not swim and had been terrified of water since the time he had almost drowned as a child – an extraordinary fact, given what he was attempting to achieve.

The book also smoothed over the moment when Herman Watzinger was airing his sleeping bag and the wind pulled it from his hands. He ran after it, slipped and fell overboard. Knut Haugland grabbed a rope, jumped in and swam to his friend, and pulled him to safety.

From the outset, Heyerdahl had wanted to take the raft to Easter Island, and the Marquesas. He had spent time on the Marquesa Islands not long before the *Kon-Tiki* expedition and had read an article about Easter Island when he was 12 or so, and had said to one of his pals, Arnold Jacoby, 'One day I will solve the mystery of Easter Island.' The statues inspired the *Kon-Tiki* experiment, as they reminded him of statues he'd seen in South America and made him think that, maybe, the South American natives had travelled across the Pacific to Polynesia.

However, once the raft was upon the ocean, the Humboldt Current had other plans, and the raft drifted elsewhere. One night, Torstein Raaby was on night watch, and decided to change their course, giving up on Easter Island and the Marquesas and heading towards the Tuamotus archipelago so that they would find land more quickly. Heyerdahl woke up to find they were totally off track from what he had planned. He decided it was best to stick with the change. In the logbook in storage he discusses the pivotal moment, but he skipped it in the published book.

In the logbook, Heyerdahl at times shows his anxieties and doubts, whereas in the dramatized version he does not. The logbook is more intimate and private: it is the only place where you can read the world of Heyerdahl, as he was.

In 2004, Heyerdahl's grandson, Olav Heyerdahl read the logbook and started to plan an expedition, *Tangaroa*, to follow the trail of *Kon-Tiki* and see how much things had changed in the past 60 years. In 2006, he and five others left from the same location, on the same day of the year as the *Kon-Tiki*, in a raft made of balsawood, only with a bigger sail.

He describes how 'in the Humboldt Current, we crossed this patch of garbage. Plastic floating all around our clean and 100% natural raft. Shocking experience! At that time I did not know that all these plastic parts were floating around. Nothing of this was described in the KT logbook.' He had been excited about filming and diving with the sharks his grandfather had described, but 'in total we saw 4 sharks! 4 sharks in almost 2.5 months at sea! If people continue eating sharkfin soup, the oceans will be clean. The sharks will for sure not survive.' While his grandfather supped on healthy shoals of tuna fish, 'We caught one tuna across! We are misusing our planet. There will only be leftovers for generations to come.'

[The *Plastiki*]
The *Plastiki*, a boat made from 12,500 plastic bottles, sailed from San Francisco to Sydney, passing through the Great Pacific Garbage Patch, a big soupy mess six times the size of the UK, made up of bags, bottles and other plastic waste.

Sailing through the Great Pacific Garbage Patch, a big soupy mess six times the size of the UK, made up of all those thrown-away carrier bags, plastic bottles and pieces of packaging that have not been recycled, must have been a devastating experience. It encouraged him to set sail aboard *Plastiki*, a 12-ton catamaran made entirely out of 12,500 recycled plastic bottles. I saw *Plastiki* being made in a warehouse in the Embarcadero in San Francisco, and followed its trip in the news as it sailed along the same route as *Kon-Tiki* and on to Australia. The aim of the trip was to highlight the damage that plastic waste is doing to the oceans and the creatures that live there. The crew hoped to inspire people to use less of the stuff and to dispose of what is used more carefully so that it doesn't end up in the ocean.

Back in the museum, the logbook is slowly being digitized, and bits of it are being put online. This began when the Thor Heyerdahl Archives were inscribed into the UNESCO Memory of the World list in 2011. The museum then decided that if the logbook was a world treasure, people really ought to be able to read it. The original will, of course, be kept safely upstairs in the museum, next door to a cold store filled with 1,300 photographs from the *Kon-Tiki* expedition and 100,000 others from Heyerdahl's later voyages. I put on a warm jacket and stepped inside to see them. I pulled a strip of negatives out at random and held it to the light. It was a row of black-and-white images of Lorita, the *Kon-Tiki*'s pet parrot. She fell overboard and was eaten by a shark, and became the only casualty of a daring and inspiring venture across the Pacific Ocean.

[*Kon-Tiki* logbook]
I turned the pages of the weathered exercise book filled with tales of adventure on the high seas.

Wally Herbert's
SLEDGE

[Location]

The SCOTT POLAR RESEARCH INSTITUTE
Cambridge, England

'MEET WALLY HERBERT!'

said Kay Smith, curator at the Scott Polar Research Institute (SPRI)

AS WE FLEW THROUGH the MUSEUM

AND CAME TO A PAUSE BEFORE

A BEAR-SIZED SNOWSUIT MADE OUT OF REINDEER,

SEAL AND OTHER ANIMAL FURS.

THIS BIG, FLUFFY SUIT BELONGED to Sir Wally Herbert – the first man officially to walk to the North Pole. Behind it, on the other side of the display case, is a miniature version, a tiny girl's snowsuit that belonged to Wally Herbert's daughter, Kari, who lived with her parents in an Inuit family for several years when she was young. The snowsuits are the only artefacts belonging to Wally and Kari Herbert on display. Wally's photographs, maps, drawings and the wooden sledge that took him and his crew, with their supplies, to the North Pole, pulled by 15 dogs, are in the vault of the museum. The museum would love to exhibit the sledge. 'It's one of our treasures,' Kay tells me, 'but we just don't have the space.'

The sledge lives, wrapped in plastic, on a shelf in Museum Store A, which contains piles of polar kit: binoculars, scissors, tools for measuring sunshine, a bag of arrows made by Arctic tribesman – even a pair of string underpants (no one is quite sure where they came from). It is on a bottom shelf because it takes six strong men to lift it. On Wally's expedition to the North Pole, it would have been piled high with provisions, attached to a pack of dogs and pulled across the snow and ice. Sometimes one of the team would catch a lift on it – standing on it like you would catch a lift on a trolley in an airport or supermarket – and ride northwards.

[Wally Herbert's sledge]
Sir Walter William 'Wally'
Herbert became the undisputed
first man to walk to the North
Pole in 1969. He led his team,
with this sledge, on a 15-month
journey, which has never been
repeated.

[Wally Herbert with his dogs]
After reaching the North Pole
Wally Herbert returned to
Portsmouth aboard the HMS
Endurance. Here he is with two
of the expedition's huskies,
Eskimo Nell and Apple Dog.

Wally Herbert became a polar explorer because of what happened one rainy day when he was 20 years old: 'I was sitting in a bus; my raincoat was soaking wet. [The bus] lurched and a newspaper fell off the luggage rack smack into my lap.' The newspaper landed open at a page that had an advert for team members to join an expedition to Antarctica.

The word 'expedition' touched the romantic in him. He got a place on the trip … and then on another one, then another. Over the 50 years he worked in the polar regions, where he travelled over 37,000 kilometres, mapping vast swathes of the snowy waste and painting the scenery.

The most famous of these travels is his North Pole adventure, in which he led his team, with this sledge, on the first surface crossing of the Arctic Ocean by its longest axis from Canada, to Svalbard and to the North Pole, via the alarmingly named Pole of Inaccessibility.

It was a 15-month journey of around 6,000 kilometres, which has never been repeated. In the winter of 1966–67, in preparation for the expedition, he and two team mates lived with the Inuit in Greenland for four months then travelled 2,414 kilometres by dog sledge to Canada. At the end of Wally's stay, the Inuit group he lived with pinned a map to the door of his hut, marked with all the places Wally was most likely to die.

Wally planned it all perfectly, including delivery of pipe tobacco all along the route. However, he liked to be led by intuition and would sometimes set off in a direction in the morning based on the dreams he had had the previous night. He took lots of photographs and drew maps en route. Reaching the North Pole was a remarkable achievement. Sir Ranulph Fiennes described him as 'the greatest polar explorer of our time', and Wally was knighted in 2000.

If Wally Herbert was the first to the North Pole, then why hasn't everyone heard of him? Well, it was all in the timing. Just as the press were waking up to his arrival at the North Pole, two men stepped on to the moon.

Also, his adventure took place a long time after Scott and Amundsen's race to the South Pole, which has become the stuff of legend. Interestingly, the two record-breaking trips are linked. Many people had tried to get to the North Pole before Herbert. In 1909, exactly 60 years before Wally Herbert officially reached the North Pole, Robert Peary and James Cook claimed they had made it, but neither had enough evidence to certify their claims. At the time, however, the two men's tales were enough to change history.

Roald Amundsen (after whom Roald Dahl was named) had been planning an expedition to the North Pole; when he heard about the controversial journeys claimed by Peary and Cook, he decided instead to turn the map around and turn south, to claim the title of first to the South Pole, beyond any doubt. Captain Robert Falcon Scott also changed direction, and the race to the South Pole began.

Everyone knows that Scott made it to the South Pole shortly after Amundsen, on the *Terra Nova* Expedition. It ended tragically, as Scott, Oates, Bowers, Evans and Wilson froze to death on their return journey to base camp. Scott's diary has become legendary, telling the story of how Captain Oates went out into the snow to die rather than slow down his team mates. The final words of his diary, written on 29 March 1912, are heartbreaking: 'It seems a pity, but I do not think I can write more. R. SCOTT. For God's sake look after our people.'

The diary is in the British Library, but thousands of objects relating to the *Terra Nova* Expedition are in the SPRI. They own Bowers's diary and 1,701 (I love the precision of that number) glass plate images taken by the Terra Nova's photographer, Herbert Ponting, as well as his camera. When I visited, the institute was about to acquire hundreds of photographs taken by Scott on the expedition which until then had been in private hands, as well as his writing desk, upon which he wrote the famous diary.

[**Wally Herbert (1934–2007)**]
With his family in 1972.

In another museum in Cambridge, the Sedgwick Museum of Earth Sciences, there is a letter from Marie Stopes, campaigner for women's rights, to Scott. She was also a palaeobotanist, and was interested in the idea that the world's continents were once one supercontinent called Gondwanaland. She wrote to Scott asking if she could go with him to Antarctica. He replied saying she could not, but he promised to bring back fossil samples to help with her theory. He had the fossils she had asked for on his body when he was found.

'We're still very much connected with the explorers through their families. We are in touch with children, grandchildren, even great-grandchildren. They come to look at their family's things – journals, clothes – and then they get involved in things we're up to' explained Heather Lane, Librarian and Keeper of Collections at the SPRI. The day I visited they were getting ready for an exhibition of Scott's granddaughter's paintings, created in Antarctica when she was the artist-in-residence aboard HMS *Scott*.

Down in storage there is a pair of skis worn on Scott's Discovery Expedition; they are on a shelf just above Wally Herbert's sledge. Before his death in 2007, Wally Herbert was known to visit the SPRI, and it was he who donated his North Pole sledge to the museum. 'He probably had it in the garage at home and wondered what to do with it, and so gave it to us,' said Kay. 'We also have a lot of his furs, radio equipment and photographs from the expedition.' They just don't have the room in their museum to display very many things.

As we walked back upstairs into the museum, I was told how the SPRI works. The museum is just one part of it. The institute is devoted to the polar regions and so is filled with polar books, ethnographic objects made by native people, animal specimens, thousands of photographs and a lot of data collected by the earliest explorers up to the most recent. 'The early data is a baseline and still informs expeditions now,' Heather explained. 'We have over 250,000 maps useful for planning expeditions. You name a polar explorer, they'll have been here.'

Heather showed me a big, brass ship's bell from Scott's vessel *Terra Nova*. It is kept on a small wooden stool, halfway up the stairs that lead from the museum floor up to the curators' offices. Each day, at 10.30 a.m. and 4 p.m., the bell is rung according to ship time. In the morning it is rung five times, and in the afternoon eight – just as it would have been rung by Scott and his team on the *Terra Nova*.

In the SPRI, the bells are a signal to everyone that it is teatime – a chance for whoever is in the institute – researchers, scientists, writers, curators – to get together for a nice cup of tea. Heather said, 'If you watch Herbert Ponting's film about *Terra Nova* called *The Great White Silence*, you can hear the ship's bell being rung. None of us can watch it without thinking of teatime; it's a Pavlovian response.'

I wasn't there during either teatime, but I didn't leave empty-handed – a curator gave me some rhubarb he had grown in his garden. I took it to my grandparents' house in Norfolk to eat with them. My grandpa had a copy of Scott's diaries, and a copy of Herbert Ponting's film, so we settled down to watch it.

The bell ringing is the first sound you hear in the film. It reminded me of the SPRI and its hidden treasures. It also made me want to put the kettle on, but I didn't want to miss the film.

SONG 21

[Location]

The CANADIAN MUSEUM of CIVILIZATION
Ottawa, Canada

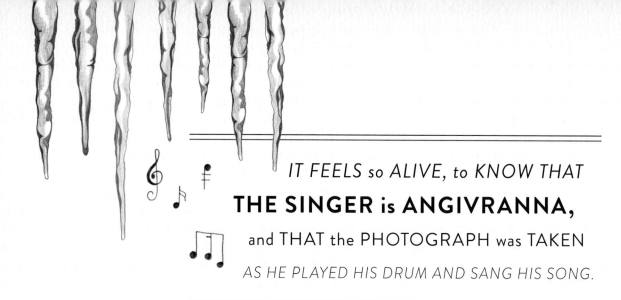

IT FEELS so ALIVE, to KNOW THAT

THE SINGER is ANGIVRANNA,

and THAT the PHOTOGRAPH was TAKEN

AS HE PLAYED HIS DRUM AND SANG HIS SONG.

[Angivranna]
Angivranna singing and
drumming at Berens Islands,
Coronation Gulf, Nunavut.
28 May 1915.

THIS WAX CYLINDER IS A piece of intangible cultural heritage. Hidden inside it is a beautiful song, sung by a man named Angivranna in 1915. He is the man in the photograph, sitting holding his drum. He is no longer alive, and many of his people also died, soon after first contact with the white men who came to their land in search of furs to make themselves rich. Those that lived had their lives totally transformed by contact with the outsiders. So this song will never be sung in the same way again.

The wax cylinder is stored behind the scenes at the Canadian Museum of Civilization. It is too fragile to display and risk damaging the unique, irreplaceable song that it contains.

'Song 21' is one of 137 songs collected by ethnologist Diamond Jenness while he was part of the Canadian Arctic Expedition of 1913–18. Others on the expedition spent the years looking for new lands and new species. Diamond Jenness, meanwhile, made contact with the Inuit, and was adopted by an Inuit family for two years, in order to learn as much as possible about how they lived.

His new mother was called Icehouse, or Higalik; his father, Ikpuck; his brother, the Runner; and his little sister, one of the happiest girls in the Arctic, Jenny Sunshine. He wrote a wonderful book, *The People of the Twilight*, about his time with the charming, funny, welcoming family and their extended tribe.

At first everyone watched him closely. 'They remembered the legend which said that Eskimos, Indians and white men were originally brothers,' Jenness wrote. 'Their mother was a beautiful woman who rejected every suitor until her father's dog metamorphosed into a handsome young man, visited her and won her love. She herself went down to the ocean floor to preside over the waves, the fish and the sea animals; but her children scattered in all directions. Only the Eskimos remained human; the Indians kept their human forms but became like wild beasts at heart; and the white men degenerated into monsters even in outward appearance.' His adopted mother asked him whether white men had arms that trailed to the ground and whether his real mother had hair.

Over time, he earned the family's trust. He shared his food, they shared theirs; he traded his things – fish hooks, needles, pans and, later, bullets and guns for hunting – for theirs: lamps, pots and clothes and, later, for stories and songs: his 'specimens', which are now in the museum's collection. After six months, his adopted mother, having come to love her son, told him, 'You white men are just like us'. She still couldn't be sure about white women, because she'd never met one.

Diamond Jenness loved to record Inuit songs on his Edison phonograph. At first, they were nervous of the machine: 'The first man who sang into it shivered with apprehension when he heard his voice come back to him out of the horn, and asked in an anxious whisper, "Is there a spirit concealed in the box?" Nothing would induce him to sing again, and for a time I feared this first record of their music would also be my last.'

However, Jenny Sunshine found the whole thing a lot of fun and 'sang half a dozen chants and made the house ring with laughter when we played them over again'. From then on, he had no trouble finding singers and recorded 150 songs for future study.

The machine still sometimes amazed them. One afternoon, Jenness played them a song that was sung by the expedition's guide, an Inuit man named Paleak. Everyone listening knew he was 21 kilometres away across the ice – they had seen him that morning, and then travelled onwards, leaving him behind. So how was he singing to them now? It must be magic.

I chose 'Song 21' from all of the songs and incantations recorded by Jenness that are in storage at the museum because they also own a photograph of the man who sung it. It feels so alive, to know that the singer is Angivranna, and that the photograph was taken as he played his drum and sang his song.

[Wax cylinders]
These cylinders contain songs recorded by ethnologist Diamond Jenness.

[Edison phonograph]
Diamond Jenness loved to record Inuit songs – like 'Song 21' – on an Edison phonograph like this one. At first they were nervous of the machine, and thought it was magic, but over time Jenness earned their trust and recorded dance songs and incantations that will never be sung in the same way again.

All the songs Jenness recorded were dance songs and incantations to the weather. Dance songs were sung in a dance-house, where everyone wore their best clothes, adorned with trophies like the teeth or claws of a polar bear, or the knuckles of a seal. Whoever was dancing would usually wear a cap with a bird's bill on top, as well as gloves and boots.

The people Jenness lived among travelled with the seasons, and a dance-house would be built from snow and animal skin wherever they settled. They would leave it behind, along with the other houses, when they moved on. Inside the dance-house, every piece of news, every event, every emotion was recorded in dance and song. Jenness described the dance-songs as being a bit like the local newspaper.

They were sung to tell the story of adventures when a group had been away hunting, to welcome guests, to pass stories from tribe to tribe, as lullabies to send babies to sleep and to pass the evenings in winter. The songs changed as they went from singer to singer, a bit like Chinese Whispers.

Their only instrument was the drum, like the one Angivranna is holding, made from wood and deerskin. Children liked to flip their fingernails against their teeth to make music. Usually, the singer would drum with the instrument held above their head, and sing while moving from foot to foot, swaying and circling around. Everyone would join in loudly. When the singer yelled with joy everyone would cheer.

I find it wonderful to listen to Diamond Jenness's voice at the beginning of the recording of 'Song 21'. He introduces it, saying: '4C57 Dance song by Angivranna, Coppermine River man.' The gramophone recorder whirs into action and the song begins: 'Ai yai ya ai ya qa-ai yei ya …'

Imagine it being sung across the ice of the Arctic nearly a hundred years ago as Diamond Jenness hovered close by, hoping the recording would turn out well.

Jenness explained how, with each song, the Inuit helped to transcribe the words. 'They jostled my arm as they crowded around, talked incessantly all at the same time, and laughed at the babble of their own voices. But they were always good-natured, and genuinely interested in helping me in my work.'

The translations weren't perfect. Angivranna's song seems to be about trying to remember the right words to the song, while running around hitting a seal, a bear, and then spearing a fish. But to Angivranna and his tribe, its meaning would have been crystal clear as they leapt around the dance-house singing stories in time to the drum.

Much as Jenness loved collecting the songs for the museum, he didn't always have fun in the dance-house: he describes how one night 30 people banged his frying pans, while snow melted from the ceiling and dripped ice on to his head. 'The din and odour were terrific, more than flesh and blood could endure,' so he went outside and 'gradually regained my senses'.

In his book, Jenness describes how even the children at play would create dance-houses and pretend to be people inside singing and dancing. They also played at catching caribou and shot arrows for fun. The Inuit taught him how they fish, hunt, sew clothes, sing and dance. In return, they learnt about things he could do, like swim, which was something they never imagined was possible.

When, a year into the expedition, Jenness and his team first heard about the war that had been raging far away from the Arctic, he explained it to his family: 'Ikpuck would not believe our western natives when they told him that the white men were killing each other like caribou, and my own explanation mystified him deeply.' He thought about it for days and wondered whether the ancient story was true, for using their knowledge in such a way was really 'unnatural and inhuman'. Perhaps white men had become monsters, just as the legend foretold.

News of the war didn't interrupt the expedition. Jenness carried on trying to find out about the Inuit and, at night, 'they gathered around my phonograph and filled the house with song'. There were no love songs, for relationships were practical; there were no war songs, for they avoided the Indians far to the south who were the only ones who could cause trouble. Their songs were prayers, and the dance-song was their form of storytelling. Jenness writes, 'However harsh their voices, their melodies revealed a deep sense of musical beauty.'

In July 1916, having woven themselves into the fabric of Inuit daily life, it was time for Jenness and his companions to leave. He gave his family useful things: a frying pan, needles, thread, scissors, a fishing rod, a tent, a canoe and, controversially, a gun for hunting in winter. Then he packed his songs and other 'specimens' into bags and loaded them on to the ship. His mother asked him to 'Harken to our call', should she ever call to his

[Alert]
Alert, Nunavut, is the most northerly inhabited settlement in the world. With coordinates 82°28' N, 62°30' W, it is only 817 kilometres away from the North Pole. This is the Canadian Forces Station in Alert, covered in the names of visitors' home cities and the distances to them.

spirit in need. His father and Jenny came to the beach to see the boat off. 'I am going,' he said. 'You are going,' they replied in unison.

Five years later, a missionary who had been working with the Inuit knocked on Jenness's office door, back in Canada. His Inuit mother had sent him a message. She had heard her son had married and longed for a picture of the strange white woman who was now her daughter. She also wanted a big bowl.

Three years later, his Inuit father sent another message. 'Jenny, your sister, is married and has a son. But I am growing old. Come back and stay with me once more before I die.' Jenness knew the Arctic was changing, mostly for the worst. The caribou herds had been devastated by guns and the Inuit were catching diseases they had no name for and working for wages rather than to support the tribe. 'Whither will it lead?' he asked. 'Were we the harbingers of a brighter dawn, or only messengers of ill-omen, portending disaster?'

In the heart-wrenching epilogue, written in 1958, Diamond Jenness answers his own question. His mother died of influenza, brought into her homeland by the white men. His father died while hunting caribou. His sister Jenny Sunshine had caught tuberculosis; it had already killed her tiny son and later killed her husband too. Her generation's life was changed forever, as 'the commercial world of the white man had caught the Eskimos in its mesh, destroyed their self-sufficiency and independence and made them economically its slaves.'

Today, Nunavut is a native-ruled territory. Its creation in 1999 was a landmark moment for the Inuit, granting them self-governance. It is one of the most remote places in the world, with a tiny population of 31,000. The northernmost permanently settled place in the world is there: Alert.

It's so sad, knowing all that, to listen to this song. But it's wonderful that we can. The fact it has been recorded means it is still part of what anthropologist Wade Davis has called the 'ethnosphere': 'the sum total of all thoughts, dreams, ideas, beliefs, myths, intuitions, and inspirations brought into being by the human imagination since the dawn of consciousness'.

[OBJECT 29]

EXU BOCA de FOGO

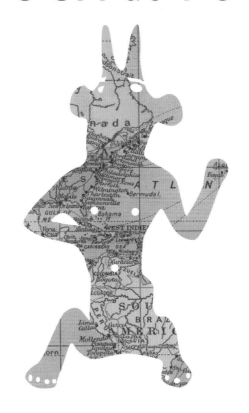

[Location]

Museu AFRO-BRASILEIRO
SALVADOR de BAHIA, Brazil

EXU might look INTIMIDATING TO PRUDISH CHRISTIAN EYES **but really he's IRREVERENT and PLAYFUL** *and, like all the orixás,* **he has GOOD and BAD sides, just LIKE a HUMAN.**

SALVADOR DE BAHIA IS A dazzling coastal city. From the sixteenth to the eighteenth century, it served as the capital of the General Government of the Portuguese colony. Now it is hot and hectic, the host to a seemingly endless succession of festivals.

Once the Portuguese established themselves in Salvador they began to import slaves from Africa. From the middle of the sixteenth to the middle of the nineteenth century, around 4 million Africans were brought to Brazil as slaves. Salvador was the principal point of arrival. It was the first sight of Brazil for millions of African people, the first place the varied African cultures began to take new shape on Brazilian soil. It is this culture that is the focus of the Afro-Brazilian museum in Salvador.

A big feature of the museum is the religion of Candomblé, which means 'dance in honour of the gods'. It evolved as millions of people from different parts of Africa began living together, as slaves, in Brazil. Of course, the Catholic Portuguese suppressed it, so its evolution was shaped by secrecy, but it survived and now flourishes throughout Salvador and Bahia.

In the storeroom of the museum is the curators' much-loved statue of Exu, a god of Candomblé. The curators excitedly led me into their archives, and pulled out a sliding drawer. 'Here is our Exu,' they said, and looked at me for my reaction to the little creature, with his big red mouth and tongue, who had popped out of storage to say hello. I thought he was great!

In Bahian Candomblé there is one all powerful God, Oludumaré, who is served by lesser deities called orixás (which means 'owners of heads' in the Yoruba language of west Africa). Back in Africa, each area had its own orixá. In Bahia, all the gods came together as people from different African nations lived alongside one another. The hundreds of African orixás were reduced to just 27, 12 of whom were really important. These 12 orixás are all over Salvador; they each have a day, a colour and an area of life they are responsible for.

Exu is one of the most important orixás. He is in charge of movement, communication, paths, crossroads and decisions, and is the main link between the dead and the gods. He is vitally important: he is the animating force of human bodies and, without him, life would not have begun.

People who follow Candomblé believe that he lives outside their house, in the street, and before any party or gathering in their home they make offerings to him to make sure everything goes well. The 2 million people around the world who worship the orixás do so through offerings, prayers and ceremonies. During a Candomblé ceremony, orixás possess the people as they dance, drum and sing for days on end. Offerings to Exu are the starting point of any Candomblé ceremony, to ensure its success.

There are two representations of Exu on show in the museum. The first is a bronze figure of him in his usual pose – with his penis sticking out, holding a three-pronged fork. The second is in the highlight of the museum, a wood-panelled room filled with intricate wood carvings of each of the 27 Bahian orixás. Some are inlaid with shells, another with turquoise, others with mirrors and metals. Ossaniyu, the medicine man orixá, who uses leaves to heal, is carved out of wood like the others, and represented as a tree. So what is this particular Exu, the third the museum owns, doing nestled in a sliding drawer inside a secure cabinet in the storeroom?

[Candomblé]
The name Candomblé means 'dance in honour of the gods'. Worshippers sing and dance to music, possessed by the orixás.

I asked Graça, one of the museum's lovely curators, why it was in storage. She screamed, 'He is too scary! The children will be scared!' She thinks that if this horned creature with his vivid red, sticking-out tongue were on show she might have crying children on her hands (and she doesn't want that).

The other reason for hiding the statue away is that Exu is misrepresented as a devilish creature. He looks menacing, has horns, hooves and a curly tail. Christian religious figures have often confused Exu with the devil, because he's tricky, sensual and provoking and, as I mentioned, usually depicted with his penis sticking out, holding a fork. But this isn't what Exu is about at all.

Exu might look intimidating to prudish Christian eyes but really he's irreverent and playful and, like all the orixás, he has good and bad sides, just like a human. Exu and all the orixás are there to help each person to fulfil his or her destiny to the fullest, regardless of what that is; they don't judge things as 'good' or 'bad'. This statue of Exu might give people who didn't know anything about Candomblé the wrong impression, so – as much as the curators love him – they have chosen not to put him on display to the public.

It was interesting to see the zany little wooden Exu, having seen the elaborate religious object, the precious gem-studded cross in storage in the Museu de Arte Sacra on the other side of the city. Both Catholicism and Candomblé were imported into Brazil and evolved in Bahia, and both thrive there and across Brazil still.

Once I had seen the statue of Exu, I looked deeper into the archive, uncovering clothes worn for Candomblé, including an intricate lace dress too delicate to display, and a symbolically powerful wooden rattle used in its ceremonies. Graça also showed me a beautiful silver crown, which would be a security risk if it were on show; it isn't valuable in monetary terms, but it is culturally. Graça thinks someone might try to steal it. She says the museum has opponents; some people think there shouldn't be a museum devoted to Afro-Brazilian culture and that they might try to cause trouble. The rest of the archive was filled with drums, ceramics and other African and Brazilian creations donated by African countries, international institutions and local Brazilian people.

Afterwards, I was sitting in the curators' office chatting. A lovely smiling lady named Gilcelia Oliveira Pinto (or Gil) came in. I told her I was going to write about the statue of Exu in the archive, and she invited me to her home. She makes clothes worn for Candomblé ceremonies and wanted me to see her work.

[The orixás]
On the way over to Gil's house I passed a lake, filled with huge sculptures of the Bahian orixás dancing on the water.

I went over that evening with Graça. On the way there I passed a lake, filled with huge sculptures of the Bahian orixás dancing on the water. When we arrived Gil was in the shower. She was laughing from behind her shower curtain, saying how happy she was and welcoming us to her home. We had coffee and sweetcorn cake and talked in a mixture of Portuguese (her) and English (me) with a lot of help from Graça. I marvelled over the beautiful white cloths she has been making since she was 12 years old. I was taken aback by the craftsmanship, the level of skill and the level of dedication: for the most ornate piece of lace cloth, she told us she might work on it every evening for two years. She loves her creations, and pointed out each of the different stitches, each representing a different orixá.

Each month, Gil wraps herself in the white cloths she has handstitched and goes to a Candomblé ceremony one and a half hours away by bus. During it, she becomes possessed by the orixás, and people in the ceremony take care of her, taking off her white clothes and dressing her in the clothes of the orixá who has inhabited her body. Women are extremely important in Candomblé worship and often hold the highest positions. Ceremonies are usually led by a woman, known as 'mother of the saint' and they are responsible for training future priestesses. During the ceremonial feasts, food sacred to each orixá is served in large leaves. It is believed to have healing powers.

Gil told me she always leaves an offering to Exu at the beginning of a party or gathering. As we sat at her kitchen table, she pointed out the door into the street – 'he lives there, just there, outside my door.' His spirit is all over Salvador de Bahia – as are each of the orixás.

From the beginning of the slave trade, Christian slave owners and Church leaders tried to convert the enslaved African people, to make them more submissive and to sever the links to their shared past. Many slaves practised Christianity outwardly, praying to the saints, but secretly worshipping the orixás and their ancestor spirits. Candomblé followers were violently persecuted right up until the 1970s, when the law that required police permission to hold a Candomblé ceremony was lifted.

The popularity of Candomblé surged. Around 2 million people in the world now follow it, and many people from African countries visit Bahia in order to learn more about the faith of their ancestors. There is no holy scripture, so you can only learn from looking and listening to other people, like Gil and Graça.

Oxum, a female orixá who loves beauty, love and fertility, is said to take care of the city of Salvador, as well as newborn children, until they are four years old. If you visit her city filled with music, dance and life, be sure to say hello to Exu. Pay your respects, and he will take care of you.

[OBJECT 30]

LIVINGSTONE and STANLEY'S HATS

[Location]

The ROYAL GEOGRAPHICAL SOCIETY
London, England

'Dr
LIVINGSTONE,
I presume?'

THIS HAS GOT TO BE one of the most famous lines in history. It was uttered by a journalist called Henry Morton Stanley, who was on a job for the *New York Herald*. He was looking for David Livingstone, a missionary and explorer who was in Africa trying to find the source of the Nile.

When they met, each man was wearing a hat. The two hats are now side by side in the archive of the Royal Geographical Society (RGS) in London.

In *How I Found Livingstone* (1872), Stanley's account of their meeting in Ujiji, deep in the heart of what is now Tanzania, he describes how they doffed these hats to one another:

> *As I advanced slowly toward him I noticed he was pale, looked wearied, had a gray beard, wore a bluish cap with a faded gold band round it. ...*
>
> *I walked deliberately to him, took off my hat, and said, 'Dr Livingstone, I presume?'*
>
> *'Yes', said he, with a kind smile, lifting his cap slightly.*
>
> *I replace my hat on my head and he puts on his cap, and we both grasp hands, and I then say aloud, 'I thank God, Doctor, I have been permitted to see you.' He answered, 'I feel thankful that I am here to welcome you.'*

The hats – a sailor's cap that belonged to Livingstone and a pith helmet that belonged to Stanley – are in front of me now, on a table at the RGS. A tailor named Hawkes made Stanley's pith helmet and another named

[**Henry Morton Stanley (1841–1904)**]
His real name was John Rowlands.

Gieves made Livingstone's cap. This was before the two tailors joined forces to become the famous tailoring firm of Gieves & Hawkes. Their current shop at 1 Savile Row was once the headquarters of the Royal Geographical Society, before it moved out to South Kensington. The tailors had kitted out so many explorers over the years that the building felt like home, so when the Society moved they bought it for themselves.

Livingstone was very fond of his hat and is usually depicted wearing it: at the RGS there is a painting of him with it on, and the statue of him outside the building also shows him wearing it as he gazes out towards Hyde Park, above an old milestone measuring the distance to London (1 mile to Hyde Park Corner) and Hounslow. Have a look if you are walking past.

The hat reminds me of another piece of Livingstone memorabilia, held by the Hope Entomological Collection in Oxford, the second largest collection of insects in the UK. It is the 'type' or standard example of a tsetse fly. This small fly, little realizing how famous it would be in the future, landed on Livingstone's arm. He swatted it, then scraped its squished body and two others like it on to a piece of card, labelled the card 'Setse: Destroys horses in Central Africa', and sent it home to his entomologist friend, Frederick Hope (1797–1862), in Oxford, who was probably delighted to open it over breakfast one morning. The first curator of Hope's insect collection, John Westwood (1805–93) described the tsetse fly from this specimen and added it to Hope's collection of almost 5 million insects (it's unlikely anyone will ever count them all).

But Livingstone didn't go to Africa just to collect scientific samples. He went as a missionary, though only managed to convert one person to Christianity during his 33-year career with the London Missionary Society. Even that person was only a brief convert; the African chief lapsed shortly afterwards, due to 'the temptations of polygamy'. What really drove Livingstone was exploration. He became the first European to cross Africa from the Atlantic coast to the Indian coast. He renamed Victoria Falls after the Queen (they were originally called Mosioatunya, 'the smoke that thunders', by the people who lived there) and, with the help of the RGS, went on an expedition along the Zambezi River. In 1844 he was mauled by a lion and survived.

[Victoria Falls]
Livingstone first saw the falls in November 1855. He named them after Queen Victoria. They already had a local name, Mosioatunya. He was inspired to write: 'No-one can imagine the beauty of the view from anything witnessed in England...scenes so lovely must have been gazed upon by angels in their flight.'

[Livingstone and Stanley's hats]
When the two men met each was wearing a hat, which they doffed to one another. I saw the two hats, side by side, in the archive of the Royal Geographical Society in London.

He is best known for his final expedition, sponsored by the RGS, to find the source of the Nile. He set off in 1866 determined to solve the mystery, though several others, including the translator of the *Kama Sutra*, Sir Richard Burton, had failed before him. Seven years later, he still hadn't found it and the world had lost all contact with him. In 1872, Henry Stanley, a journalist, was sent to find him.

Stanley's real name was John Rowlands. He was born in Wales and grew up in a Denbigh workhouse after his parents abandoned him. At 17, he joined a ship and jumped off in New Orleans, where he met Henry Stanley, who was a local cotton magnate. Rowlands pretended to be his son and took his name. He joined the army but deserted and became a journalist. The *New York Herald* paid him to look for Livingstone. He set off from near Zanzibar in 1871. On his way, Stanley encountered cannibals who shouted, 'Niama, niama,' ('Meat, meat'). After one violent clash, according to his diaries, those left on the battlefield had their faces, genitals and stomachs boiled and eaten with rice and goat meat.

It has been suggested that Stanley made up the line 'Dr Livingstone, I presume?' for his article in the *Herald* in August 1872 and then repeated it in his biography. Whatever the truth of the matter, it makes for a good story and has been reported ever since.

Livingstone died within a year of their first meeting. All the years of travelling had made him sick, and he died, aged 60, while kneeling in prayer. His heart was buried under a mvuli tree and an African man named Jacob Wainwright carved the inscription 'Livingstone May 4 1873' into its bark. Livingstone was laid in state at the RGS at 1 Savile Row before being buried in Westminster Abbey. The inscribed bark was brought back to England two decades later when the tree was cut down. It is in the RGS archives, along with his letters, diaries, maps and more. In 1902, the Livingstone Memorial was built to mark the spot where he died.

The RGS keeps the things belonging to Livingstone and Stanley in the 'hot' archive, which contains artefacts brought back by explorers who had adventures in hot parts of the globe. There is also a 'cold collection'. The 'coolest' object I saw was a Burberry balaclava that once belonged to explorer Sir Ernest Shackleton (1874–1922). He may first have worn it between 1901 and 1904 during the *Discovery* Expedition, when he and Captain Robert Falcon Scott sledged in Antarctica to 82 degrees south; the furthest south anyone had been at that time. Shackleton was sent home early from that trip on health grounds. Inspired by his first taste of Antarctic exploration, he returned to Antarctica in 1907 as leader of the Nimrod Expedition, in part sponsored by the RGS.

Nimrod was the name of the boat he took to Antarctica. He set off with it from New Zealand. On board the ship from England to collect *Nimrod* in the Antipodes, he met a theatre impresario called Frank Thornton who was on his way to Australia to produce a play, *When Knights were Bold*. The two became friends and Shackleton gave Thornton his balaclava as a keepsake. He wrote a message upon it:

> *To Frank Thornton: I give this helmet though it is not of any use in his combat in 'When Knights were Bold' it may be liked as it was worn 'When Nights were Cold' when the most Southerly point in this world was reached by man. With kindest wishes from E. H. Shackleton 19/01/1907.*

In January 1909, Shackleton made it even further south, just 180.6 kilometres from the pole. He was disappointed not to get to the Pole, but his wife, Emily, later recorded: 'The only comment he made to me about not reaching the Pole was "a live donkey is better than a dead lion, isn't it?" and I said, "Yes, darling, as far as I am concerned."' In 2010, five crates of Mackinlay's Rare Old Highland Malt Scotch whisky left behind by Shackleton's team were found, and Whyte & Mackay, who own the Mackinlay brand, have now successfully recreated it by matching it, using chemical analysis. Frank Thornton's play went on a successful tour of Australia and Tasmania.

If you want to see the hats, you can. The Royal Geographic Society is happy to show people their collections. They haven't a museum, so it's all in their archive of over 2 million items (including a million maps and half a million images), but they'll happily retrieve things for you. While you're there, look out for modern-day explorers planning their trips or regaling people with stories of their latest travels.

[Burberry balaclava worn by Ernest Shackleton]
He wrote a message on it and gave it as a gift to Frank Thornton, whom he met on the boat out to the Antipodes to collect his ship, *Nimrod*.

[OBJECT 31]

Hawai'ian Feather
HELMET

[Location]

PEABODY MUSEUM of ARCHAEOLOGY and ETHNOGRAPHY

Harvard University, MA, USA

IN THE EIGHTEENTH CENTURY,

*FEATHERS in HAWAI'I WERE like **GOLD** in **EUROPE**,*

or turquoise in Mexico.

BIRDS were BELIEVED to be SPIRITUAL MESSENGERS,

BRIDGING THE GAP BETWEEN
the **GODS** and **MANKIND**.

'WE HAVE OVER 600,000 CATALOGUE records – 75,000 of those are ethnographic specimens collected from living people – then there are several million archaeological artefacts, so working out how many objects we have in the collection sort of depends on how you count,' said the Peabody Museum's curator, Susan Haskell, as she led me up the stairs to the storage rooms in the roof of the museum building. As the air conditioning hummed, she turned off the alarm that protects the archives, unlocked a low, brown door with a 'watch your head' sign above it and showed me into the first room, which was lined with white shelves and ethnographic objects.

We headed for the Hawai'ian area, to a box that contains a beautiful, rare Hawai'ian feather helmet made in the eighteenth century. It's in mint condition, all three types of red, black and yellow feathers still carefully preserved on the crested helmet. It lives in storage, where few people ever see it. Susan told me its story.

Columbia, under Captain Gray (1755–1806), was the first American ship to circumnavigate the globe. On its journey, it stopped in Hawai'i in 1789, where the ship's crew met the royal family. The ship continued on across the Pacific, before returning home to Boston. This was a big deal. Before the Revolutionary War (1775–83), the British did not allow Americans to trade in the Pacific. So, the minute the war was over, the Americans had set off

[Captain Gray (1755–1806)]
Gray was an American merchant sea captain who led the first American voyage around the world aboard the *Columbia*.

from Salem and Boston and all the ports along the East Coast and headed for the Pacific. The *Columbia* was the first to make it there and back.

On the way home, Captain Gray and the *Columbia* picked up the crown prince of Owyhee (now Hawai'i) and sailed with him to Boston. When they arrived there, a big parade was held in the streets of the city.

The crown prince marched up the street, with Captain Gray at his side, and the crew of the *Columbia* behind them, to meet the Governor of Boston. The crown prince was wearing this feather helmet, and a beautiful feather cape.

Two years later, his costume was presented to President Washington by the 'gentlemen adventurers' of the voyage. He, in turn, gave it to Rembrandt Peale (1778–1860), founder of the Peale Museum in Baltimore, for safekeeping. The helmet was the first deposit in the museum. Years later, the helmet was given as a gift to the Peabody Museum at Harvard University, where it has been carefully stored and preserved. It was once on exhibition, but now it is considered too fragile to display.

It is exquisite. The helmet was made to fit the crown prince perfectly. It is made of a basket woven from bark fibre and encased by a net, into which the feathers have been pressed. The crest swoops over the top of the head of the helmet, like a Mohican. It looks heavy, but since it is made out of bark and feathers, it is very light.

Around 10,000 tiny feathers decorate the helmet. They were collected from the three different types of bird by specialist bird catchers. Several hundred people probably collected them – unless they were made from feathers collected over several generations and stored until needed. The red feathers probably come from the Hawai'ian honeycreeper, the yellow feathers from the honeyeater. The bird from which the black feathers came hasn't been identified yet.

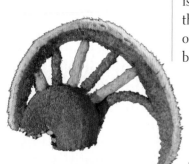

[Hawai'ian feather helmet]
It is in mint condition, all three types of red, black and yellow feathers still carefully preserved on the crested helmet.

In the eighteenth century, feathers in Hawai'i were like gold in Europe, or turquoise in Mexico. Birds were believed to be spiritual messengers, bridging the gap between the gods and mankind. So when a Hawai'ian chief wore a piece like this (known as *mahiole* in Hawai'ian), he was connected more closely to the gods, and believed he could communicate more clearly with them. A helmet like this was worn for sacred ceremonies, as well as in times of danger, like going into battle, or in times of change. It was both a piece of art and a display of prestige, and worn only by Hawai'ian royalty.

The helmet and the feather robe must have made a huge impression on the locals of Boston as the Prince of Hawai'i strode down the streets of their city. The high crest of the helmet would have stood out, above the heads of the others in the parade. It's strange to think that more people saw it that day than have ever seen it since, but that is the best way; if it had been exhibited for all those years, it would not be in the perfect condition it is now. I saw a few others in storage that looked worn, and I could see the basket beneath the feathers clearly.

Offering a helmet like this was a huge step for a Hawai'ian royal. Interestingly, 16 helmets were given to another man, Captain James Cook (1728–79) when he first landed in Hawai'i just over a decade earlier. His arrival coincided with a festival called Makahiki dedicated to the god of peace, Lono. Cook was welcomed and given gifts, and spent a peaceful time on the island.

Then he set sail to continue his journey. He was driven back to Hawai'i by a storm. This time, he arrived during a ceremony of war. The locals stole one of his boats and he decided to take a chief hostage until the boat was returned. His idea backfired and Cook ended up dead; parts of his body were eaten.

One of the helmets presented in friendship by those who murdered him is now on display in the British Museum. Another, which the Hawai'ian chief placed on Cook's head, is in the National Museum of New Zealand, Te Papa Tongarewa.

Today, this helmet, the first feathered object like it to come to America, is shown only to those who ask to see it. Most of the requests come from Hawai'ian people, particularly native Hawai'ians who want to learn how to do featherwork. They come to see this beautiful example of traditional work, still in mint condition.

It is significant that more helmets like this one exist outside of Hawai'i than at home, where they were created. For some Hawai'ians, their featherwork treasures in museums around the world are a potent symbol of all the Hawai'ians lost through their interaction with Europeans from Cook onwards – the final consequence of which was annexation by the United States. They have lost their nation, their chiefs, their way of interacting with the universe. However, those who seek independence from the United States see the feathered helmet and other feathered objects like it as symbols of what could be regained in the future in Hawai'i.

[*Mahiole*]
Painting by Rembrandt Peale of a member of the chief class of Hawaii wearing a Hawai'ian feather helmet. Most of the requests to see the helmet in storage come from Hawai'ian people who want to study it as a perfect example of traditional feather work.

[OBJECT 32]

THE LIENZO
of TLAPILTEPEC

[Location]

The ROYAL ONTARIO MUSEUM
Toronto, Canada

THIS BEAUTIFUL LIENZO,

which lives wrapped in pillows,

is the LARGEST, MOST COMPREHENSIVE

AND MOST HIGHLY PRIZED of THEM ALL.

THE LIENZO OF TLAPILTEPEC IS a long piece of cloth covered in glyphic drawings and tiny black footprints that was created by the Mixtec people. The word 'lienzo' comes from the Spanish word meaning 'painted cloth', and the one I saw, in a back room at the Royal Ontario Museum (ROM) comes from the village of Tlapiltepec in the Coixtlahuaca valley, Oaxaca State, Mexico. It tells the story of the rulers of the illustrious city of Coixtlahuaca, from their mythological beginnings to around the time the Spanish arrived in Mexico (1519–21).

The lienzo lives in the archives of the museum in Toronto, folded up, cushioned by pillows and carefully tucked up inside a drawer. It can't be exhibited because it is very sensitive to light. The once vibrant colours of the drawings have already been burned almost to oblivion by the hot Mexican sun during the years it hung in the Mixtec equivalent of the village hall in Tlapiltepec. The ROM, of course, wishes to preserve what is left of its colours by keeping it out of the light, behind the scenes.

The day I visited the ROM, Arni Brownstone, who curates the museum's Latin American collection, had woken the lienzo up. He unrolled the entire history of the Mixtec people and laid it out on a long table for me to see. It's 3.97 x 1.7 metres, so stretched the length of the room we were in. It is made from three pieces of cloth – each one the breadth of the weaver's shoulders – that have been sewn together. It is covered

[The lienzo of Tlapiltepec]
The lienzo is covered in glyphs, which represent people, towns, landmarks, churches and historical dates in the Mixtec calendar. Little black footprints and red and black lines link the pictures together. It is 3.97 x 1.7 metres in size.

in glyphs which represent people, towns, landmarks, Christian churches and historical dates in the native Mixtec calendar, with black and red lines and little black footprints linking the pictures together. We walked from one end to the other, looking at the images, and Arni told me the story of the precious lienzo.

The tale begins inside the cave of origins known as Chicomostoc. In the drawing, the first one on the lienzo, the cave looks like the open jaws of a monster. Out of the cave appears the god of the Mixtec people, Quetzalcoatl, an Earth-bound snake covered with the feathers of a sky-soaring bird. The next drawing is of a kneeling priest twirling a stick on a bone to start a fire. This scene symbolizes the bringing of the cult of the god Quetzalcoatl to the Coixtlahuaca valley and the founding of the valley's ruling lineages.

Smoke rising from the point of the turning stick leads the eye to the first lords and ladies. Then, from this first couple run lines of couples, along the length of the lienzo. There are 21 generations of ruling couples drawn in total, and these are the actual rulers of Coixtlahuaca from the eleventh to the early sixteenthth centuries. Their names are written alongside their picture. The names are the same as their date of birth in the ancient Mexican calendar – each birth date is made up of the name of the day plus a number. The numbers are represented by coloured circles, which look a bit like a sign for traffic lights you might draw if you were writing down directions for a friend.

The red lines and black footprints run across the lienzo in lots of directions; they show rulers' movements, their spheres of influence and their genealogical ties. One ruling couple's power was felt all the way to Tenochtitlan, the heart of the Aztec empire, now Mexico City.

The glyphs of places on the lienzo have been matched up to towns and villages of today, and their arrangement on it corresponds to their arrangement in the actual landscape: the lienzo is also a map. Some of the rulers' buildings and churches drawn on this one still exist today.

The whole thing was created by the Mixtec to record the story of their people, to show that their rulers were legitimate, and that their power had been felt in the area right back to the beginning of time. It was created around the time the Spanish conquistadors arrived in the country, in response to the dramatic changes this caused in the region. Neither the Aztec conquest of the region (1458–62) nor the Spanish conquest (1519–21) is drawn on the lienzo.

Until the Spanish arrived, the Aztecs had ruled over the Mixtecs, demanding tribute from them in the form of gold, turquoise, woven clothing and quetzal feathers. When the Spaniards came, they embarked on a profound reorganization of the native culture, including their religion and settlement patterns. They also brought awful diseases. Recent archaeological research suggests the population of Coixtlahuaca may have dropped during the sixteenth century from perhaps 75,000 to just a few thousand people. (Today, the valley holds only small villages, since many native people have decided to migrate elsewhere.)

There are 11 extant lienzos from this area of Mexico, painted by the valley's Chocho and Mixtec inhabitants in the decades after the Spanish conquered Mexico. They were created because the ruling houses were trying to preserve their status and hold their communities together in the face of all the turmoil created by outsiders. This beautiful lienzo, which lives wrapped in pillows, is the largest, most comprehensive and most highly prized of them all.

When the ROM purchased it from Constantine Rickards, the British consul general, they did not know it had been stolen. It came into their collection in 1919 and for a long time its origins were obscure. Decades later, a music journalist from Toronto, Ross Parmenter, became interested in the lienzo and decided to work out where it was from. He ended up in the village of Tlapiltepec, where an elderly man remembered it having been stolen by a legal assistant who had been working on a land dispute case between the village and two neighbouring villages. The lienzo was key evidence. The legal assistant stole it and sold it for 400 pesos to Rickards, who sold it on to the ROM.

They recently decided to create a lifesize version of it, as it would have looked, in its original colours, so that visitors to the ROM would be able to learn about the lienzo that lives in storage. This was a tricky task, as the colours have faded so much that today all you can see on the original are the black outlines of the glyphs, drawn in soot made from burnt bones or wood.

They also used a 1910 tracing of the lienzo they had found in Berlin, and technology developed by NASA called 'decorrelation stretch'. This software is used to fill in missing colours in pixel images taken from space by exaggerating colour differences. Hidden details of the original painting and rich colour passages were drawn out of the sun-bleached lienzo to create an illustration, close to how the original lienzo would have looked when first painted.

It turned out that the black outlines were originally filled in with two shades of yellow – a strong yellow for jaguar-headed serpents, a light yellow in the reed mats under ruling couples; blue for water and women's shirts; red for buildings; brown for flesh; grey for eagles and green in the hills. Two copies were made, one for Tlapiltepec, one for the ROM.

The ROM made contact with the people of Tlapiltepec to find out how they would feel about having their lienzo copied and displayed. Arni explained to me that, given that the lienzo had been stolen from the village, 'it was a strange situation. I was kind of nervous about the village asking for it back. I kept wondering if there was resentment or animosity there about the lienzo having been taken from them, but there doesn't seem to be any. They still think of the lienzo as important, but maybe they don't feel empowered enough to ask for it back. We hope they feel it's being well looked after here.'

The new illustration is on show in the ROM, hung vertically on a specially constructed freestanding wall of its own. The people of Tlapiltepec wrote back to say that the ROM's decision to share their knowledge of the lienzo with the public was to perform 'activity we consider to be one of the most noble that human beings can realize, and it fills us with pride to know that the lienzo of Tlapiltepec stands among the cultural expressions that are displayed over there.' While the original slumbers in storage, the colourful copy is being woven into the history of the world.

[The Royal Ontario Museum]

[OBJECT 33]

MIXTEC TURQUOISE
Mosaic Shield

[Location]

NATIONAL MUSEUM of the AMERICAN INDIAN
Washington **DC, USA**

IT'S AMAZING that this SHIELD has SURVIVED

IN SUCH INCREDIBLE CONDITION,

HIDDEN in a CAVE,

DURING ALL the CENTURIES of CHANGE.

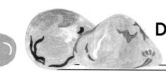

[Mixtec turquoise shield]
Mixtec craftsmen made this shield using 14,000 turquoise pieces sourced from far and wide. It's not on display because the glue in the shield is centuries old, and the sound of turquoise tinkling as it hits the museum floor is the last thing a museum curator wants to hear.

THIS INTRICATE SHIELD, MADE FROM 14,000 fragments of turquoise, is one of the most exquisite things I have ever seen. It is quite small, only 31.8 centimetres in diameter (about the size of a pizza), but its impact is impressive. The shield shimmers, even here in the high-security vault in the storage facility of the National Museum of the American Indian.

The Aztecs commissioned its creation. When they used it in ceremonies to venerate their ancestors, it must have been spectacular. Each of the 28 holes around the outside would have contained an eagle feather. Imagine it, held high, surrounded by people drumming, singing and celebrating.

The shield wasn't made by the Aztecs but by Mixtec craftsmen, with turquoise pieces sourced from far and wide, perhaps in exchange for parrot and macaw feathers. It was made to order. The Aztecs were in charge at the time, a full century before the Spanish conquest of the sixteenth century. They demanded tribute from their subjects, including the highly skilled Mixtec people (who also made the lienzo stored in the Royal Ontario Museum).

We don't know what happened to it next. It disappeared for centuries, until, some time between 1906 and 1908 when a respected German botanist named Carl Albert Purpus (1851–1941) was out looking for plants near Acatlán, in Puebla, Mexico, and wandered into a cave. There he unwittingly found a treasure trove of Mixtec turquoise creations – this shield, several less striking ones and some ritual masks.

The shield (and other artefacts) came to the attention of George Gustav Heye, founder of the National Museum of the American Indian's predecessor, the private Heye Foundation Museum in New York City, in 1920. George Heye sent Marshall H. Saville, a well-known scholar and a member of the museum staff, to Mexico to meet Purpus, evaluate his collection and arrange for its purchase and shipment to New York.

The shield has been in storage since Heye's collection became the National Museum of the American Indian. It can't be hung permanently on exhibition because the turquoise pieces have a tendency to fall off. The glue holding them in place is centuries old. The sound of 400-year-old turquoise tinkling as it hits the museum floor is not what any museum curator wants to hear.

I visited the shield on the same day I saw the spacesuits (the two museum storage facilities are a short drive away from one another). I met Pat Neitfield, the collections manager of the National Museum of the American Indian, and she took me to see it.

On our way to find the shield we walked up through three storeys of artefacts. There were shelves holding kayaks, canoes and reed boats, the way rowing boats are stored in a boatshed. Nearby were headdresses, clothing and several totem poles made by the Haida, Tlingit and Kwakiutl peoples of British Columbia and south-eastern Alaska.

We stopped to look closely at a Seneca Iroquois log cabin built on the Tonawanda reservation in New York state. Pat isn't sure it will ever be reassembled, but it's being stored as lumber because it is the only one that still exists.

We also saw a Tli'cho (Dogrib) tipi – one of only two known to be in existence – made from 42 caribou and thousands of other things packed away in boxes.

Pat unlocked the high-security vault containing the Mixtec turquoise sun shield. There were lots of beeps as alarms were turned off. We walked inside and carefully lifted the shield down from its shelf, on to a table. It is stunning.

Thousands of tiny pieces of turquoise have been carefully shaped and polished, then glued, using resin or gum, on to a round wooden base, to create an intricate mosaic made from ripples of greens and blues.

A few little pieces of turquoise that have fallen off are stored in a glass vial nearby.

[**Moctezuma II (c.1466–1520)**]
Ruler of the Aztecs.

In the mosaic, I could make out the sky, the sun, the sun's rays and a person – a warrior or a god (no one is sure which) – falling from the sun, towards a hill, with two warriors flanking the falling being on either side. The hill stands for the ancient town of Culhuacán, the mythical homeland of the Aztec people.

There is a lot of debate about what is going on in the scene depicted. It seems to be an Aztec creation myth, and it has been suggested that the falling figure is a female, one of the warrior goddesses who descend with the sun from noon to sunset. The two figures beside her are males, holding staffs and blowing on conchshell trumpets.

For the Aztecs, the sun was the symbol of their ruler and the state, and it is represented in turquoise, a stone that was as precious in Mexico as gold was in Europe. They called it *teoxihuitl* – turquoise of the gods. The Aztec ruler Moctezuma II wore a turquoise nose plug, a loincloth made with turquoise beads and a turquoise diadem when sacrificing humans to the Aztec gods.

There are some turquoise mosaics in the British Museum, including a shield a little like this one but with shell and beads, not just glittering turquoise. The British Museum's shield is on display. It shows a solar disc, created from red shell, with four rays beaming out, dividing the world into quarters. Inside each quarter is a sky bearer with its arms in the air; these are the gods who support the sky. There is also a tree made from mosaic with a snake wrapped around it. The tree represents a point of union between the underworld, the Earth and the celestial realms.

The British Museum think the Aztecs gave their shield to Hernán Cortés (1485–1547) as tribute when he arrived in the New World and took control of their empire. The Aztecs were accustomed to demanding tribute from their dominions so, when the strange Spaniards arrived, they imagined that this was what they would want as well and packed up boats full of turquoise and gold and silver treasures to send back to Europe. The Spanish accounts say that Moctezuma believed Cortés was an incarnation of the Aztec god Quetzalcoatl, as their legends told them that the god would one day return as a fair-skinned man. Of course, this might just be Spanish propaganda but, either way, when presented with booty galore, the Spanish could hardly believe their luck. They shipped the treasure back to Europe to show what they had found.

People back home were impressed. This was their first taste of the New World. It must have been mind blowing for them to see the work of a completely unfamiliar civilization, from far across the sea.

The artist Albrecht Dürer wrote in his diary:

All the days of my life I have seen nothing that has so rejoiced my heart as these things. For I saw among them strange and exquisitely worked objects and marvelled at the subtle genius of the men in distant lands.

As he wrote these words, the mighty empire was being smashed to pieces by the invading Spanish.

The Mixtec who created the sun shield would not have had an inkling of all the upheaval that was about to happen in Mexico. In the end, they joined with the Spanish, preferring their rule to that of the Aztecs, and the Aztec empire was reduced to ruins. Many of the local Mixtec people were also wiped out by European diseases, like smallpox. It's amazing that this shield has survived in such incredible condition, hidden in a cave, during all the centuries of change.

Today, the Museum of the American Indian concentrates on collecting native contemporary art, but the Mixtec turquoise shield will always be one of its most precious treasures.

[Hernán Cortés with Montezuma II]
The Aztecs were accustomed to demanding tribute from their dominions so, when the strange Spaniards arrived, they imagined that this was what they would want as well and gave them all kinds of treasures to send back to Europe.

[OBJECT 34]

ALICIA (1965–67)
MURAL by JOAN MIRÓ
and Josep Lloréns Artigas

[Location]

The SOLOMON R. GUGGENHEIM Museum
New York City, USA

IF YOU GO TO AN EXHIBITION AT THIS *FABULOUS MUSEUM, IMAGINE IT THERE,* BEHIND the FIRST PIECE of ART, or the FIRST PIECE of TEXT, TWINKLING BEHIND the WALL AS YOU ASCEND THE GUGGENHEIM SPIRAL.

THE SOLOMON R GUGGENHEIM MUSEUM

THERE IS A CELESTIAL WORK of art inside the Guggenheim Museum in New York that is always there, hanging on the wall of the gallery just at the beginning of the spiral that runs up through the museum. Although it is a permanent feature of the collection, very few people know it is there, and even fewer people have been lucky enough to see it.

Alicia is a large, painted tile mural created by the Spanish surrealist artist Joan Miró with the help of his friend the ceramicist Josep Lloréns Artigas and his son. It is made out of 190 ceramic tiles, and is fairly large: taller than you, and far wider – it is over 2.5 metres high and nearly 6 metres wide.

So, if it is so big, and adorns the wall at the entrance to the museum, how is it possible that so few people know of its existence? Well, it lives hidden behind a white wall, where the curators of the museum keep an eye on it through a secret window, to make sure that it is okay.

Why have a beautiful artwork if it can rarely be seen? It wasn't always hidden: when the piece was first created, it was seen all the time.

Its life began with Harry F. Guggenheim, then the president of the Solomon R. Guggenheim Museum. (Solomon was the uncle of both Peggy Guggenheim and Harry F. Guggenheim).

[The Guggenheims]
When Alicia Patterson Guggenheim died at the age of 56, her husband, Harry F. Guggenheim commissioned a brilliant memorial to his wife.

[**Joan Miró i Ferrà
(1893–1983)**]

Miró agreed to create something
magical that would reflect Alicia
Guggenheim's spirit.

In 1963, Harry F. Guggenheim decided to commission a brilliant memorial to his wife, Alicia Patterson Guggenheim, who had died that year at the age of 56. He asked the museum's director, Thomas M. Messer, to ask Miró whether he would create something that would reflect Alicia's spirit.

The museum owned a lot of the artist's work, including *The Tilled Field* (1923–24). Miró was excited by the idea, and began to discuss ideas with Artigas. The two artists were lifelong friends and collaborators. They had met in 1912 when Miró was an art student in Barcelona and began working together in 1944. At first Miró painted on Artigas's vases, then Miró began to make his own sculptures; Artigas would then translate Miró's sculptures into clay.

Thomas M. Messer, Miró and Miro's dealer, Mr Pierre Matisse, exchanged letters as the *Alicia* project progressed. Today, these letters are in the archive of the museum. Reading them gave me a fascinating insight into the creation of the work. Miró was excited about creating the piece, and in 1964 he visited New York with his wife, Pilar, to see the space the mural would fill. The couple had supper with Harry Guggenheim. Then there was a lull. It seems that 1964 was a bad year for Miró, but in May 1965 he wrote expressing his wish that the year to come would 'bring us a big smile'. It seems that, as he had hoped, things picked up.

In the summer of 1966, Miró wrote to Messer, 'I am delighted to tell you that the great mural has already been started. I am very hopeful about the results of this first stage. Let's hope that our great friend Fire will also bring us his richness and his beauty for the next steps.' He left it to the elements to add the finishing touches to his surrealist work, and may have enjoyed the element of surprise.

Once it was finished, he and Artigas signed the mural on the bottom right. Artigas's son travelled to New York with the tiles and hung them in the gallery, where they have been ever since. The mural delighted everyone. Messer immediately sent a telegram to Miró, who was in Mallorca, saying, 'Overwhelmed by the beauty of your mural stop hope very much that you may be present at its unvailing [sic] May 18th.'

A party was thrown on 18 May 1967 to celebrate the mural, which was officially unveiled at 9.30 p.m. Miró was there. Harry F. Guggenheim paid tribute to his wife and said how instrumental she had been in shaping the growth of the museum when it first opened. Thomas Messer observed,

'Besides enriching the collection, the mural, through its permanent place on the first wall encountered in ascending the museum's spiral ramp, will ever remain a dramatic visual accent.' A former colleague of Alicia's wrote an article in the magazine *Newsday* that Miró's colours and shapes brought 'a light-hearted, gay sort of innocence to his highly sophisticated work. In short, I can't think of any artist better suited to do a mural dedicated to "Miss P".'

After the ceremony, Messer wrote to Miró, 'to confirm once again how proud and happy we are to count the *Alicia* mural among the museum's treasures.' To Artigas, he wrote how 'moving' and 'satisfactory' the unveiling occasion had been and how well the mural worked in the museum: 'The somber monumental surface glows from the white walls of the building, creating a strong and completely resolved unit of its own.'

For many years, the mural was the first thing visitors to the museum would see. Anyone who knew that *Alicia* was a tribute to Alicia Patterson Guggenheim may have wondered why Miró had woven the name Alice into his abstract creation of shapes and colours, rather than Alicia. Miró was quite mysterious about this.

I read letters that discussed the decision to include Alicia's name in the mural, as Guggenheim had suggested. Messer had nervously asked, by letter, 'whether the "A" of Alicia's name might be allowed to enter your thoughts to perhaps find its way into the surface of the world in ever so discreet, indirect and elliptical a manner'. To his relief, Miró replied right away, 'I myself feel that inscribing the name Alice on this fresco offers me new possibilities and new means of expression … we will soon begin the work.'

Messer did later suggest to Miró in a letter that he had misspelt Alicia's name: 'Before it is too late, could you allow me to bring again to your attention that the desired name is Alicia. I am sure that this will make little difference to your compositional and formal explorations, and of course matters a great deal to us.' Miró didn't reply, but clearly wasn't up for changing anything. When Messer once asked him about it in person, 'He merely returned a puckish smile accompanied by an indefinable grunt.' In the end, it did not matter: everyone loved the mural.

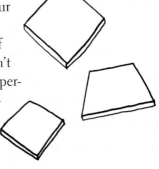

In 1969, it was covered over with a temporary wall so that it would not disturb the aesthetics of an exhibition. Because the red, black, blue and grey mural with its spirited motifs is such an impressive, timeless piece, and is in such a prominent place, it is difficult to exhibit it without it taking over the space. The curators at the museum prefer to have a blank canvas of white wall for their exhibitions and usually hang the first artwork, or introductory text of each exhibition, on the temporary wall that covers the precious mural.

Occasionally, though, it does come out of hiding. The last time was in 2003, for the 'From Picasso to Pollock' exhibition. It fitted the theme of the exhibition, so the wall in front of it was knocked down and it was displayed in all its playful, colourful glory for several months. That was the first time it had been seen in over a decade, and it has not appeared since.

If you go to an exhibition at this fabulous museum, imagine it there, behind the first piece of art, or the first piece of text, twinkling behind the wall as you ascend the Guggenheim spiral. I love the shapes, the colours, the stars and inventiveness of the piece. I think that, even if you can't always see it, it's nice to know it's there, secretly existing behind a wall, a monument to the love her husband felt for Alicia, rendered in colour and shaped by two friends who met long ago in Barcelona.

[OBJECT 35]

An Unopened Book

[Location]

ISABELLA STEWART GARDNER Museum
Boston, USA

If you ever visit Naples and see pilgrims travelling

TO THE SHRINE OF THE MADONNA DELL'ARCO,

CARRYING POLES with the SACRED IMAGE ON TOP,

THINK OF THE HUGE BOOK IN BOSTON,

DECORATED WITH THE IMAGE

of the Madonna, her child and the ball

THAT CHANGED EVERYTHING.

[Hans Guggenheim's well from Mali]
He keeps this in his living room, along with shelves full of African artefacts.

I WAS AT A DINNER party in Boston, where I met an 82-year-old man named Hans. I started chatting to Hans right away and told him I was writing a book about treasures you'll never be able to see. With a twinkle in his eye, he said, 'How wonderful. I have just the friend for you. He'll know of some hidden treasures. I'll introduce you by letter. He and I travelled together in Mali when we were 19; his name is David Attenborough.' Hans is my kind of man.

I think, had he lived a century ago, Hans and Isabella Stewart Gardner (1840–1924) would have been good friends. She was a zestful, curious, travelling sort just like him and used Boston as a base from which to explore the world, collecting artefacts and friends, just as he does. Like Isabella, Hans's home is a cabinet of curious things; he has a well from Mali in his living room, a photograph of himself with the Dalai Lama, and shelves full of artefacts from all over Africa. Recently, he donated three Dogon sculptures to the Israel Museum in Jerusalem.

Isabella Stewart Gardner began adventuring in earnest when her only child died, aged two. She and her husband set off for Europe to revive her saddened heart. This was the beginning of a lifetime of travelling, writ-ing, collecting and entertaining.

Her favourite place in the world was Venice. She and her husband, Jack, would stay at the Palazzo Barbaro on the Grand Canal, a gather-ing spot for American and English expats. The couple spent their days buying art and antiques, and their evenings at the opera, or dining with artists and writers.

Back in Boston, she built a replica Venetian palazzo to house her collection, in an unpopular area surrounded by a marsh. No one could believe she had moved there. 'What will you do for company?' they asked. 'Oh! People will come to me!' she replied. Or so I was told at dinner.

She was right. The museum in the reclaimed marsh is now in a popu-lar part of Boston, down the road from the Museum of Fine Arts and Fenway Park, home of the Red Sox, and people flock to wander around it and see the treasures she picked up on her travels.

It is the world's only private art collection in which the building, col-lection and installations are the creation of one individual, and a woman at that. It houses the first paintings by Botticelli and Piero della Franc-esca to come to America and her Titian *Europa* is considered one of the most important paintings in any American museum. Nothing has a label beside it: Isabella Stewart Gardner insisted this is how she wanted her collection to be displayed. Nothing has been moved; even empty frames remain on the walls after paintings valued at $500 million were stolen. Entry is free to anyone called Isabella, or who visits on their birthday.

The archives of the museum are stuffed with over 7,000 letters thank-ing Isabella for dinners and concerts thrown for her friends, including one from the writer Henry James and another from the artist John Singer Sargent. 'Has the music room dissolved, this morning, in the sunshine? I felt last night as though I were in a Hans Anderson Fairy Tale, ready to go on a flying carpet at any moment,' wrote the American novelist T. R. Sullivan on 10 January 1902. Alongside the letters are 28 travel journals she wrote and shelves packed with rare books.

I visited the museum to see one particular book, which is actually on display in the museum. Anyone who visits the museum can see it, but they will never see it open. For decades, not even the curators had a clue what was inside it. Its contents are a hidden treasure.

[The mysterious book]
It looks like a book of spells.

[The Gothic Room]
The final exhibit in the dark Gothic Room is the portrait by John Sargent of Isabella Stewart Gardener. It hangs like a goodbye from the museum's creator. Below her portrait is a wooden chest, and on this chest sits an enormous book that takes three people to open.

I wasn't prepared for how beautiful Isabella's museum would be. I walked into a flower-filled courtyard and looked up at the Venetian-style palazzo. It reminded me of being in Italy, where you can push open a plain wooden church door to find a dazzling feast of colour and beauty.

To see the museum, you visit each uniquely styled room in turn, twice climbing stairs and circling the central courtyard. I wandered through them all, including a tiny chapel, until I reached the final gallery of the museum – the Gothic Room – and the book I had come to see.

The final exhibit in the dark Gothic Room is a portrait by John Sargent of Isabella Stewart Gardner. It is the most prominently displayed image of her in the museum and hangs like a goodbye from the museum's creator. Below her portrait is a wooden chest, and on the chest sits an enormous book that takes three people to open. Almost none of the curators who walk past it each day as it lies quietly closed inside the Gothic Room is sure what is inside. It looks like a book of spells.

The day I visited, the book was to be opened. It was heaved into a corner of the Tapestry, a big open room on the first floor of the museum, and placed on a lectern on the floor, under a spotlight. The area in which the book lay was roped off, like the VIP area of a nightclub. A cameraman started snapping away at the cover as the entire curatorial and conservation teams of the museum and their artist in residence assembled to watch. It was like a film set, complete with museum visitors peering from behind the rope to catch a glimpse of the star: a book.

When the cameraman was ready and everything was still, three conservators in white gloves gently and slowly opened the book. They were so careful, so curious. As a curator said, 'It's like it's breathing … and we're not,' for we were all holding our breath in excitement. I think if Mrs Gardner could have seen the reverence in which her museum treasures are held and the curiosity of everyone watching, she'd have been leaping with joy.

Page one was a beautifully illuminated hymn. It was written by hand to be sung annually on 30 November, the feast of St Andrew. Hidden for decades, the song, in spirit at least, leapt off the page, and almost into sound.

Once everyone had taken in the colourful hymn, the pages of the book were turned and its illuminated pages photographed. As we watched the pages turn, the curator of rare books, Anne Marie Eze, a modern Miss

Marple, told us everything she had been able to find out about the mysterious manuscript.

When Anne Marie was hired to research the vast collection of rare books in the museum and archive left by Isabella Stewart Gardner, all that was known about the old book sitting on the chest in the Gothic Room was that it was probably eighteenth century and Spanish, a present from Isabella's brother-in-law, George. There was a story about it having been rescued from a shipwreck in Naples – there is a lot of water damage on the pages – but no one knew much more than that. Anne Marie/Marple began her detective work by looking at an inscription inside: 'I brother Girolamo da Nola from the Province of St Catherine wrote this book in the year …' He hadn't finished the sentence. Still, Nola is near Naples, and so Anne Marie trawled through publications on Neapolitan illuminated manuscripts until, by luck, she found an identical book that had been scribbled in by the same Girolamo da Nola. Only, this time, he had finished: '… for the convent of Santa Maria dell'Arco in the year 1614'.

Santa Maria dell'Arco is an important pilgrimage site near Naples and has been since Easter Day in 1450. On that day, some men were playing handball in the street. On the wall where they played there was a fresco of the Virgin Mary. One man threw the ball at a tree in anger. It bounced off a branch and hit the left cheek of the Virgin Mary. She began to bleed. The little shrine quickly became a sensation. Pilgrims arrived from far and wide to see the miracle. A church was built to accommodate the pilgrims and, in 1593, a medal was struck to commemorate the laying of the first stone of the sanctuary of the Madonna dell'Arco. The image on the medal is of Mary and Jesus – and in his hand is the fateful ball. This same metalwork image is on the upper cover of the binding of the book in the Gardner Museum.

Once Anne Marie had discovered the provenance of the book, she uncovered ten companion volumes – that makes 11 in all – each bearing the same image of the Madonna dell'Arco with the Christ child holding the ball. Two books had always been kept in the convent in Naples. Eight had somehow ended

[Inside the book]
Hidden for decades the songs, in spirit at least, leapt off the page and almost into sound.

up just up the coast from Boston, at the Hispanic Society of America in New York. They, perhaps realizing the books in their collection weren't Spanish, sent them to be auctioned at Christie's in 2009. The sale never happened, because the convent heard about it and asked for the books to be given back to them. The books were brought home to Naples for a triumphant exhibition held in April 2010. Local Italian newspaper clippings show that the exhibition was a hit.

Each of the 11 manuscripts is a choir-book containing Gregorian chants for the feast days of the church's calendar. This particular volume runs from 30 November to 26 June, celebrating saints from St Andrew to the Holy Martyrs, John and Paul. The other books cover the rest of the liturgical year.

The books were created between 1601 and 1615 in Naples for the choir of Santa Maria dell'Arco monastery. They are enormous – the volume at the Gardner measures 70 by 44 by 17.5 centimetres – because, like the Gutenberg Bible in the Morgan Library (Gardner referred to Morgan and Frick as 'squillionaires', for they could spend more on their collections than she could on hers), they were designed for big groups to read, or in this case, sing from, at the same time. The monastery's choir would have gathered around the appropriate book for the day, in the church, to sing their hearts out.

The musical notes are written in neumes, big square notes, unlike the chubbier, round notes we are more familiar with. The music and the Latin text were written by Fra Girolamo da Nola, a scribe-monk from the town of Nola. At certain points in the book, he wrote one word vertically at the bottom of the page. He wasn't odd: the vertical words are called 'catchwords' and are like our page numbers: they told the binder in which order to gather the pages for the book. Girolamo signed each book at the end and handed it over to a workshop of artists run by the painter Giovan Battista Rosa, who created thick, vivid, gold, red and blue illuminated images of the saints.

How nine of the books left Naples and ended up on the East Coast of America is a mystery. Anne Marie thinks that George Gardner may well have bought this book in 1887 when staying in a monastery near Naples during a tour of Europe. He said it had been rescued from a shipwreck, and the water damage suggests this is possible – but where was the ship going? We don't know yet. But we do know that the eight volumes in New York are now back in Italy and this book in the Isabella Stewart Gardner Museum in Boston is the only one we know of that is away from its home in Santa Maria dell' Arco.

So, if you ever visit Naples and see pilgrims travelling to the shrine of the Madonna dell'Arco, carrying poles with the sacred image on top, think of the huge book in Boston, decorated with the image of the Madonna, her child and the ball that changed everything. Or, if you visit Isabella Stewart Gardner's museum, her homage to beauty, study her portrait, then look at the wooden chest below. On top of the chest, the book will sit, firmly shut – unless you're lucky and visit a rare books evening at the Gardner, where, maybe, it might be open for an hour. Now you have glimpsed inside it and know its hidden story, and how one day it was opened with much ceremony and its songs burst forth in beauty.

[OBJECT 36]

THE DIAMOND SUTRA

[Location]

THE BRITISH LIBRARY
London, England

IT HAS the DATE it was PRINTED MARKED ON THE LAST PAGE: AD868. *THIS DATE MAKES it a WORLD TREASURE,* because it is the **EARLIEST DATED PRINTED BOOK in the WORLD.**

I FIRST HEARD THE WORDS of the Diamond Sutra on Radio 4's *Desert Island Discs*. Frances Wood, curator of Chinese works at the British Library, was the guest and she chose, as her first disc, a recording of Buddhist monks and nuns singing it.

I had the radio on in the background, but when I heard the enchanting sound of clanging bells and soulful song I stopped to listen carefully.

Before long, the show's presenter, Kirsty Young, piped up: 'That was a recording of Buddhist monks and nuns of the Fo Guang Shan temple in Taiwan singing the Diamond Sutra … You said, Frances Wood, that we accrued merit just by playing this?' Frances confirmed, 'We did indeed.'

Frances went on to talk about the British Library's copy of the Diamond Sutra. It has the date it was printed marked on the last page: AD 868. This date makes it a world treasure, because it is the earliest dated printed book in the world.

The Diamond Sutra is a teaching given by the Buddha to his disciple Subhuti. 'Sutra' is the Sanskrit word for teaching, and the Buddha asked Subhuti to name the lesson 'The Diamond of Transcendent Wisdom'. He said the words of the sutra would cut like a diamond blade through worldly illusion to teach those who read or chanted it what is real and everlasting. In the teaching, the Buddha explains that chanting the sutra creates merit, or good fortune.

[The Diamond Sutra]
This is the frontispiece of the Diamond Sutra, one of the most beautiful images I have ever seen. It shows the Buddha, in a garden, teaching his disciple, watched by Buddhist beings and angelic creatures on clouds.

Perhaps listeners to Radio 4 that morning felt better for hearing it. I know I did, which is why I wrote 'The Diamond Sutra' down on a piece of paper and gave Frances Wood a call. She kindly agreed to let me see the beautiful work of art at the British Library.

Usually it is kept in a vault in the library but, as luck would have it, Frances was planning to get it out to show to a group of Asian art students from the School of Oriental and African Studies (SOAS) in London. She invited me to join them, and the following week there we all were, gathered around seven beautiful printed pages.

The Diamond Sutra is not a book in the way we normally encounter them: it's a scroll nearly 5 metres long. The first page, or frontispiece, is a wonderful and intricate drawing of the Buddha in a garden, giving the Diamond Sutra teaching to Subhuti. Watching over them are two lions and a group of Buddhist beings, including two angelic creatures on clouds. It is a very gentle, intricate scene, one of the loveliest images I have ever seen.

The six pages that follow are the teachings the Buddha gave to Subhuti in the garden, laid out in beautiful, delicate Chinese characters on yellow, mulberry paper. The characters, like the frontispiece, were created with woodblocks – they were carved into wood and then printed on to paper. Some of the SOAS students were Chinese, and they remarked on how beautifully shaped the characters are. They were really happy to see the Diamond Sutra and posed for photographs to show to their families.

The Buddha gave the teaching in India, in a language called Pali. His lessons were passed on first of all by word of mouth, then gradually some of his teachings were written down, first in Pali and then in Sanskrit. This version of the Diamond Sutra was translated from the Sanskrit into Chinese by one of the best Buddhist scholars and translators in China at the time, Kumārajīva. He wasn't really a fan of translated works, even though this was his skill. He said that reading texts in translation 'was like eating rice someone else had already chewed'.

In the Diamond Sutra, the Buddha is thought to be trying to help Subhuti let go of his limited notions of reality and enlightenment. In four lines near the end, the Buddha talks about impermanence:

All conditioned phenomena
Are like dreams, illusions, bubbles, or shadows;
Like drops of dew, or flashes of lightning;
Thusly should they be contemplated.

It's best to listen to the sutra or, if you can, chant it, as otherwise it's like reading a musical score without playing the music. You need to hear it aloud or sing it yourself to really feel the effect it has on your consciousness. One of the SOAS students had an app called 'iDharma' on his iPhone, so we listened to the Diamond Sutra being chanted as we looked at it. It was a magical moment.

In China, when a cat purrs, the Chinese phrase is 'the cat is reciting the sutras' and, just as a purring cat is a lovely sound to hear, so too is the Diamond Sutra. Why not have a listen?

Buddhists all over the world chant the Diamond Sutra today, in the same way it has been chanted for over a millennium. They do this to create merit.

Within the text of the Diamond Sutra, the Buddha says, 'If a good son or good daughter dedicates lifetimes as many as the sands in the River Ganges to charitable acts, and there were another person who memorized as much as one four-line verse of this scripture and taught it to others, the merit of the latter would be by far greater.'

This is also the reason why this particular version of the text was made. On the back page, there is a dedication, which reads:

Reverently made for universal free distribution by Wang Jie on behalf of his two parents on the 15th of the 4th moon of the 9th year of Xiantong [11 May 868].

Wang Jie – we do not know who he was – created this version, and probably many others just like it, which have not survived, to create good fortune for his parents.

If there were once lots of copies of this exact version of the Diamond Sutra made in AD 868, why is this the only one that survives? This is what I find really interesting. This world treasure only exists today because it was considered to be in too poor a condition to be used in a temple.

The Caves of Dunhuang
The cave was part of a network of caves called the 'Caves of a Thousand Buddhas', filled with thousands of other Buddhist texts, sculptures and paintings.

It was found in a cave near Dunhuang, a town on the old Silk Road in north-west China. The cave was part of a network of caves called the 'Caves of a Thousand Buddhas', filled with thousands of other Buddhist texts, sculptures and paintings.

No one knows for sure why the creations were put into the caves, but one likely explanation is that these Buddhist works of art were no longer of good enough quality to be used in the local temples but, as they were religious items, they could not be thrown away. Instead, they were hidden, walled up and forgotten about for centuries. We don't know this for sure, but it is what Frances Wood believes to have happened.

As time passed, the contents of the cave, once not fit for use, became rare and precious treasures, and are now conserved in libraries and museums. The Diamond Sutra, because of its date, is the most important object from the caves.

It made its way from China to England because of an archaeologist called Sir Marc Aurel Stein. He heard about an Aladdin's cave of Buddhist treasures on the grapevine and managed to find it in 1900. He bought the scroll and a hoard of other delights from a monk guarding the caves, and carried them across land by camel and yak, to London. His contemporaries described what he did as 'the most daring and adventurous raid upon the ancient world that any archaeologist has attempted'.

Initially, the Diamond Sutra was kept in the Natural History Museum, but it was moved to the British Museum, where many of Stein's treasures are still store, in the vaults – silk paintings, carved tablets, pots and figures – and then to the British Library.

For the first hundred years after its arrival in London, the sutra was in poor condition. Then, about 20 years ago, the British Library decided to restore it. Mark Bernard, the conservator, used a brilliant technique. He took tiny strips of paper, laid them out on his desk – Frances said they looked like millipedes – and used them to protect the back of the thin paper exactly where it needed it, rather than simply backing up the entire scroll with fresh paper.

Before he would allow himself to touch the Diamond Sutra, he practised for years on manuscripts of less importance from the same Chinese cave: he wanted to understand perfectly the fibres of the paper.

Then he spent a thousand painstaking hours working on the Diamond Sutra, mostly at weekends so he wouldn't be disturbed. He removed glue and watermarks, and repaired tiny holes in the paper so that now it is in almost as good a condition as it would have been when it was first used in a temple in China in the 800s. As Frances told Kirsty and the Radio 4 listeners – and pointed out to us in the British Library: 'You can even see a trace of an indent of the wooden block that had been pressed down when it was first created.'

You can see a copy of it online, and virtually turn the pages. It might go on display occasionally, but it's not likely to stay out for long. Paper is a delicate material and doesn't react well to light, so it is best if it's kept inside its wooden box in a special vault – where gas rather than water is sprayed in the event of a fire – kept company by the other most precious books in the British Library.

It is strange to think this exquisite Diamond Sutra, the oldest dated printed book in the world, only survived for 1,145 years because, back in the late 800s, it was considered too worn-out for everyday use. Its adventure is somewhat similar to that of the cuneiform tablets from King Ashurbanipal's library, now in the British Museum stores – they only survive today because they were set on fire by the Babylonians millenia ago.

The tales of the ancient library and the Diamond Sutra remind me of a story my meditation teacher tells called 'Good Luck, Bad Luck, Who Knows?'

When a farmer's horse runs away, all his fellow villagers exclaim 'What bad luck!' Much to the villagers' confusion, the farmer replies, 'Good luck, bad luck, who knows?' A week later, his horse returns with a whole herd of horses it has recruited while wandering in the hills. The villagers exclaim in wonder, 'Oh, Farmer! What good luck!' The farmer just shrugs and simply says, 'Good luck, bad luck – who knows?' The story continues like this, with a series of things happening to the farmer and his son. The moral of the tale is that what might seem awful could be good fortune in disguise and we should take things as they come, without judgement.

[OBJECT 37]

TIBETAN ABBOT's
Costume

[Location]

The VICTORIA and ALBERT Museum
London, England

THE COSTUME I SAW IS INTERESTING

BECAUSE OF ITS STORY,

and there isn't room to tell that story

on a SMALL MUSEUM CARD.

AFTER I LEFT SCHOOL I lived in India to 'teach' in a school in a village in Himachal Pradesh. I loved it. The village was filled with fantastic characters, the countryside around it was lush and green and the children were adorable. At the weekends my friends and I would jump on a bus and head to Dharamsala, home of the exiled Dalai Lama. The town was full of monks dressed in their robes, walking the streets, sitting in cafés talking about Tibet and showing photographs of themselves on their travels. We could walk up to their temple to watch them meditating and chanting. It was heaven for me, even though I wasn't into meditation then.

Anyway, meeting Tibetan monks during those months in India is probably the reason I fell for a Tibetan costume and picked it out from the epic swathes of costumes from every era and every continent stored in the Victoria and Albert Museum.

When I saw it, it lived in the Asian costume storage room inside the museum itself where the museum keeps its vast collection of textiles and paintings that are light sensitive and can't be on permanent display. But by now it has probably been moved to the V&A Museum's storage rooms in Blythe House. When I visited, the V&A was planning to move the entire Asian and western textile collection to new storage rooms there, called the Clothworkers' Centre for Textiles and Fashion Study and Conservation, due to open in 2013. There the garments will be stored according to type of clothing, rather than geography so that the researchers,

[The Tibetan abbot's costume]
This sleeveless outer wool and brocade jacket is part of the costume I saw in storage at the V&A that belonged to the last abbot of Tengye Ling monastery in Lhasa. The abbot was involved in a plot to kill the young, 13th Dalai Lama, and so he was sent to prison, and his monastery was dissolved.

artists and designers who ask to delve into the storehouse can easily find the clothes they'd like to see.

As they packed the costumes in preparation for the move, the curators told me that they are uncovering new things all the time. They had just found some wall hangings that had once belonged to Marie Antoinette.

John Clarke, a curator who looks after Himalayan, Burmese and Thai treasures, offered to show me the Tibetan costume.

After he had buzzed me through into a study room behind a wooden door just at the end of the café, I found myself in a high-ceilinged room. Two people were working on the costumes up on a mezzanine level and, down below, where John and I stood, there were shoes laid out on racks. He explained that a jewellery designer who likes shoes had just been in to study different styles for a collection she was working on.

He took the costume out to show me and laid it carefully on a table. It is a Tibetan abbot's costume made up of several different pieces: a heavy woollen skirt; a jacket with a museum number sewn into it showing it came into the museum in 1930; a pair of red velvet boots with woven soles; a wonderful yellow headdress, the colour of the Dalai Lama's sect of Buddhism; a monk's robe, which is wrapped around the body; a vibrant red over-jacket beautifully tailored with red cotton and wool and a ceremonial water bottle. The whole lot is stored, like so many hidden treasures, inside a grey box with its catalogue number on it, and kept on a shelf.

This costume hasn't ever been on display, because the museum owns another, better preserved example of a Tibetan abbot's costume from the same era; however it might one day be included in future shows about Tibetan clothes. The costume I saw is most interesting because of its story, and there isn't room to tell that story on a small museum card.

It belonged to the last abbot of Tengye Ling monastery in Lhasa. This was quite an important monastery in Tibet, because it was the one from which the regents of Tibet were chosen.

The regents ruled Tibet in between Dalai Lamas, while the next reincarnation of the Dalai Lama was being found to take over from where he had left off in his previous lifetime. The regents were also reincarnated, but they were easier to find, as they tended to turn up in this particular monastery in Lhasa. The abbot of the monastery who owned this costume had been regent until the 13th Dalai Lama was appointed.

[The 13th Dalai Lama]
He was enthroned at the Potala Palace in Lhasa in 1879 aged 19, and so became the temporal and spiritual ruler of the Tibetans.

The 13th Dalai Lama's name was Thubten Gyatso. He was enthroned at the Potala Palace in Lhasa in 1879 aged 19, and so became the temporal and spiritual ruler of the Tibetans. The ruling Chinese Qing officials were not happy, however. The previous Dalai Lamas, from the fifth until Thubten Gyatso, had all mysteriously died before they reached the age to take the throne. However, the 13th had survived, and was a strong, healthy and energetic young man. A Chinese official was quoted as saying, 'Affairs had been managed very badly,' in the case of Thubten Gyatso. What could they do?

Their solution, some speculate, was to ask the abbot who owned this costume, Demo Rinpoche, to try to bump him off.

The abbot sewed evil charms into the soles of a pair of boots very similar to the ones in storage at the museum today and gave them to Terton Sogyal – a close confidant of the Dalai Lama, who was very spiritually accomplished, especially in relation to Shinge, the Lord of Death. The abbot thought this would bring them close enough to the Dalai Lama – the boots would walk in the same rooms as him each day. Then he waited for the hidden charms to work their dark magic.

Sure enough, the Dalai Lama began feeling terribly ill. He consulted an oracle. The oracle said that there was a plot on his life. A pair of boots was to blame. An investigation was made and Terton Sogyal said that the abbot had given him a new pair of boots as a gift and, funnily enough, every time he wore them he got a nosebleed.

The boots were torn open and inside one of the soles was a scrap of paper with the Dalai Lama's name on it and a black magic symbol. These were the deadly charms that were casting a spell on the Dalai Lama.

The abbot, his brother, his minister, his wife and their associates were arrested, and the National Assembly sentenced them to death. Of course, this was a step too far for the benevolent 13th Dalai Lama, so, instead, he had them punished. Each of them had pieces of bamboo jammed under their fingernails – which makes me wince even to think about it. The chief minister's wife, who was in on the trick, was made to sit in the street, where all of Lhasa could see her, wearing the cangue, a big bit of wood, across her shoulders. Then she and her husband were sent into exile. The abbot who once wore this costume drowned in a copper vat of water while in prison, which sounds very suspicious to me.

[Flag of Tibet]
The 13th Dalai Lama predicted
the Chinese invasion of Tibet.

Tengye Ling monastery was closed, and the monastery's lineage was no longer recognized. There would be no more reincarnations of regents from the monastery. Later, the monastery supported China in its repression of Tibet. Because of these two disgraces, the monastery was emptied and everything was sold on the street.

The costume was donated to the Asian collection of the Victoria and Albert Museum by a friend of the 13th Dalai Lama, David McDonald, who lived in Tibet. His job was to look after British Indian trade between Tibet and India. His mother was from Sikkim, then a kingdom in northern India, and his father was Scottish. McDonald was so accepted in Tibet that he had a Tibetan name: Dorje.

The 13th Dalai Lama had to deal with a British invasion of Tibet in 1903 and 1904, and then a Chinese invasion in 1910. To escape the latter, he went into exile for two years in Darjeeling, in India. McDonald helped him to get safely out of Tibet. It's possible that McDonald was given the costume by the Dalai Lama as a gift of thanks, or else he bought it from someone who acquired it in the street during the monastery's closing-in-disgrace sale.

When the 13th Dalai Lama returned to Lhasa in 1913, he assumed the spiritual and political leadership of Tibet, declared its independence from China, created the Tibetan flag as it is today and introduced secular education, postage stamps and banknotes into the country. Before he died, he predicted:

Very soon in this land (with a harmonious blend of religion and politics) deceptive acts may occur from without and within. At that time, if we do not dare to protect our territory, our spiritual personalities, including the Victorious Father and Son [Dalai Lama and Panchen Lama], may be exterminated without trace, the property and authority of our Lakangs [residences of reincarnated lamas] and monks may be taken away. Moreover, our political system, developed by the Three Great Dharma Kings, will vanish without anything remaining. The property of all people, high and low, will be seized and the people forced to become slaves. All living beings will have to endure endless days of suffering and will be stricken with fear. Such a time will come.

He predicted the Chinese would invade and take over Tibet, and said he would die early so that his reincarnation, the next Dalai Lama would be old enough to lead the Tibetan people when that time came. His successor is the current Dalai Lama, the 14th, who has lived in exile since 1959, when he left Tibet with 80,000 Tibetan refugees. He has worked all his life for the welfare of Tibetans inside and outside Tibet, somehow managing to chuckle with joy all the way.

I didn't see him in Dharamsala when I was there, as he spends so much time travelling and teaching, spreading his messages of hope that the twenty-first century will be a century of peace, tolerance and dialogue. I once saw him speak at the Albert Hall in London. Although I couldn't understand much of what he was saying as the sound wasn't great, the atmosphere was one of the most incredible I've ever felt inside the Albert Hall. He radiated love.

[His Holiness the 14th Dalai Lama]
Tenzin Gyatso, 14th Dalai Lama. He is in the Gelug, or 'Yellow Hat', branch of Tibetan Buddhism.

[OBJECT 38]

TWO GOLDEN BEES,
from the Glass Palace in Burma

[Location]

The Victoria and Albert Museum's Object Storage
Blythe Road, London, England

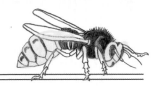

IT'S LUCKY THAT THESE LITTLE CREATURES,

MEMORIES of a REVERENTIAL, GRACEFUL TIME,

WERE TAKEN OUT OF THE PALACE

– probably because they were easy to carry –

AND MADE IT into a MUSEUM,

WHERE THEY COULD BE CONSERVED.

THE VICTORIA AND ALBERT MUSEUM's Asian object storage in Blythe House is filled with lots of objects from among the museum's Asian treasures which it doesn't permanently display. Anyone who would like to visit can do so by appointment, and it's used a fair bit by researchers and designers. The Asian textiles, paintings and sculptures are stored in other locations in Blythe House, and in the museum itself.

The Asian object store is a large room, but far smaller than some of the warehouses I've been to. It is lined with grey metal and glass cabinets, filled with things from India, Burma, Tibet, Bali – in fact, from all over Asia. On the walls there are nineteenth-century copies of the paintings inside the Ajanta caves in India, and inside the cabinets are armour, shields, jewellery from India, furniture from Burma, Indian and Southeast Asian sculptures and most of the Tibetan Collection.

In among all these things can be found two golden bees the size of rabbits. They're tubby things, with their wings folded on top of their bodies. They are carved from red wood, lacquered, and gilded all over with crushed-up gold. I saw them in a glass cabinet, on a shelf, but once upon a time they adorned the Bee Throne in the Glass Palace in Mandalay, Burma.

[Two golden bees and a golden camari]
These three creatures once adorned thrones in the royal palace in Mandalay, Burma: the bees were tubby things, with their wings folded on top of their bodies. The camari is a mythical creature invented by the Burmese.

[The palace at Mandalay]
There were eight thrones inside the Glass Palace and a ninth was just outside. Each was decorated with its own auspicious and symbolic animal carvings.

The Bee Throne was one of eight thrones in the palace complex (a ninth was just outside). Each was decorated with its own auspicious and symbolic animal carvings. There were the Lion Throne, the Duck Throne, the Conchshell Throne, the Elephant Throne, the Deer Throne, the Peacock Throne, the Lily Throne and, of course, the Bee Throne. The most important was the Lion Throne, which had a double door at the back, so the king could climb into it without being seen clambering up. He sat upon it to receive his most important subjects, twice a year, when they swore allegiance to him. The king was protected by a carved sea of magical lions, ancestral figures and worshipping pageboys. The figures enhanced the mystique and prestige of the king, grounding him in a mythical, magical world. The carvings were also a practical way to put off any potential assassins, particularly superstitious ones. A lot of the rulers of Burma met sticky ends, but none while sitting upon his throne.

The Bee Throne, on which the big bees I saw lived, was placed in the Glass Palace, the most beautiful part of the Mandalay complex, and it was where the king and queen sat to welcome in the New Year. The princesses sat there too, protected by bees, when they had important ceremonies to take part in: maybe they were having their ears pierced that day, or perhaps they were receiving gifts – say, an orchard, an elephant or a servant – bestowed upon them by their parents.

When the throne was in the Glass Palace there were 36 bees, just like these two in their glass cabinet in London. Now, only the two before me in the V&A storage survive. They are kept company by an extraordinarily beautiful praying pageboy and a slightly bonkers camari, a mythical creature invented by the Burmese. It has cloven hooves, wings, a snub nose, pointy ears, a painted red tongue, tufts on its head, antlers and a goatee beard. Each of the four creatures is golden and red, because the gold has rubbed off in parts over the years to show the red lacquer base beneath. The pageboy has a red chest, red wrists and bits of red showing all over his body.

A palmleaf manuscript written in 1816 tells how each of the 659 sculptures that decorated the thrones, including these four, was carved simultaneously. An astrologer had decreed the optimum moment for their creation. Each was carved from beautiful trees without blemishes which grew in 'untainted ground'. Musicians and dancers performed while the carvers worked.

The thrones themselves were adorned with jewels and gilded with gold leaf. Once all was ready, ceremonies were performed to encourage lucky deities to move in and to keep incumbent spirits happy. Each throne was a focal point during different ceremonies throughout the year. As the king sat upon a throne, he would see the carvings of the animals upon it and be reminded of his different duties, represented by different animals.

On all four corners of each throne sat a camari, like the one in storage. He was a good symbol for the king to have on each throne because it was said that the camari was so proud of its bushy tail, it would fight to the death to defend even a single hair upon it. The figure on the throne reminded the king to act like the camari, and fight to the death for his kingdom and for justice.

Another thing all the thrones had in common was a row of eight carved, golden, naked pageboys standing before it. These pageboys (*thu nge daw*) each faced the king with arms lifted in worship. The whole setting must have been a sight to behold. Sometimes, so the story goes, these boys came to life: this was said to have happened in 1819, for example, when the boys in front of the Conchshell Throne started squabbling, much to the surprise of the courtiers who 'saw' it happen.

What are the bees, the camari and worshipping boy from the Glass Palace doing here? I first read about the exiled Burmese royal family in the beautiful novel *The Glass Palace* by Indian writer Amitav Ghosh. I was captivated by the story of King Thibaw, his wife Queen Supayalat and their daughters, the princesses, and their shocking 30-year exile from Burma, by the British, to Ratnigiri, southern India.

The king – known as the White Umbrella of State – was undermined, and the mystique of the royal family was destroyed. King Thibaw came from a dynasty of kings known as the 'Kings Who Rule the Universe'; they were treasured as demi-gods by their subjects. When the royal family left their home, in November 1885, the golden figures were taken as trophies by the British Army, then troops were billeted inside the palace. Later, during the Second World War, Japanese troops used the palace as a supply depot, and the wooden palace was bombed by the Allies and burst into flames.

[The Lion Throne]
This was the most important of all the animal thrones in the palace. It had a double door at the back, so the king could climb into it without being seen clambering up.

Only one of the nine thrones has survived, and that is in a museum in Yangon, Burma. It's lucky that these little creatures, memories of a reverential, graceful time, were taken out of the palace – probably because they were easy to carry – and made it into a museum, where they could be conserved. The British Museum and the Pitt Rivers in Oxford each own a medium-sized lion – the smaller ones could well be hiding unrecognized on a family mantelpiece. The two museums also own a pageboy each. The boys are sculpted in the same pose as the child I saw, their arms in prayer in front of their heads, but each one is very slightly different, probably each made by a different artist. No deer, peacocks, conches, lilies, ducks or elephants have turned up yet.

The bees arrived at the V&A with a note: 'This gilded beetle [sic] is from the throne of Theebaw, last King of Burmah, & was brought from Mandalay by the late Major General Elphinstone Waters Begbie CB, DSO, in 1899.' They are kept in storage, as the museum can't display everything, although these bees are very rare and, ideally, will be on show in the future. There are two others in Oxford but, otherwise, there really is nothing else like them in the world.

[OBJECT 39]
Slap-Soled
SHOES

[Location]

BATA SHOE MUSEUM

Toronto, Canada, kept in a storage facility in England

'Whether they are OBJECTS of BEAUTY or INSTRUMENTS of TORTURE, SHOES are SURELY SIGNS of the TIMES.'

IN 1987, MRS BATA, FOUNDER of the Bata Shoe Museum, received a phone call from Sotheby's in London. She tells me, 'They had a very rare pair of slap-soled shoes from the mid-1500s, supposedly owned by Queen Elizabeth I. They asked whether I would be interested to view them. Of course I was, and on my next trip to London I made a special appointment to examine these shoes.'

She was shown a large nineteenth-century glass case 'with a pair of magnificent slap-soled high-heeled ladies' shoes inside. They had an engraved bronze sign stating that they had belonged to Queen Elizabeth I.'

Slap-soled shoes were a high-heeled fashion of the seventeenth century. When the heel was first introduced into western dress at the end of the sixteenth century men, who were the first to wear the new style, often slipped their heeled footwear into a pair of flat-soled mules so that their heels wouldn't sink into the mud. When the mules and heels were worn together they made a 'slap slap slap' sound when the wearer walked. When women fancied a pair of these shoes too, a fashion began for a style where the heels of their shoes were affixed to the soles of the mules so that they could pad around noiselessly. Even though the shoes no longer slapped as they walked, the name stuck.

[The slap-soled shoes]

Mrs Bata and her museum specialists decided to buy the shoes and investigate the story behind them. They found out that the shoes were more than likely made in Italy, for indoor wear only, as a gift for Frances Walsingham (or a member of her family). Walsingham (1569–1631), was a lady in waiting to Queen Elizabeth I. Her father was Sir Francis Walsingham, Elizabeth I's most trusted advisor. He was head of her spy network, and was responsible for foiling a number of assassination attempts on the queen, orchestrated by angry Catholics. Mrs Bata told me she thinks Frances Walshingham would have worn the slippers to a wedding or other special occasion.

The shoes are made from cream-coloured kid leather, elaborately decorated with gold and silver braid, sequins and pink ribbon trims and once had big ribbon rosettes on the instep. They are a really extravagant pair of slap-soles and among the last to be made in the style. Since buying them, the museum has collected more and more, but these are the most richly decorated.

Frances Walsingham had three husbands. The first was Sir Philip Sidney, a soldier, courtier and poet whom she married in 1583 but who died three years later. In 1590, she married Robert Devereux, 2nd Earl of Essex. Queen Elizabeth was very fond of Robert and so was not pleased about the match. Robert was executed in 1601. Frances's third husband was Richard de Burgh, Earl of Clanricarde and St Albans. They had two children. The shoes remained in the family of Robert Devereux until they were handed to Sotheby's to auction and Mrs Bata decided to buy them.

Although they are a part of her museum's collection, Mrs Bata keeps them under lock and key, not in her museum in Canada, but in England, because they are a part of England's cultural heritage so they can't leave the country for long. When she first bought the shoes, she sent them to Hampton Court for conservation, and since then they have appeared in major exhibitions in the museum in Toronto, or been kept in a safe in England.

When I visited the Bata Shoe Museum's archives in Toronto, the shoes happened to be there, in the stores, in an archival box, as they had just been on display. But they were about to be shipped back home.

The archives are filled with the collection of shoes put together by Mrs Bata. She has so many that only four per cent can ever go on display at one time. Her background is in architecture. She married into the Bata family, who make shoes. If you've ever been to India, you'll see Bata shoes being sold everywhere: flip-flops, plastic shoes – all styles. Bata's flip-flop, at the time of its launch, was the most affordable shoe ever sold and became, for many, the first shoe they had ever worn.

Shoes began to intrigue Mrs Bata; she wondered 'why people with the same feet wear totally different things on them'. She began collecting – in China, Japan and the Arctic – and, by the 1980s, she had a huge collection. People asked to see them, so she started to hold little exhibitions and, in 1995, built the museum. Today the museum has the largest collection of shoes in the world.

I asked Mrs Bata what her favourites were. 'Oh, whatever the last shoes to come in were,' she told me. 'At the moment I have someone collecting shoes in Mongolia, along the old Silk Road. She's going into Buddhist monasteries, buying shoes and filming the people who made them, so that we have a record of traditional shoe-making techniques in the area.'

I wanted to know what shoes Mrs Bata likes to wear. 'I used to wear only heels and elegant shoes, but now I wear loafers for comfort, except when I'm going to a cocktail party,' she laughed. If she wanted, she could take her pick from every type of shoe and boot in the world, just from the ones stored in the basement of her museum.

The rooms filled with footwear make a colourful, visual feast. One room is lined with Native American shoes, which are stored according to their geographic position, from South to North America. At the southern end of the room there are shelves full of moccasins and, further along the room, reflecting the cooler climate further north, ankle boots become the norm until, right up the far end, there are rows of seal, salmon and polar bear boots from Alaska. These have to be kept at 16°C (60.8°F): any colder and they would become brittle; any warmer and they'd go mouldy. As well as the boots, there are lots of straw insoles that go inside them.

As well as ethnographically interesting shoes, the archive also contains pieces of shoe history. It contains a wooden pair of sandals made in Egypt in 2500 BC, Napoleon's socks, Nelson's shoe buckles and a letter

[Nelson's shoe buckles]
Another piece of shoe history stored at the Bata Museum.

written by Wellington in April 1815 ordering a pair of (Wellington) boots. The handwritten, signed letter reads: 'Mr Hoby – The last boots you sent me were still too small in the calf of the leg & about an inch and a half too short on the leg. Send me two pair more altered as I have above directed. Your most faithful sevt. Wellington.' It is dated Brussels, 11 April 1815. The Battle of Waterloo took place in June of that year.

[**A letter handwritten by Wellington (1796–1852)**]
He wrote this letter ordering a pair of (Wellington) boots, a few months before the Battle of Waterloo.

Perhaps the most unexpected shoes in the collection are the ones that were made for the Chilean miners who were trapped in 2010. I didn't know this, but a limited edition of shoes was quickly made for them, shoes that could be rolled up and sent down into the mine. Mrs Bata collected a pair to go in her vast museum storage facility.

She explained how her collection all fits together. 'On the surface, shoes are an indication of personal taste and style, but a closer examination yields a different picture. If you look at the development of shoes chronologically, you notice the subtlest shifts in a society's attitudes and values. Footwear illustrates entire ways of life, indicating the climate, religions, professions, attitudes to gender and social status of different cultures through the ages.' She concludes: 'Whether they are objects of beauty or instruments of torture, shoes are surely signs of the times.'

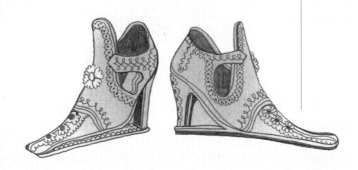

[OBJECT 40]

BLOOD's DAGGER

[Location]

The TOWER of LONDON
London, England

STRANGELY ENOUGH

BLOOD REQUESTED an AUDIENCE
with **KING CHARLES II**,
with NO ONE ELSE allowed in the room.
The KING GRANTED his WISH.
BLOOD was PARDONED,
with NO PUNISHMENT,
and **INSTEAD** was offered a **PENSION.**

WHAT DID HE SAY

TO GET HIMSELF OFF THE HOOK?
WE WILL NEVER KNOW.

IN 1671, COLONEL THOMAS BLOOD (1618–80) used this dagger, now stored in the archives of the Tower of London, to steal the Crown Jewels. The aptly named Blood made friends with the elderly Keeper of the Jewels, Talbot Edwards, by posing as a wealthy man who was offering his (non-existent) nephew as a husband for Edwards's daughter.

Edwards kindly invited Blood to come over and take a look at the Crown Jewels. Blood accepted the invitation and took along his son, and a Mr Perod. He carried a cane, inside of which he had hidden this dagger. When Edwards let the threesome in, they tied him up, knocked him out and stabbed him. Then they leapt into the vault containing England's Crown Jewels.

Blood squashed the Imperial State Crown – by bashing it with a mallet – to make it easier to hide underneath his cloak. His son started sawing the Royal Sceptre in half and Perod stuck the Orb down his breeches. Just as they were about to make a get-away with as many jewels as they could possibly carry, Edwards's son popped over to his father's quarters in the Tower, found him in a terrible state and raised the alarm. Blood pulled a gun but didn't manage to get away with his jewels. This dagger was taken off him and he was arrested. He and his son were imprisoned in the Tower.

Strangely enough, Blood requested an audience with King Charles II, with no one else allowed in the room. The king granted his wish. Blood was pardoned, with no punishment, and instead was offered a pension. What did he say to get himself off the hook? We will never know.

[Blood's dagger]
The dagger is kept in the Royal Armouries archive. It is a ballock dagger; its name comes from the hilt's phallic appearance. It is dated to 1620 and was made in England or Scotland. It isn't on display in the Tower of London museum, as no one is quite sure who owns it.

The Crown Jewels are kept in cases, guarded by men with guns. Meanwhile, the dagger that was used in the attempt to nick the lot is in the Royal Armouries archive. It is a ballock dagger; its name comes from the hilt's phallic appearance. It is dated to 1620 and was made in England or Scotland. It isn't on display in the Tower of London museum, as no one is quite sure who owns it. It came to the Tower Armouries in 1926, as a gift from the Royal Literary Fund, who were given it by Thomas Newton, a relative of Sir Isaac Newton. The Tower Armouries don't exhibit it because they figure they have a better chance of keeping it if it's tucked away on a shelf in storage rather than out on display where other departments might notice it.

To see it, I was taken up a winding staircase within the Tower. It wasn't really my kind of place: there were a lot of guns, some belonging to Henry VIII, a jousting kit and a mummified cat that used to be kept inside the roof of the Tower. I found a pile of medieval castle decorations made entirely out of scrap pieces of weapons – bullets, knives and swords. They aren't displayed any more at the museum, as they are out of fashion at the moment among the curators. There was one I liked, a snake made solely from bullets, but I wouldn't put it up at home ...

What interests me about the Tower, not being so keen on weapons and prisons, is that for over 600 years it was home to a royal menagerie. Founded by King John in the early 1200s, it filled up with exotic animals given as royal gifts for the entertainment and curiosity of the court. The first animals to arrive were lions, an elephant and a polar bear, which would hunt for fish in the River Thames. Later came tigers, kangaroos and ostriches.

The menagerie was as big a tourist attraction at its height as the Crown Jewels are today. However, it closed in 1835, as the Duke of Wellington couldn't stand the smell and the animals in the Tower became the first animals in London Zoo, in Regent's Park.

The skulls of two male Barbary lions from North Africa, once kept as royal pets and now an extinct subspecies, were found in the moat surrounding the Tower of London. They have been carbon dated, one to 1280–1385, and the other to 1420–80, making them the first lions to live in Britain since the Ice Age. The skulls are in the archives of the Natural History Museum in London.

I also saw a stuffed Barbary lion in the vaults of the Swedish Museum of Natural History. It's not on display because it's in an unnatural, quite camp pose – paw lifted off the ground – unbecoming of a ferocious lion. It's mane runs half way along its body and it has a golden halo around its face. The lion is part of a genetic study called The Barbary Lion Project which is trying to work out the genetic code of the species and then use living lions, in zoos, which are genetically close to the Barbary lion, to selectively breed back the species.

[The menagerie]
This was as big a tourist attraction at its height as the Crown Jewels are today. However, it closed in 1835, as the Duke of Wellington couldn't stand the smell, and the animals in the Tower became the first animals in London Zoo.

Nowadays, the Tower of London's most famous animals are the ravens. 'If the ravens leave the Tower, the kingdom will fall …' is the old superstition. However, the earliest reference to a raven in the Tower dates back only to 1885 (a picture in *Pictorial World* newspaper). Today, seven ravens (including Baldrick and Marley) are kept at the Tower. They each have a wing clipped to ensure they can't fly far, although one – Grog – made it as far as a pub in the East End in 1981 on foot – or claw. All but one of the Tower's ravens died from stress during the Blitz. A piece of the bomb that fell on the Tower of London during the Blitz is in the Royal Armouries archive beside Blood's dagger.

[OBJECT 41]

TELL HALAF
Sculptures

[Location]

THE PERGAMON MUSEUM

Museum of the Ancient Near East, Berlin, Germany

IMAGINE SITTING DOWN TO DO

a 3D JIGSAW PUZZLE of 27,000 PIECES.

WHERE WOULD YOU BEGIN?

PROBABLY by TIPPING all the PIECES

ON TO THE FLOOR.

A TEAM of ARCHAEOLOGISTS FROM

THE PERGAMON MUSEUM in BERLIN

DID JUST THAT.

THEY TOOK AN ENORMOUS PILE of rubble made up of fragments of 3,000-year-old sculptures and laid it out on a warehouse floor. Nine years later, they had completed the puzzle and 30 magical sculptures of scorpion-men, griffins, gods and goddesses which once adorned a great palace were brought back to life.

The sculptures were built in what is now Syria at the beginning of the first millennium BC. They stood inside and guarded the gates of the palace, which was built by Kapara, an Aramaean ruler in an area now known as Guzana.

In 1899, Max von Oppenheim, a banker's son from Cologne (1860–1946), was working as a diplomat in Cairo. He was taken by a Bedouin guide to a mound the locals called Tell Halaf. He started to excavate the site and immediately found a wall with relief slabs and the remains of great sculptures. He had stumbled across the ancient palace, covered over by the sands of time.

In 1910, he left his job and started excavating the site in earnest. Over the years – interrupted by the First World War – sculptures, pottery, inscriptions and colourful reliefs appeared out of the earth.

Uncovering the treasure cost Oppenheim a fortune. He gave some of the sculptures and other finds to a museum he set up in Aleppo, and brought the rest to Berlin. The Pergamon Museum could not afford the price he was asking, so he opened his own Tell Halaf museum in Charlottenburg, Berlin, on 15 July 1930, his birthday.

Samuel Beckett visited, as did Agatha Christie. Oppenheim showed her and her archaeologist husband around. She wrote in her diary that he stopped during the tour to stroke his 'enthroned goddess' sculpture, cooing, 'Ah, my beautiful Venus.' He was so fond of this sculpture the excavation team nicknamed her his 'bride'. Agatha got museum legs during the trip: 'there was nowhere to sit down. My interest, at first acute, flagged, and finally died down completely.' She was there for five hours.

When the Second World War broke out, museums in Berlin generally moved their collections to safe storage vaults. The Tell Halaf sculptures were too big to move and they had to take their chances with the civilian population. In November 1943, the museum suffered a direct hit. Everything made from limestone, including reliefs that showed the colours of the Tell Halaf palace, was utterly destroyed. The sculptures were made

[Max von Oppenheim with his 'bride']
Agatha Christie wrote in her diary that Oppenheim stopped while showing her around his museum to stroke his 'enthroned goddess' sculpture, cooing, 'Ah, my beautiful Venus.'

[After the war]
Chin up! *Bon courage!* And don't lose your sense of humour!' This was the motto of Max von Oppenheim.

[The 'enthroned goddess']
A restorer works to rebuild the sculpture of the 'enthroned goddess'. It took nine years to recreate each of the sculptures, piece by piece.

of basalt. They broke apart, and when fire hoses sprayed water on to the baking, damaged statues, they shattered into thousands of pieces, seemingly beyond repair.

'Chin up! *Bon courage*! And don't lose your sense of humour!' This was the motto of Max von Oppenheim. He hoped the fragments could be gathered up and taken to the National Museum of Berlin and there, eventually, reassembled. 'But what a horrendous task that would be,' he wrote to a friend, 'given that this collection has been smashed to smithereens. What I want most of all, of course, is to save the great enthroned goddess.' That was the one he had stroked when showing Agatha Christie around. He died three years later, in 1946, never knowing that his dream would eventually be realized.

Throughout the Cold War, the pieces of sculpture were stored in the vaults of the Pergamon Museum in East Berlin. Lutz Martin, who is now the curator of the Near East collection at the Pergamon, visited as a student and thought there was no way to reconstruct them. Little did he know he would one day become their curator and spend nine years proving his student self wrong.

I met him at the Pergamon Museum. We jumped on a train out to the warehouse in Friedrichshagen where the fragments of rock were laid out on the floor and the sculptures were slowly rebuilt. Here they remain, in storage.

We hopped off the train half an hour later and walked along a peaceful suburban street to the warehouse. Lutz bumped into a friend who was cycling along the road. He knows a lot of people around here, as he has been coming for nearly a decade, checking up on the progress of his sculptures. We came to the warehouse. It was just off the street, surrounded by trees. The air was filled with birdsong. There was nobody inside, so we let ourselves in.

Dappled sunlight streamed through the tall windows of the warehouse, bathing the majestic gods and mythical creatures. I spotted the 'enthroned goddess', the love of Oppenheim's life. She looks like a work of ancient Cubism, sitting upon her throne. Once, she would have held an offering bowl in her hand, in which the Aramaean people put gifts for the dead. Beside the goddess is the weather god, Teshub. He was head of the pantheon of gods in Tell Halaf.

The Aramaean gods lived in families, like humans. In the palace, Teshub would have stood upon a bull, with his wife, the sun goddess, and their son beside him, standing on lions. One of these lions was the first piece to be reconstructed, as it had the largest fragments of all the exploded sculptures. Beside the lions stands a wonderful, big-beaked griffin, made up of 2,600 fragments of broken basalt, and two scorpion-men who once guarded the gateway to the palace.

Teshub looks a little forlorn these days. He is stored in two halves. His head and chest are one half, his body and legs the other. The halves are next to each other, placed on wooden platforms and secured in place by blue straps. It's the best way to store him for now. It's as if he is resting. After all those years of being worshipped each day, in the language that Christ spoke, being asked to bring good weather, he spent millennia in the ground. Then, he was dug up, brought to Germany, bombed, reduced to rubble and, at last, restored. These statues are real survivors.

Lutz Martin told me the restorers began by sorting the pieces into piles: corner and edge pieces; carved surfaces; pieces with relief decoration and, finally, those from the interior of the sculpture. As a reference guide to what went where, all they had were Oppenheim's photographs of the Tell Halaf museum that was bombed and the excavation site in Syria. At first they thought they'd use a computer, but human brains turned out to be more efficient.

The team loved it, Lutz explained. 'I thought it was impossible and not my work to do, but every day we had success. So satisfying!' He continues: 'At first we found homes for 30 or 40 fragments a day, then it got harder. As we continued, we got a feeling for the stone, so that after a year and a half of working with the material we could identify the pieces of the inner parts of the sculpture. It was like doing a jigsaw puzzle: you have to get your eye in.' Once everything was in place it took a year to firmly glue everything together. The fragments that could not be placed were laid in boxes labelled with blue stickers. Then tar from the fire was cleaned off the sculptures with high-pressure dry ice.

I could clearly see each individual fragment that makes up each sculpture. There has been no attempt to pretend the bomb never happened. The sculptures look very out of place in the warehouse in suburban Berlin. It felt magical to be standing beside them, thinking of all they had

[The warehouse in Friedrichshagen]

Lutz Martin told me the restorers started piecing together the bombed statues by sorting them into piles: corner and edge pieces; carved surfaces; pieces with relief decoration and, finally, those from the interior of the sculpture. Slowly the sculptures were brought back to life.

endured. How lucky they were that a team of restorers was excited enough to spend nine years restoring these beauties, piece by piece, just as Oppenheim had hoped, so they could rise like a phoenix out of the ashes.

Relief slabs, stone tools, stone vessels and column bases were reconstructed too. Some engravings were found along the way. Lutz read me the cuneiform writing on the sculpture of the weather god, Teshub: it says, 'Kapara has built this palace and anyone who destroys his name from this inscription is cursed.' Lucky for Lutz and his team that they are the ones who restored the engraving.

Some of the restored sculptures were displayed in a brief exhibition in 2011. Then they disappeared back into the depot. I like to think of them resting there in the tall, windowed rooms, surrounded by trees and birdsong. They must need some peace after all they've been through.

Their rest will not last for ever. The Pergamon is building a new wing for them, due to open in 2025. Then they will go on display. I asked Lutz whether he would be happy then. 'Oh yes,' he said. 'That's when I plan to retire.'

[OBJECT 42]

Alfred Nobel's
WILL

[Location]

THE NOBEL MUSEUM
Stockholm, Sweden

Nobel had a vision of a future
THAT MIGHT BE,
and DECIDED to CHANGE his DESTINY.

[Alfred Nobel (1833–96)]
When he invented dynamite, Nobel never imagined how it would be used. Referring to his dynamite factories he said: 'Perhaps my factories will put an end to war even sooner than your congresses; on the day when two army corps will be able to annihilate each other in a second, all civilized nations will recoil with horror and disband their troops.'

THE NOBEL PRIZES HANDED OUT every year to leaders in the fields of chemistry, physics, physiology or medicine, literature and world peace are Alfred Nobel's best-known legacy to the world. However, it was nearly a very different story. Over a cup of tea in the museum café, Olov Amelin, the curator of the Nobel Museum in Stockholm told me the story of how the prizes came into being.

The Swedish inventor and businessman Alfred Nobel invested in armaments and had factories that produced dynamite. At first dynamite was used for mining, creating tunnels and channels, but before long it was adapted for warfare. In 1864, his brother Emil and four others were killed by a spontaneous explosion caused by nitroglycerine separating out of dynamite. Nobel invented gelignite, a more stable explosive material, to stop this from happening again. A later, most deadly, invention of Nobel's was ballistite (smokeless gunpowder), which he saw used during his lifetime, to create havoc and misery. By the time of his death Alfred Nobel had amassed a considerable fortune from destructive forces.

When his brother Ludwig passed away in 1888, the French press mistakenly thought that it was Alfred who had died. Alfred Nobel had a large house in Paris, and so the story was of considerable interest to French journalists. *Le Figaro* wrote a most uncomplimentary article about him, calling him 'the Tradesman of Death'.

Nobel was shocked to read how he would be remembered. Or so the story goes. It seems a little neat, but you never know. When Olov told me the story I was reminded of the tale of Scrooge in *A Christmas Carol*: Nobel had a vision of a future that might be, and decided to change his destiny.

He thought for a while about what to do. Then, on 27 November 1895, he took action. He went to the Swedish Norwegian Club in the Marais in Paris, sat down at a writing desk – which is still there (the venue is now called simply the Swedish Club) – and wrote his last will and testament.

Over four pages, he set out what he wanted to give to his relatives – he had no children – and to his staff. He asked that the rest of his estate be invested into a fund, 'the interest on which shall be annually distributed in the form of prizes to those who, during the preceding year, shall have conferred the greatest benefit to mankind'.

The interest was to be divided into five equal parts and each part given to the person who had made the most important discovery each year in four fields and, finally, 'one part to the person who shall have done the most or the best work for fraternity between nations, for the abolition or reduction of standing armies and for the holding and promotion of peace congresses' – the Nobel Peace Prize.

He had no legal assistance, he kept everything very simple, asking four men who happened also to be in the Swedish Norwegian Club that day to witness the document.

Nobel's last will and testament is kept in a vault at the Nobel Foundation in Stockholm, based just ten minutes' walk from the museum. The vault contains several locked cabinets filled with artefacts that belonged to Alfred Nobel. His death mask is there, which still has bits of beard hair inside it – there has been talk, jokingly, of cloning Nobel from his beard. Inside a box within one cabinet is the will, its pages covered in right-slanted writing in black ink. These words, which he wrote long ago in Paris, marked a fresh start to the way Nobel would be remembered in history.

His will has never been on display. The museum is too small to fit the kind of secure, atmospherically controlled cabinet required to display it safely. The museum is planning on moving to bigger premises in 2018, and hopes to be able to show it one day but, for now, it remains unseen. I find it wonderful that these four pages, down in a dark vault in Stockholm, have a staggering impact on the world each year.

Alfred Nobel had entrusted Ragnar Sohlman, his assistant, to be executor of his will. When Nobel died, in 1896, Ragnar was only 25, so this was quite a job for him, but he raced around Paris in a horse-drawn

[Nobel's will]
Kept in a vault in the Nobel Foundation these four pages, written in the Marais in Paris, are responsible for the yearly Nobel Prizes.

carriage, collecting cash, papers and bonds from different banks. He packed everything into boxes and shipped it to Sweden, from the Gare du Nord, Paris, as registered luggage. Back in Sweden, he began slowly to sell Nobel's shares, so the companies he had invested in didn't crash.

When Nobel's will was read for the first time, there was lots of resistance to his wishes. For starters, his family was shocked and surprised – they hadn't known about his plans. The Swedish royal family accused Nobel of being unpatriotic for not supporting just Swedes but, instead, insisting that nationality was not to be considered when choosing the winners of the prizes. And, of course, everyone who was to be involved knew it would take a huge amount of organization each year, and Nobel hadn't considered the admin costs.

Still, there was also a great deal of support for Nobel's idea. The Olympics were happening in Greece in 1896 and there was a general sense of wanting to create a world family and to honour people who were helping mankind. Ragnar found more and more support as he worked steadily to set up the Nobel Foundation, and to make Nobel's wishes a reality. In 1901, five years after Nobel's will was first read, the first Nobel Prizes were awarded in Sweden and Norway. A century later, the museum opened in Stockholm.

Each year a ceremony is held in Sweden at the same time as the Nobel Peace Prize is awarded in Norway. The prize itself consists of a medal, a certificate and around 10 million Swedish kronor (the exact amount varies depending on how well the Nobel Foundation has done that year). After the ceremony there is a banquet, held simultaneously in both countries. When Nobel wrote his will, the two countries were one. Norway controlled interior policy and had its own parliament, the Stortinget, whose opinions on peace issues impressed Nobel, which is probably why he gave Norway responsibility for the prize.

The first Nobel Peace Prize, in 1901 was awarded to both Henry Dunant, who founded the Red Cross, and Frédéric Passy, an economist who worked for international peace. In 1991, Aung San Suu Kyi won it while under house arrest in Burma. In her acceptance speech, which she gave when she was finally free in 2012, she talked about how she felt when she had first been awarded it. At the time, she had felt unreal, disconnected from the world, but 'as the days and months went by, and news of reactions to the award came on the airwaves, I began to understand the significance of the Nobel Prize. It had made me real once again; it had drawn me back into the wider human community.'

Olov's favourite Nobel-winner's story is that of is Pyotr Kapitsa, who won the prize for physics in 1978. He was born in Russia, but in 1921 moved with his family to Cambridge to work. He returned briefly to Moscow in 1934, invited as a special guest of Stalin in recognition of his work; however, once he was there, Stalin would not let him leave. He moved his family to Moscow, and set up a laboratory in the city. Kapitsa was asked to work on the atom bomb. He refused and was sent, with his family, to live in Siberia. He might have been awarded the Peace Prize for his refusal, but his Nobel Prize was awarded for physics, for the research he worked on in Cambridge before he was forced to live in Russia.

Olov explained that, of course, there have been controversial prize-winners: 'Kissinger, Arafat spring to mind'. I wondered if any had been revoked? 'No, the Nobel Foundation can't take any prizes back,' he answered.

He has had the privilege of meeting several Nobel laureates. He met Aung San Suu Kyi last year, and had tea with the Dalai Lama, right where he and I were sitting in the museum café. 'That was great,' he said. 'We sat surrounded by monks, chatting, and the Dalai Lama laughed a lot.'

[Pyotr Kapitsa (1894–1984)]
Olov's favourite Nobel-winner's story is that of Kapitsa, who won the Nobel Prize for physics.

[OBJECT 43]

Sketches of
CHURCHILL

[Location]

The NATIONAL PORTRAIT GALLERY
London, England

He asked Sutherland at the outset
'HOW ARE YOU GOING TO PAINT ME?
AS A CHERUB, OR THE BULLDOG?'
to which Sutherland replied:
'IT ENTIRELY DEPENDS ON
WHAT YOU SHOW ME, SIR.'

CREATING A PORTRAIT, ON CANVAS or on film, is an intimate act. The sitter must trust the artist. The artist must capture the essence of the sitter. The relationship and the creation of the portrait can so easily go wrong. But then again, after hours of trying ideas, looking intently at the sitter, feeling for their character, sketching, thinking of how best to express their form, the portrait can click into place, with the press of the camera button, or the stroke of a brush dipped in paint.

It's the portraits that went right that the National Portrait Gallery seeks to collect. I met Dr Tim Moreton, who has been overseeing new acquisitions at the gallery since 1980. He is so intrinsic a part of the gallery that his own portrait is in the collection. 'Whatever the mysterious magic is that gives a portrait a charge, that is what the National Portrait Gallery is after,' he explained. Of course they only collect portraits of people who have contributed to the nation, and when they know the portrait – in the case of a painting – was created while the artist was in the same space as the sitter.

Collecting images that contain a certain magic has been the secret to the success of the gallery since its creation. Every portrait that comes into the collection – they're acquired four times a year – is noted down in a vast ledger book. Whose portrait was the first in the collection? It was William Shakespeare's.

[Sutherland painting Churchill]
As an 80th birthday gift to the
prime minister, Winston Churchill,
members of the House of Lords
and House of Commons
commissioned Graham Sutherland,
an artist aligned with Surrealism,
to paint Churchill's portrait.

When I visited, in June 2012, the gallery was on number 6,942 in the book. However some numbers can be entire collections so there are thousands more portraits than that in the total collection. These are the paintings and photographs that made the grade, and will be kept safe for the future.

However, in the back rooms of the gallery are the sketches of a portrait that isn't in the collection, by an artist who really missed the mark, as far as the sitter was concerned. The sitter was a wordsmith, like Shakespeare. He used his words to win the Second World War. That man was Winston Churchill.

In 1952 Churchill turned 80. He was still the prime minister. As a birthday gift, members of the House of Lords and House of Commons past and present commissioned Graham Sutherland, a modernist artist aligned with Surrealism, to paint Churchill's portrait. He had painted the writer Somerset Maugham as his first portrait five years earlier so, despite his surreal painting style, the MPs thought he would do a good job.

Churchill was also an artist. Many of his paintings still hang in his studio, in his former home, Chartwell, in Kent, now owned by the National Trust. He must have understood the process of creating a portrait because he had painted some, and because he had sat for over a hundred of his own. He asked Sutherland at the outset, 'How are you going to paint me? As a cherub, or the Bulldog?' to which Sutherland replied: 'It entirely depends on what you show me, sir.' Sutherland later told Lord Beaverbrook: 'Consistently … he showed me the Bulldog.'

Churchill sat patiently, several times, for Sutherland, as he sketched the prime minister, in Chartwell. Sutherland took all of the sketches back to his studio and probably pinned them onto the canvas as he worked, creating his portrait in oil paint.

However, somehow the magic of the sketches can't have translated into the painting for when Churchill was presented with the final, life-size portrait of himself he was furious. He said it made him look 'half-witted'. However, he graciously, perhaps with gritted teeth, went along with the MPs' desire to present the offending item to him as a birthday gift on 30 November 1954, in Parliament. The prime minister said wryly: 'The portrait is a remarkable example of modern art. It certainly combines force and candour …' He took it home with him, and the painting disappeared. It is generally thought that, after it had hung around their house annoying everyone and upsetting Churchill, his wife threw it on a bonfire in their garden.

Only the sketches and two preparatory studies in oil still survive. One of the oils is on display in the gallery and the other is hanging in the Churchill War Rooms, among other treasures belonging to Churchill – speeches, letters to his wife Clementine, a cigar and his red velvet 'Siren Suit', which is a precursor to a onesie; he had several of these made in Savile Row, in different colours, and loved to wear them as they were so comfortable.

The oils and sketches were found lying around Sutherland's studio when he died in 1980, 28 years after he created them in 1952. Perhaps he kept them for sentimental reasons, or maybe he just hadn't got around to clearing out his studio in a long while, but luckily his wife donated them to the gallery.

I went to see them at the National Portrait Gallery's prints and drawings storage on Orange Street in London. An underground tunnel filled with framing studios links the building with the gallery itself. All of the collection's prints and drawings that aren't currently on exhibition are in here, in controlled conditions inside green boxes, in drawers and stacked against the side of the wall. The sculptures and oil paintings are kept in Southwark.

Tim and his colleague, Rab MacGibbon, who is the gallery's associate curator, pulled the three sketches of Churchill, and one sketchbook that also belonged to Sutherland, out of their different green boxes and spread them out on top of a chest of drawers.

We looked at the sketchbook first. Sutherland had ripped a lot of the pages out, but a few quick sketches of Churchill's left arm remain. The sketchbook was a tool; in the pages Sutherland began to work out the angles of his portrait. It was interesting to see his brain in action, trying out ideas on the page.

Once he'd nailed it, he moved onto the next sketch, beside it, a full study of a hand, in pencil and ink. It has criss-cross pencil lines across the page, which was useful for scaling the study up in size later on. Sutherland probably pinned this one onto his canvas to work from as he painted.

[Churchill's birthday gift]
He was presented with the portrait on his birthday, 30 November 1954, in Parliament.

[**Preparatory sketch**]
There is a sense of melancholy, a trace of the 'black dog' Churchill said followed him around, right there, in the lines of the chalk.

[**Fourth sketch**]
Legs astride, feet planted on the ground, this is the classic Bulldog.

The third sketch I looked at is the one I really like. It's a sketch in chalk, of Churchill's face, with a thick line around the profile. There is a sense of melancholy, a trace of the 'black dog' Churchill said followed him around, right there, in the lines of the chalk. It is an intimate sketch, drawn as Churchill sat, thinking, perhaps talking, in his iconic gruff voice, a few steps from Sutherland's easel. It felt very personal, to look so closely at a sketch of his face, created when he was right there. I liked his wispy, slightly mad-looking eyebrow. The sketch is framed but there is no mount, so you can see the edge of the paper, which is frayed, where it has been ripped out of a sketchbook.

The fourth sketch is the largest, and latest, and by this time Sutherland has worked out exactly what he wants to paint. Churchill is enthroned in a chair, legs slightly astride, feet firmly planted on the ground, in a pose akin to the one he was captured in for the final portrait. His character pours forth from the page, the classic Bulldog. This is the Churchill who won the Second World War with his words. This is the look of the man who addressed the nation, on Sunday evenings, when crisis demanded. This is the face of a man whose speeches still echo in the minds of those who were there, and millions who were born once victory for the Allies had been won. Even now his words give you goosebumps. 4 June 1940:

We shall go on till the end. We shall fight in France. We shall fight on the seas and islands. We shall defend our island whatever the cost may be …

Or days later, as the Battle of Britain is about to begin:

Hitler knows that he will have to break us in this Island or lose the war. If we can stand up to him, all Europe may be free and the life of the world may move forward into broad, sunlit uplands.

But if we fail, then the whole world, including the United States, including all that we have known and cared for, will sink into the abyss of a new Dark Age made more sinister, and perhaps more protracted, by the lights of perverted science.

Let us therefore brace ourselves to our duties, and so bear ourselves that, if the British Empire and its Commonwealth last for a thousand years, men will still say, 'This was their finest hour.'

It seems to me that Churchill, after all he did for humanity, really ought to have received a portrait he liked for his 80th birthday. Maybe a gift wasn't the right vehicle for Sutherland to present his idea of the 'real' Churchill. That's why I like these sketches. I feel like the sparkle of possibility for a great portrait is in them.

How lucky the sketches survive as a memory of a controversial moment in twentieth-century portraiture. Maybe if Churchill's wife had come across them, she would have burnt them too, but I don't think she would. I think she and her husband would probably have liked them.

[A full study of a hand in pencil and ink]
The lines across the page were useful to Sutherland later when he scaled the study up in size.

FRIENDSHIP BOOK

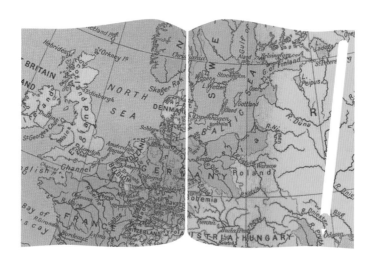

[Location]

ANNE FRANK HOUSE
Amsterdam, The Netherlands

'DEAR JUULTJE,

What shall I write here?

WAIT, DEAR JUUL, I HAVE AN IDEA:

GOOD HEALTH and ALL THE BEST!

BE GOOD and FULL of ZEST,

And WHATEVER FATE MAY BE DIVINING,

REMEMBER, EVERY CLOUD has a SILVER LINING.

IN MEMORY OF YOUR FRIEND

ANNE FRANK'

[Friendship book]

Poësiealbums were a tradition in
Holland. This one, in the archives
of the Anne Frank House,
belonged to Juultje, a friend
of Anne Frank. On page three
of the book Anne glued in a
photograph of herself, and in the
corners wrote 'For-get-me-not'.
On page four she wrote her poem.

ANNE FRANK WROTE THIS POEM for her friend Juultje Ketellapper in a friendship book that lives in the archives of the Anne Frank House in Amsterdam.

Erika Prins, who is a historian working in the Collections Department of the Anne Frank House museum, lifted the book out of its
storage box and laid it on a pillow.

It is now rather scuffed but, once, the cover was of clean cream
linen. It has green leather edging and a buckle to fasten it closed.
On the front in red is the word 'Poësie'.

Poësiealbums were a tradition in Holland among schoolgirls well
before the days of email and Facebook. Every girl had one. You
would buy a book and hand it around to your parents, teacher and
your friends, and each person would write a verse inside. Maybe you have
a book like this too? I know I do: an autograph book from Disney World
filled with poems and messages from my friends when we left primary
school aged 11.

Anne Frank and Juultje were just like every other schoolgirl. They were
in a class together at the Montessori school in Amsterdam in 1939 and
went to each other's birthday parties. In a photograph of Anne at her tenth
birthday party, on 12 June 1939, you can see Juultje and another friend of
Anne's, Kitty Egyedi. In the same month, Kitty gave Juultje the album I
saw in the archives. It was a present for her 11th birthday.

On the first page, Juultje wrote;

*I was given this album by my friend Kitty Egyedi on my birthday
and I hope I'll have happy memories of everyone who writes in it.
Amsterdam 26 June 1939.*

She handed it to Kitty, and then to Anne. Anne wrote on pages three
and four of the book. On the right hand page she wrote her poem; on the
left hand side, she glued in a photograph of herself; and, in each corner
of the left-hand page, she wrote the words 'For-get-me-not.'

I could imagine Anne sticking in that photograph of herself – that
same fun, expressive face, now so famous – then carefully writing her
words into her friend's book. Her writing was very neat.

Erika still has two of her own albums from school. She explained that
girls would take a lot of care when writing in each other's books – 'We

used to draw pencil lines, then write our poem, then rub the pencil out so our writing was in straight lines.'

Anne Frank's poem was written when Jews were (more or less) treated like other citizens in Amsterdam. Anne Frank's family was Jewish and had left Germany to escape persecution. They had grown to love their new country. Anne had lots of friends and, as her determined poem shows, she was full of optimism, believing that life was going to offer her adventures.

The words are written in Dutch, so Erika read the words aloud to me in translation. 'Remember, every cloud has a silver lining.' Knowing Anne's fate, as we do now, the words are desperately sad. She never had a chance to blossom in life. She died, of typhus, starving and alone, three months before her 16th birthday, in Bergen-Belsen concentration camp.

Her story is world famous because of her diary, which is filled with closely observed detail about her life in hiding, and with self-reflection. It is a must-read. She pours her heart on to the pages, describing how she feels during those two years. Anne Frank often felt misunderstood by her mother, she adored her father (who she called Pim) and she longed to feel closer to her sister, Margot. She was irritated by the German dentist whom she barely knew and with whom she had to share a room. In her diary, she names him Dussel, which translates as 'numbskull'. That tells you what she thought of him.

Slowly, she begins to fall in love with the son of the family the Frank family shares their annexe with: Peter van Daan. She describes in intimate detail what went on day to day among the eight residents of this secret annexe until they were tragically betrayed, discovered by the Nazis and taken to concentration camps.

Of the eight people who hid in the secret annexe only Otto, Anne's father, survived the camps. When he made it back to Amsterdam he was given his daughter's diary papers by Miep Gies, one of the small group of employees and friends who had helped, fed and kept the Frank family and their fellow hideaways undiscovered for so long.

She had rescued the diary, and some stories Anne had written, from the secret annexe, hoping to return them to Anne after the war. She gave everything to Otto Frank, with the words, 'Here is your daughter Anne's legacy to you.'

Otto knew about the diary: Anne had kept it in his briefcase at night.

[Anne Frank's tenth birthday]
From left to right: Lucie van Dijk, Anne, Sanne Ledermann, Hanneli Goslar, Juultje Ketellapper, Kitty Egyedi, Mary Bos, Letje Swillens, Martha van den Berg.

[Anne Frank's bedroom]
The pictures Anne pinned on her
bedroom walls are still there.

He had promised her he would never read it, and he never had. It took him a great deal of courage to do so, knowing she was no longer alive. He had to read it in short bursts, because the memories were so painful.

Although he recognized a lot of the scenes she described, and even some of the lines she wrote – as she had sometimes read bits of her diary aloud to everyone in the annexe – her father was surprised by the depth of emotion she described. He hadn't known how she really felt, or how self-critical she was.

In talking about her diary, he said, 'My conclusion, as I had been on very, very good terms with Anne, is that most parents don't really know their children.'

He did know one thing for sure, though – that she would have wanted her diary to be published. Within its pages, she wrote: 'You've known for a long time that my greatest wish is to be a journalist and, later on, a famous writer. In any case, after the war, I'd like to publish a book called *The Secret Annexe*.'

He hesitated to publish his daughter's diary, but he finally decided to fulfil her wish.

Before long, the diary was a sensation. Across the world, people got to know Anne Frank intimately through her own words, and everyone was moved by the story she told. A Broadway play based on her diary opened in 1955, and was shown in Germany the following year. A reviewer wrote, 'In Berlin, after the final curtain, the audience sat in stunned silence. There was no applause. Only the welling sound of deep sobs broke the absolute stillness. Then, still not speaking and seeming not to look at each other, the Berliners filed out of the theatre.'

Otto Frank wanted Anne's diary to be a message to humanity: 'I hope Anne's book will have an effect on the rest of your life so that, insofar as it is possible in your own circumstances, you will work for unity and peace.' This was also his motivation for making the secret annexe into a museum.

At the museum's opening ceremony, he could not finish his speech: 'I ask forgiveness because I can no longer speak of the events that took place here during the war. It's too hard for me. I can't.' He hoped that the house would be 'an earnest warning from the past and a mission of hope for the future'.

Today, over a million people a year visit the Anne Frank House. I was very moved when I went there and walked through the secret annexe. The events of 70 years ago seem so immediate. Anne's words are written on the walls of the rooms; her feelings pervade the space. The pictures she pinned on her bedroom wall are still there: beautiful brunette film stars, sweet blonde girls and reproductions of paintings. Next door, in her parents' room, are the pencil lines they made to mark how tall Anne and Margot were at various ages. I was surprised by how high the top lines were drawn. I hadn't imagined Anne as a tall teenager, but of course, six years had passed since she wrote in the friendship book kept in storage.

Anne died, tragically, a month before the Allies liberated the Bergen-Belsen camp. Margot had already died, and Anne had no idea whether their parents were still alive.

Hanneli Goslar – a schoolfriend of Anne who is also in that tenth-birthday photograph and also wrote a verse in the album in the archives – was one of the last of Anne's friends to see her, in the camp. Hanneli said after the war, 'I have always thought that if Anne had known that her father was still alive, she would have found the strength to go on living.'

Anne Frank's story is one of the best-known stories of anyone who lived through the Second World War. She has become a symbol for the lost Jewish children of her generation. But she is only one of over a million children who, like her, were wrenched from happy childhoods, into hiding, into exile, or to their death.

I wondered what had become of her dear schoolfriend Juultje Ketellapper, the owner of the poësiealbum. Erika told me. It was not a happy tale.

While Anne's family went into hiding, Juultje's family, also Jewish, went on living in Amsterdam, hoping for the best. Their lives, lived out in the open, were very restricted and unsafe. As Jews, they were banned from riding bicycles, taking the tram, driving a car. They had to wear a yellow star, which of course Juultje didn't like at all – neither had Anne before she went into hiding. People were disappearing all the time; taken to concentration camps.

[Entrance to the secret annexe]
The steps that led up to the secret annexe were hidden behind a moveable bookcase.

Juultje hadn't a clue that her friend was living above Otto Frank's office by the canal in secret. She believed the Franks had escaped to Switzerland. A year after Anne Frank went into hiding, a friend of Juultje's family, a girl named Lineke van der Valk, was riding her bike one Sunday morning and headed out of Amsterdam. She came to a roadblock and saw there was about to be a raid on Jewish homes. She quickly cycled back to warn her friends. Juultje gave Lineke her poësiealbum for safekeeping. This is how the book survived when Juultje did not. She and her family were taken from their home.

Juultje and Anne's Montessori schoolteacher saw the raid happen, as did a neighbour and friend, Lilian van Delft. Lilian had often shopped for the Ketellapper family, as Jews were not allowed into shops, and she watched in horror as her neighbour, whom she said she loved for her honesty and openness, was taken away, wearing a backpack, a warm wind jacket, a skirt and a pair of good shoes: clothes Lillian had bought for her. Nobody could do a thing to help.

Three weeks later, Juultje was murdered; gassed in Sobibor in occupied Poland with her father, mother and sister. Many of her family members from her mother's and her father's side were also killed.

Years after the war was over, in the 1950s, Lineke van der Valk met Kitty Egyedi (also Jewish), who had survived the war, and returned the poësiealbum to her. Kitty remembered giving it to Juultje at her birthday party, before the war began and, years later, she gave it to the Anne Frank House.

When Erika showed it to me, gently resting it on a pillow, I felt incredibly moved. I was looking at a true hidden treasure: a memory of a happy time when Anne Frank was a spirited girl writing a poem to her friend. I thought back to that photo of Anne's tenth birthday. Then, Anne, Juultje, Kitty and their friends were normal, gorgeous girls at the beginning of their lives, all with a future to look forward to.

Anne would have had her own poësiealbum just like it, filled with messages from her friends, but, unlike her diary, it wasn't saved.

I don't want to have lived in vain like most people. I want to be useful or bring enjoyment to all people, even those I've never met. I want to go on living even after my death!

Anne Frank, 5 April 1944

Torah Ark
CURTAIN

[Location]

JEWISH MUSEUM
Berlin, Germany

It is **QUITE AMAZING**

that such a FRAGILE OBJECT

HAS SURVIVED IN SUCH GOOD CONDITION

– with a lot of help from conservators –

FOR SO MANY CENTURIES, AND IN SO MANY INCARNATIONS:

FIRST as a ROLL of SILK,

THEN as a WEDDING DRESS,

a TORAH ARK CURTAIN and a DISPLACED REFUGEE IN EXILE,

UNTIL IT WAS REDISCOVERED AND REBORN,

brought back to life by

COLLECTORS and CONSERVATORS at the MUSEUM.

As his name suggests, from the moment Moses Mendelssohn (1729–86) was born, his family expected him to become a rabbi, but he followed his teacher to Berlin, which was then under the enlightened rule of Frederick II. He read the works of writers of the Enlightenment and turned all he learnt towards his religion, urging his fellow Jews to leave behind superstition and engage with modern culture. He translated the Bible into German and argued that the religious truths of Judaism were the same as the fundamental truths accessible to anyone, as demonstrated by philosophy. He believed that the soul is immortal and that God exists; and he championed religious tolerance.

In the collections of the Jewish Museum in Berlin is a treasure that belonged to him and his wife, Fromet Guggenheim. It is a delicate, white, silk Torah Ark curtain embroidered with flowers, two lions and decorative motifs. He presented it to a Berlin synagogue in 1774 or 1775. It was a very personal gift, for it was made from his wife's wedding dress and may have been given to the museum to celebrate the birth of their daughter, Henriette.

For many years, during the two most important Jewish festivals of the year – the New Year Festival and the Day of Atonement – the Berlin synagogue hung it in front of their Torah cabinet containing the Torah scrolls. The scrolls in any synagogue are handwritten copies of the Torah, the Jewish sacred scriptures, made up of the Five Books of Moses. They are stored in the Torah Ark, built along the wall that faces Jerusalem, and are usually veiled with a decorative curtain, like this delicate silk that was once a wedding dress.

Several years after Moses Mendelssohn's death, Fromet went home to Hamburg and took her transformed wedding dress with her. She gave it to a synagogue in Altona, where it remained hanging for nearly 150 years.

Then troubles began for the Jewish people. From 1938, they were no longer safe in Germany and elsewhere, and thousands upon thousands of Jewish people fled from Germany. One refugee took the precious silk with them to Antwerp, where it was used in a makeshift prayer room set up by refugees. In the evenings, the community warden, Leo Rothschild, kept it in his home. In May 1940, the Nazi Party occupied Belgium, and Leo's wife, Betty, gave the precious silk to a family friend, who hid it in a wash basket filled with dirty clothes. Betty and her two sons were murdered in

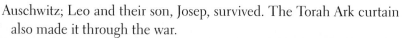

Auschwitz; Leo and their son, Josep, survived. The Torah Ark curtain also made it through the war.

It was found in terrible condition, in New York. It was in a 'genizah', a storage place where Jewish religious items are put when they are no longer in a good enough condition to be used in rituals. The Jewish Museum in Berlin bought it and decided to conserve it.

The museum is quite new – it opened on 9 September 2001. For a few years before they opened they began buying interesting treasures, the Torah Ark curtain was bought in 1997. When the museum first opened, the curtain was on display. However, the opening celebrations were muted because of 11 September. The curtain did not stay on display for long – just six months – then it was put away, in a secret location in the museum, hidden in complete darkness. The museum would love to display the Torah Ark curtain, made from the dress of the bride of one of the most important figures in Jewish history, but its job is to preserve its treasures. The quality of the silk and the colours of the thread would degrade and fade in daylight.

Michal Friedlander, curator at the Jewish Museum, took me to see it. We went into a room filled with grey cabinets, and she pulled open a large, grey drawer. As the drawer rolled open, more and more of the soft silk fabric was revealed. The most striking figures on it are the two lions. They symbolize Judah, one of Israel's 12 tribes. They have their paws up on a crown, the Keter Torah, or Torah crown. Around the lions is an arch with two columns adorned with wreaths of flowers, and across the top I could see several small motifs, which Michal told me symbolize the Temple in Jerusalem. An inscription was sewn on to the curtain saying that it was a gift from the couple and asking for their protection.

It is quite amazing that such a fragile object has survived in such good condition – with a lot of help from conservators – for so many centuries, and in so many incarnations: first as a roll of silk, then as a wedding dress, a Torah Ark curtain and a displaced refugee in exile, until it was rediscovered and reborn, brought back to life by collectors and conservators at the museum.

It was briefly on show in June 2012 for a weekend to celebrate the 250th wedding anniversary of Moses and Fromet, so that their descendants could see it. It won't be displayed again. It will remain tucked away, a testimony to love, and to survival against the odds.

[OBJECT 46]

The Tower of the Blue Horses
BY FRANZ MARC

[Location]

UNKNOWN, formerly **THE NATIONAL GALLERY**
Berlin, Germany

NO ONE KNOWS WHERE IT IS;

IT IS LISTED in the GALLERY'S CATALOGUES,

and THERE ARE A LOT of RUMOURS,

but its location is a MYSTERY.

[Franz Marc]
According to his first
biographer, Alois Schardt,
Marc was so ugly at birth that
his father, when taking a first
close look at his son at baptism,
fainted. He looks alright to me.

THE NATIONAL GALLERY, ON MUSEUM Island in Berlin, is in what became East Berlin when the Berlin Wall was built in 1961, to divide the city into a western, capitalist sector and an eastern, socialist sector. When the wall went up, some of the National Gallery's collection ended up on one side of the wall, some on the other. A new national gallery – the Neue Nationalgalerie – was built to house the collection in the west. Both are still there, the old and the new.

A lot of the National Gallery's collection was taken by the Nazis in their 'Degenerate Art' campaign was in 1937. Paintings were burned or, in many cases, sold – auctioned in Switzerland and sold to buyers all over the world. Many paintings have still not been handed back: a lot of the National Gallery's collection is missing.

One of the best of these missing paintings is *The Tower of the Blue Horses (Der Turm der blauen Pferde)* by Franz Marc (1880–1916), a German Expressionist painter and printmaker. No one knows where it is; it is listed in the gallery's catalogues, and there are a lot of rumours, but its location is a mystery. We do know exactly what it looked like however, which is lucky, because it was unusual to photograph in colour at the time. The painting shows four blue horses, one above the other and they are shown in a landscape of boulder-like objects. A rainbow arcs above them, painted in bright colours of red, orange, yellow and green.

Marc was a big fan of van Gogh:

Van Gogh is for me the most authentic, the greatest, the most poignant painter I know. To paint a bit of the most ordinary nature, putting all one's faith and longings into it – that is the supreme achievement ... Now I paint ... only the simplest things ... Only in them are the symbolism, the pathos, and the mystery of nature to be found.

He painted *The Tower of the Blue Horses* in the winter of 1913. He used the colour blue to represent masculinity and spirituality, yellow for feminine joy and red for an atmosphere of violence. He loved to paint animals, for they symbolized innocence to him; he believed animals were purer in spirit than man. When he joined the First World War, he found it utterly traumatic. He began to see ugliness in animals, too: in a letter to his wife in 1915 he said that he was no longer able to see the beauty which animals had once represented for him. He adhered to a bizarre school of thought that believed war would purify the universe of all that was bad.

In 1916, he was killed by a shell splinter during the Battle of Verdun. The government had recommended that he be taken out of the army, as he was such a notable artist, but the orders for him to be reassigned did not make it in time.

One of his last letters read:

I understand well that you speak as easily of death as of something which doesn't frighten you. I feel precisely the same. In this war, you can try it out on yourself – an opportunity life seldom offers one ... nothing is more calming than the prospect of the peace of death ... the one thing common to all. It leads us back into normal 'being'. The space between birth and death is an exception, in which there is much to fear and suffer. The only true, constant, philosophical comfort is the awareness that this exceptional condition will pass and that 'I-conciousness', which is always restless, always piquant, in all seriousness inaccessible, will again sink back into its wonderful peace before birth ... whoever strives from purity and knowledge, to him death always comes as a saviour.

[*The Tower of the Blue Horses*]
The painting once hung in the National Gallery in Berlin but it was declared 'degenerate' by the Nazis in 1937 and, soon after, it disappeared. It's lucky it was photographed in colour so we know exactly what it looked like.

In 1919, the National Gallery in Berlin bought *The Tower of the Blue Horses*, and it stayed there for 18 years, until the Nazis declared it

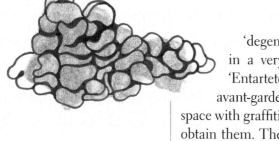

'degenerate' and took it down. It was displayed once in 1937, in a very controversial exhibition called 'Degenerate Art' or 'Entartete Kunst', put together by the Nazis to mock 'degenerate' avant-garde art. Pieces were crammed together in the exhibition space with graffiti-style comments about how much the state had spent to obtain them. The show toured Germany and Austria and three million people saw it. There were complaints about *The Tower of the Blue Horses* appearing in the show, so it was taken out. Then it disappeared, one of the many countless masterpieces that did so. It may have been destroyed. There are also rumours that it is in a Swiss vault.

In May 2012, an artist, Martin Gostner, created an outdoor installation at the Neue Nationalgalerie on the theme of the missing painting called *Der Erker der blauen Pferde (The Oriel of the Blue Horses)*. He sent out invitations to the show that featured a reproduction of the painting in an oriel, or bay window. Then, in secret, he left four pieces of blue horse dung, outside the gallery. Only some people saw them, others might not have noticed them. He wanted the sculptures to pose questions about the painting: Where is it? Does it still exist? What traces would the four blue horses leave behind? What signal could the horses give their owners?

The painting is still very much in the consciousness of art lovers in Berlin, and still considered a part of the National Gallery's collection, even though nobody knows where it is.

[Hans Scholl (1918–1943) left, and Sophie Scholl (1921–1943) centre]
Back when the painting hung in the National gallery it was a favourite of Hans Scholl, brother of Sophie. The siblings were members of the White Rose, a student group in Munich that was part of the resistance movement in Nazi Germany.

Back when the painting hung in the gallery, it was a favourite of Hans Scholl, brother of Sophie Scholl, German teenagers in the 1930s. Sophie and Hans joined the Hitler Youth, but their father persuaded them that Hitler was destroying the German people. Their father was later sent to prison for telling his secretary, 'The war! It is already lost. This Hitler is God's scourge on mankind, and if the war doesn't end soon the Russians will be sitting in Berlin.'

Hans and Sophie believed it was their duty as citizens, even during wartime, to stand up for what they believed, and speak out against the Nazi regime. They wrote a leaflet entitled 'The White Rose', along with other students and professors from the University of Munich, describing how the Nazi system had imprisoned the German people and was destroying them.

The group wrote six more leaflets and contacted resistance groups across Germany. They wrote graffiti such as 'Down with Hitler!' and 'Freedom!' in the streets. The Nazis became furious as resistance against them grew stronger. The Gestapo could not initially track down any members of the group, but after several months, Hans and Sophie were arrested at the University of Munich. Hans had a freshly printed leaflet in his pocket.

Four days later, they were put on trial. Sophie Scholl remarked: 'Somebody, after all, had to make a start. What we wrote and said is also believed by many others. They just don't dare to express themselves as we did.'

The two siblings were found guilty of 'conspiracy to commit high treason' and, that afternoon, after saying goodbye to their parents, they were led to the guillotine. Sophie was 21, Hans 24.

Copies of their final pamphlet were smuggled out of Germany and air-dropped back into the country by Allied Forces, which led to more resistance against the Nazis towards the end of the war. The Scholl siblings have gone down in history in Germany. They tell the story of the 'other' Germany, of the artists, the poets and thinkers who believed in the freedom of the human spirit.

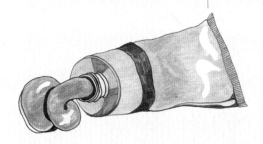

CHRISTMAS TELEGRAM
FROM AGENT ZIGZAG

TOP SECRET

[Location]

BLETCHLEY PARK
Buckinghamshire, England

In August 1938, 'CAPTAIN RIDLEY'S SHOOTING PARTY'

ARRIVED AT BLETCHLEY PARK,

A LARGE MANOR HOUSE IN BUCKINGHAMSHIRE.

THEY had been **SUMMONED** by a **TELEGRAM THAT READ:**

'AUNTY FLO IS NOT SO WELL.'

EACH MEMBER OF THE 'PARTY' was an MI6 agent. They had come to set up a base in which to make plans in the event of war.

They turned the water tower of the manor house into a listening station and called it Station X, which is what Bletchley Park itself became known as during the war. The X stood for ten, as it was the tenth such listening station established in the country.

I headed up the rickety stairs of the tower and stood inside the original Station X, soaking up the atmosphere: this is where listening in on the enemy began in Bletchley Park. The room is off limits to museum visitors.

After war broke out, more and more codebreakers joined the initial team. They were an eclectic bunch of chess grandmasters, university students, mathematicians and musicians. Some were recruited with the help of the *Daily Telegraph* crossword. Entrants sat the crossword under exam conditions, and those who completed it in less than 12 minutes were called to Bletchley Park.

At the peak of the Second World War, 9,000 people were working in three shifts around the clock, deciphering 6,000 messages a day that had been scrambled by the German Enigma and Lorenz machines. Enigma was a machine which looked like a typewriter, with keys that lit up, that was used by the Germans to encode their messages. The deciphering team was codenamed Ultra and was kept a secret throughout the war.

[Hut 3 at Bletchley Park, Buckinghamshire, 1942]
The codebreaking huts worked in pairs. The decoded messages from Hut 6 were passed to Hut 3 for translation, analysis and dispatch. There was a connecting chute between the two so that information could be sent quickly between them.

[An Enigma machine]
Enigma was used by the Germans to encode their messages. The German authorities had no idea that British codebreakers stationed at Bletchley Park understood how it worked and, with the help of Polish mathematicians, they cracked the Enigma code.

Churchill referred to them only as his 'Most Secret Source'. He once described the sharp, bright minds who worked busily at the park as, 'The geese that laid the golden eggs and never cackled.' Thanks to them his government could anticipate the movements of the enemy. It has been said that the war ended two years earlier than it might otherwise have done because of the work at Bletchley Park.

The codebreakers did not work out the initial solution for Enigma – they were given it by Poland, just before the outbreak of war. The first to work out the code, in 1932, was a young Polish mathematician called Marian Rejewski and it was he who passed on the secret to the British. The code gave everyone at the park a fighting chance of decoding the Germans' military messages, even though they changed their system of encryption every day.

The Germans had no idea their codes had been broken, even though, at times, messages were being read in England as quickly as they were by their German recipients. Even years after the war, people who worked at Bletchley Park kept their wartime lives a secret.

The ban on talking about Bletchley Park was officially lifted in 1974, but many of the 2,500 veterans still alive won't talk about what they did there. One couple met during a Scottish dancing party on the lawn of Bletchley Park. They later married but never once discussed their work there in 30 years of marriage.

I met curator Gillian Mason, who has been working on Bletchley Park's archives since 2010, in Cottage 3, the building in which the first codebreak of the war took place. She explained that the archives of Bletchley Park are still top secret, not because they are classified, but because there hasn't been time to go through all the cupboards, drawers and rooms packed with papers, telegrams and intelligence that have lain unexplored since the war ended.

At that time, Bletchley Park was abandoned. It was nearly sold to property developers in the 1990s, but was saved by veterans. It was turned into a museum, but until 2010 it was short of funding. Gillian was then hired to begin work on the huge unmined treasure trove of hundreds of thousands of maps and papers.

We had a nose around, pulling drawers open to reveal maps and books full of telegrams. Some folders stuffed full of German intelligence are

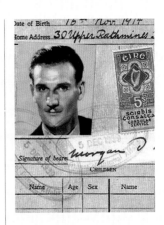

marked 'TOP SECRET' and others are marked 'MOST SECRET'. 'What is the difference?' I asked. It turns out they are the same thing, only the 'most secret' files date from before the Americans came into the war. When American codebreakers joined the effort at Bletchley Park, they weren't sure what 'most secret' meant. 'Is that, like, kind of secret, or what?' they asked. Bletchley Park agents had to get lots of new rubber stamps, this time marked 'TOP SECRET', so everything was crystal clear for their American pals.

In among all the telegrams and files was a message sent by Eddie Chapman, Britain's most successful double agent, nicknamed Agent Zigzag. Chapman had always been a bit of a bad boy. As the Second World War began, he was in prison in Jersey for a series of robberies. As a member of a 'jelly gang', he blew up safes using gelignite – invented by Alfred Nobel. Chapman had made lots of money and, before he was caught, for a while lived it up as a playboy in Soho.

[Eddie Chapman]
False identification papers issued to Eddie Chapman aka Agent Zigzag.

When the Germans occupied Jersey in 1940, Chapman was still in jail. He was desperate to get out and return to England to meet his new-born daughter. He offered his services to the Germans as a spy, saying he wanted revenge on the British, who had put him in prison. Eventually, after much deliberation and questioning, he was hired.

The German Secret Service nicknamed him Little Fritz and trained him up. They wanted him to attack an aircraft factory in Herefordshire which made Mosquito bombers. In 1942, just before Christmas, he was thrown out of a plane above a field in Cambridge and parachuted into a muddy field. Bletchley Park had been reading his telegrams and had named him Agent X. They knew he was about to arrive and had planned Operation Nightcap to find him. They didn't have to try hard, because as soon as he landed, he knocked on the door of a startled couple that lived in Ely and turned himself into the police. He then became a double agent: Agent Zigzag.

He had been trained to send telegrams back to his German bosses, with a sign that would let them know he had not been captured. The sign was five Fs – 'FFFFF' – because of his nickname, Little Fritz. It was vital that he kept using this so that the Germans would believe he was still working for them. He and the British MI5 faked an attack on the Herefordshire factory, using a magician, Jasper Maskelyne, to create an illusion. Even the

factory staff believed their workplace had been destroyed. So successful a double agent was he that Agent Zigzag, aka Little Fritz, was awarded the Iron Cross by the Germans, the only British person so honoured.

However, he nearly gave the game away shortly after his arrival in England. At 9.45 on 27 December, he sent a telegram to Germany that read, 'CALL AT 1000 IF PARIS UNABLE RECEIVE ME. OK FRITZ. HU HA HU HO.' He sat down in the kitchen to have a cup of tea, and his heart sank: he had forgotten his crucial sign, 'FFFFF'. He was terrified that his bosses back in Germany would smell a rat and he would be caught out.

He sent another message to cover up his mistake. We found the message in a book, kept in a drawer of the archives. It reads: 'FFFFF. SORRY DRUNK OVER XMAS. FORGOT FFFFF IN LAST MESSAGE. FRITZ. HAPPY XMAS.' Fortunately, that one did the trick, and he carried on his double-agent work for Britain, helping the war effort in his own way, alongside the codecrackers in Buckinghamshire.

We also found a lexicon from 1812, a sort of dictionary of code given by Lord Castlereagh, who was foreign minister at the time. Gillian liked the book, as 'it was the beginning of Britain using code for secret correspondence.'

It wasn't just coded German messages that were intercepted and deciphered – lots of people worked on Japanese messages too. Codebreakers working on those had to have a crash course in Japanese (on average, it takes two years to learn Japanese, but the codebreakers did it in six months). We found some boxes that were full of flashcards covered in Japanese characters which recruits to the park had used to learn the language.

We opened some drawers and found maps, on tracing paper, showing Japanese convoy routes, the coastline of Europe, and Hungary. Most of the maps were marked 'ULTRA'. Gillian said it was 'frustrating but exciting' to be in charge of the whole archive, because she often can't find the things she's looking for but frequently discovers unexpected gems in the process. As we were talking, she opened a drawer and said, 'Hang on – is this a map showing Bletchley Park's communication lines? That's a bit of a find.'

We stuck our heads into a room filled with wartime memorabilia: toys, clothes, uniforms, ration containers, grenades, gas masks, books – everything from the home front. New things are sent to the museum all the time.

The most touching things I saw in the archives were photographs of winter scenes at the park. In one photograph, young women skate on the lake, while another lady, all wrapped up, plays the accordion. In another photograph, codebreakers are having some time off and having a snowball fight. In the summer, the people working at Bletchley Park played rounders and tennis.

Equally lovely are programmes from shows the codebreakers put on. Some were great singers and actors, and they performed operas and plays. Some of the top codebreakers are listed in the programmes. Barbara Abernathy, one of the original members of Captain Ridley's Shooting Party, was production secretary in a performance of *French Without Tears*.

Bletchley Park is a great place to visit. You can see an Enigma machine in the bike shed where Alan Turing, one of the top codebreakers, used to work (it was quieter than his office). Something of an eccentric, he cycled around the countryside in his gas mask to fend off hayfever, and he kept a mug, still there today, chained to his radiator so nobody would steal it, leaving him short of a cup for tea. There are often veterans from the war visiting the park.

Behind the scenes, Gillian is starting to make paper files from the archives available digitally to the public. As she sorts through cupboards and drawers full of intelligence, who knows what 'top secret' information she will find and bring out into the light.

[Ice skating on the lake, 1940]
Some of the most touching things I saw in the archives were photographs, like this one, of codebreakers taking time off, skating on the lake at Bletchley Park.

[OBJECT 48]

a Channel Islands
PILLAR BOX

[Location]

The BRITISH POSTAL MUSEUM and ARCHIVE
Essex, England

WHEN YOU POP OUT TO POST A LETTER,

do you ever think of the writer Anthony Trollope?

SOMETIMES I DO, EVER SINCE I found out he was the man who introduced post boxes to England. Before that, if you wanted to post a letter, you had to queue up at the post office and ask them to do it for you.

Trollope wrote 47 novels, plus umpteen short stories and travel books. He always wrote in the morning, before setting off to work as a surveyor for the Post Office. He devoted 33 years to the Post Office, and said his greatest desire was that 'the public in little villages should be enabled to buy postage-stamps; that they should have their letters delivered free and at an early hour; that pillar letterboxes should be put up for them', and that letter carriers should earn their pay and that their working conditions should be improved.

His dream for pillar letterboxes for all came true. He suggested to his boss, George Creswell, Surveyor of the Western District, in November 1851 that he try out the idea in St Helier, Jersey. He thought that was a good place to trial them, as you could buy stamps all over town, and 'all that is wanted is a safe receptacle for letters.'

He suggested putting a box on an iron post, or sticking it on to a wall, but in the end a freestanding letterbox was chosen. It was sage green so that it would blend into the landscape. Four prototypes were tried out in Jersey, three more in St Peter Port, Guernsey (one of which is in Union Street), and another in Sherborne, Dorset, which is still in use.

One of these green boxes lives in the collection of the British Postal Museum and Archive (BPMA). They store it with their larger objects in a big warehouse in Debden, Essex. It is one of 50 differently designed post boxes they own – from this early, hexagonal one from Guernsey, to modern designs and prototypes. They are stored in two lines, facing each other. The green box is first in the line. Once everyone had got used to these funny

[**An early British pillar box**]
Still standing, on Union Street, Guernsey.

[**Anthony Trollope (1815–82)**]
His dream of letterboxes across Great Britain came true.

[**Postboxes in the archive**]
At first it was a bit of a free-for-all: every local Post Office surveyor could design a letterbox they fancied.

green boxes, got the hang of posting letters and realized they would be delivered safely, letterboxes were rolled out across Great Britain. In 1855, the first ones were put up in London. There were five green rectangular boxes: in Fleet Street, the Strand, Pall Mall, Piccadilly and Kensington.

Not everyone trusted them. Trollope mentioned this in his 1869 novel, *He Knew He Was Right*. One character, Jemima Stanbury, carried her letters to Exeter's post office. She didn't believe in 'the iron pillar boxes which had been erected for the receipt of letters … she had not the faintest belief that any letter put into them would ever reach its destination … Positive orders had been given that no letter from her house should ever be put into the iron post.'

He reassured readers that the letterboxes worked well in another novel of his, *The Eustace Diamonds*. The protagonist, Frank Greystock, proposes to Lucy Morris by post, putting his proposal in a letterbox in Fleet Street. Trollope wrote that it stayed there on Sunday, but appeared at the breakfast table on Monday, 'thanks to the accuracy in the performance of its duties for which [the Post Office] is conspicuous among all offices'.

I liked Trollope's green letterbox: it was a little piece of history. As I walked through the corridor of boxes, I saw lots of different designs. At first it was a bit of a free-for-all: every local Post Office surveyor could design a letterbox they fancied. The Scottish Suttie letterbox was my favourite; it has a gold and red crown on top. A lot of them were exported for use in India as soon as they were made. In 1883, the round box became the norm, although since then there have been lots of variations in design as the Post Office adapted the boxes to the wants and needs of the public. The only colours that seem to have been used were chocolate brown, sage green, bright sky blue for airmail letters and, of course, pillarbox red. After 1874, all were produced in that familiar colour.

There are some letterboxes that were tried out and rejected. I saw one of these experiments in the store: it is called K4 and is a huge, red telephone box, with a letterbox and a stamp-vending machine on the sides. The idea of K4 was that it would be a complete post office in one box. However, people using the phone found that if someone came to buy stamps, the clinking of the coins meant that they couldn't hear the conversation they were having, so only 50 were made.

They have shelves full of post boxes that were attached to lampposts and pigeon holes used to sort letters on board a moving train, known as Travelling Post Offices (TPOs). They also have a control panel and a driverless train (like a big green bin on wheels), remnants of the Post Office Underground Railway, latterly known as Mail Rail, which ran through a system of tunnels beneath the tube network in London. The driverless trains carried letters between the London sorting offices and railway stations.

I'd first heard about the underground mail train when I went to the London Transport Museum Depot at Acton and saw a model of Oxford Street tube station's ticket hall. Underneath the tube tunnels were some smaller tunnels, used by the Royal Mail until 2003. Funny to think that for so many years this network of trains carried letters and postcards I worte to friends, across London, even though I had no idea the system existed at the time.

Over 160 years after Trollope first wrote a letter suggesting that post boxes be used in Britain, they are still in use. I wonder what he would have made of the Royal Mail's Olympics initiative: a gold post box in the home town of every gold medallist who represented Great Britain in the London 2012 Olympics and Paralympics. I suspect he would have been very pleased.

[The first British post box]
After taking up Trollope's suggestion, the Post Office erected the first British post box in Jersey in 1852; all these years later they are still in use.

[OBJECT 49]

BUCKINGHAM PALACE
Switchboard

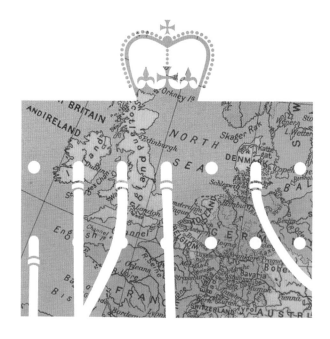

[Location]

The MUSEUM OF LONDON
London, England

AT SOME POINT,
THE SWITCHBOARD was MODIFIED,
so operators must have been listening in.
I'M NOT SURPRISED.

THE MUSEUM OF LONDON HAS 2 million pieces of London loot which it doesn't have space to display. If you include pieces of archaeological material dug up from layers and layers of earth beneath the city, then they have closer to 6 million things in storage. The archive collection is in three places: at the Science Museum store in Wroughton (where Piccard's gondola lives), at the museum itself on London Wall, and at the store which I visited, on Eagle Wharf Road in Hackney.

The Hackney warehouse is a huge space heaving with stories and swarming with archaeologists, of which the museum employs 150. Whenever they find something interesting they bring it here. Each room is filled with shelves stuffed with objects that tell the history of London. Take your pick: in the metal store, I saw a hoard of Roman copper vessels; in a general store, I saw bicycles, old televisions, washing machines and umpteen different prams. On the shelf below the prams I saw the architect's model for the Royal Albert Hall. Some archaeologists showed me certain items as they went past: a Roman brooch of Noah's Ark, for example, and a little bowl that Romans would fill with perfume and take to the baths.

I loved seeing the boxes filled with bricks that had been burnt when the Great Fire of London began, in a bakery in Pudding Lane, and then raged through the city for almost five days. Four hundred and thirty six acres of London were destroyed, including buildings such as St Paul's Cathedral, and the city smouldered for months.

[Buckingham Palace switchboard]
The switchboard is covered in jacks, with names beside each one – Privy Purse Door, Ceremonial Office ... and, in the middle, the giveaway sign, button number 65, marked 'Queen's Door'.

Plenty of objects from the Great Fire are on display in the museum, but it was all the more surreal to see these boxes of burnt bricks in storage. I picked up a few pieces and got ash from Pudding Lane all over my hands.

We continued to explore the oodles of oddities in this Aladdin's cave of London town across the years: water pipes made from hollowed-out logs of wood, things dug up under the supervision of Thomas Hardy when King's Cross St Pancras station was built, even relics from a graveyard disinterred when the Eurostar rail line was built. That seemed very wrong to me.

Then we came to one of the most cheerful things in this storage facility: a huge wooden cabinet covered in buttons and dials. It looked to me like an old mixing desk in a recording studio but, when I got closer, I saw there were names written above the buttons: Yeoman of Cellars, CHEF, Privy Purse Door, Ceremonial Office, D. of Env. Eng. Dept., Stationery Office and, in the middle, the giveaway to the origin of this strange beast – button number 65, marked 'Queen's Door'.

It is a telephone switchboard made in Coventry between 1930 and 1958 and used in Buckingham Palace until the 1960s. An operator would sit at the desk transferring calls within the palace, plugging the call into what look like buttons but are actually jacks. Before 1912, the Post Office provided staff for the switchboard for free; after that, they charged for operators, until, alarmed by the increasing costs, Buckingham Palace employed its own voluntary operators.

It can't have worked out too well, though, as the palace went back to using Post Office personnel in 1929. They took on only male operators from then on. It was suggested that the men stay for no more than two years so that none of them became intimate with the household servants, but the king wasn't sure about that idea, and asked the Privy Purse Office to write to the Post Office suggesting that two men be employed on an ongoing basis, with their jobs reviewed each year. At some point, the switchboard was modified, so operators must have been listening in. I'm not surprised.

Everywhere inside the palace that had a telephone connection is listed. You could be put through to the two entrances – the swanky Ambassador's Entrance or the more informal Privy Purse Door, the door in the north-west corner of the palace behind which the palace staff work.

You could have got through to to Sq/Ldr Checketts, that is, Squadron Leader Sir David John Checketts, who was Private Secretary to the Prince of Wales from 1970 to 1978, and Equerry to the Duke of Edinburgh before that. Or, if you'd fancied a chat with or about any of the household staff – pageboys, footmen, equerries – they are all on the switchboard, all on speed dial. In the evenings, the hotline number was the 'Pages Night ext.' In the run-up to an event, no doubt the bells of the Linen Room and the Silver Pantry sang throughout the palace. I'm hoping the Lift Engineers didn't have to be called too often. No one likes being stuck in a lift.

I can't be sure who Mr Greenwood, Miss Fowler, Mrs de Klee and Miss Colquhoun were, but they're on the list, and were probably friends of the Royal Family. 'L. Rupert Nevill' – Lord and Lady Rupert Nevill – certainly were: they threw a garden party in the autumn of 1959 at which Princess Margaret met the photographer Antony Armstrong-Jones, now Lord Snowdon, who was to become her husband.

[**Her Majesty the Queen**]
Each member of the Royal Family had their own line, and Buckingham Palace had a direct link to other royal residences.

Members of the Royal Family, including Her Majesty the Queen and the Duke of Edinburgh, had their own line, of course, as did the prime minister, and Buckingham Palace had a direct link to other royal residences, such as Balmoral Castle and Sandringham.

The first telephone exchange opened in London in 1879, to be followed a year later by the first telephone directory – an early Yellow Pages. It is only four pages long and contains 248 names, those of the first people to take the plunge into a newly linked-up world. There are some illustrious names in the mix, including Alexander Bell & Co. When Alexander Graham Bell invented his prototype telephone, he suggested that people answer with 'Ahoy, hoy.'

Bram Stoker, author of *Dracula*, had the number Victoria 1436 in 1910. Harry Houdini, who listed himself as Harry Houdini, Handcuff King, was at Gerrard 1312 in 1916. Buckingham Palace had four phone lines by then, at Victoria 1436. The royal residence upped the number of its lines quickly, discovering, as we all did, how handy it is to give someone a call rather than wait for a letter to arrive by post.

If you wanted to call Winston Churchill in 1925, what would you do? Look him up in the phone book and call Paddington 1003. He might not

[**An early Yellow Pages**]
The first telephone directory for London was only four pages long and contained 248 names, including Bram Stoker, Winston Churchill, Sigmund Freud, Marie Stopes, Virginia Woolf and Ian Fleming.

[Telephone 232CB]
To commemorate the two
millionth telephone to be installed
by the General Post Office in
Britain, the original telephone,
a model 232CB, was installed for
George V in Buckingham Palace
in June 1931.

have answered, but someone in his household, possibly his butler, would have. Sigmund Freud is in the book, too, as are Marie Stopes, Virginia Woolf and Ian Fleming – you could interrupt him writing tales of James Bond by calling Tate 2300.

In 1931, King George V was given the 2 millionth telephone in Britain. The telephone, a model 232CB, was installed in Buckingham Palace in June. There is a replica of it in storage at the Museum of London, among the millions of hidden treasures, each one telling a fragment of the story of London.

In 1953, the Queen allowed television cameras into Westminster Abbey for her coronation, and an extra half-million television sets were sold to people who wanted to watch it. There are some of these sets in storage in Hackney. There is an unusual one, a Pye television, with a curved screen filled with paraffin. It was sold with an image of the Queen inserted behind the screen, which is still there.

The Queen has always kept up with the times. Today she has a mobile phone, an iPod and is set up with an email account she uses to keep in touch with her grandchildren. She dictates her messages, uses Google, has approved a royal channel on YouTube and allowed an internet café to be set up in Buckingham Palace.

[OBJECT 50]

A Leaf of
GOAT EYE STAMPS

[Location]

The NATIONAL HISTORICAL MUSEUM
Rio de Janeiro, Brazil

IN A LOCKED DRAWER OF THE
Brazilian National Historical Museum
is the ONLY COMPLETE LEAF
of 'GOAT EYE' STAMPS in the WORLD.

[A leaf of goat eye stamps]
Brazil was the second country in the world to use national postage stamps. The goat eye was the second design. This is the only surviving complete leaf of goat eye stamps. It is so valuable that the museum has never exhibited it.

BRAZIL WAS THE SECOND COUNTRY in the world, after Great Britain, to start using national postage stamps, in 1843. Five curators led me into the storage room of the museum to see the precious leaf of stamps, printed on fine, yellowing paper and kept in a paper sleeve. It is so valuable that the museum has never exhibited it. They don't want the light to get in the goat's eyes.

The first stamps issued in Brazil were called bull's eye stamps because that's what they looked like. Apparently, these ones look like the eyes of a goat, but I can't say I've ever stared into a goat's eye, so I wouldn't really know. I'll have to take Brazil's word for it. The stamps came from Rio and, when they were printed, in 1850, each one cost 30 Reales. Today, they would cost a lot more. This entire leaf of 200 stamps is hard to put a value on, because it is the only one that survives: it would depend how much someone was willing to spend and how much competition there was to buy it.

It's interesting that Brazil introduced stamps before Portugal, its colonial ruler. This was thanks to King Pedro II, known as 'the Magnanimous', the second and last ruler of the Brazilian empire, whose reign lasted 58 years, from 1831 to 1889. His mother died when he was very young, and his father and new stepmother left him alone in Brazil while they went to Europe to try to restore his sister to the Portuguese throne when he was only five years old. Young Pedro studied from seven in the morning until ten at night, with two hours a day off for a bit of fun. Luckily, he loved to learn.

As he grew up, Pedro filled his palace with books: he had three libraries, containing 60,000 volumes, as well as a physics room, a telegraphic cabinet and an observatory. He took Sanskrit lessons and could speak several languages, including Tupi, which is now extinct but was once spoken by the Tupi people of Brazil.

Pedro liked to travel, and often came across innovations he thought would go down well in Brazil. He became one of the first photographers in the country, buying a daguerreotype camera in March 1840, and was certainly the first photographer who was also a head of state. He saw telephones in Philadelphia and brought them to Brazil and also imported rail, the telegraph and, of course, stamps.

He exchanged letters with scientists, intellectuals and artists such as Pasteur, Alexander Graham Bell, Longfellow and Wagner. He once said: 'Were I not an emperor, I would like to be a teacher. I do not know of a task more noble than to direct young minds and prepare the men of tomorrow.' He financed scholarships for Brazilian children to study in Europe and founded societies in Brazil for history, geography, music and opera, and the Pedro II School, upon which schools across Brazil were modelled.

It gets better. According to history, he was a popular, democratic ruler who wanted to understand his country, so he went walking in the street without any of his staff. He eliminated corruption from government, allowed the press freedom to write what they liked about him, listened to advisors and hired the best to advise him.

He also fought for the abolition of slavery. This eventually came about towards the end of his reign, when he was dangerously ill. He was being treated in Europe at the time, but when he was told the news it seemed to bring him back to life: 'Great people! Great people!' he said, and he began to recover, later returning to Brazil. His daughter Isabel became the regent and was supposed to have become queen after his death, but the end of slavery brought a shift to republicanism. Isabel had signed an anti-slavery law, which her father's rivals used as a way to get her, her father and their family ousted from their country, and sent into exile in Paris.

Pedro II had to leave behind a lot of his paintings and treasures, many of which adorn the walls of the museum; others are in storage. We went

[**King Pedro II (1825–91)**]
He once said: 'Were I not an emperor, I would like to be a teacher. I do not know of a task more noble than to direct young minds...'

[**Brazil's anti-slavery bill**]
King Pedro II and his daughter Isabel fought for the abolition of slavery.

[The King's clock]
When he left his beloved Brazil
for a life in exile, Pedro II had
to leave behind a lot of his
things, some of which are in
the archives of the museum,
including this clock made from
ebony with dragons carved
upon it.

to the main storage facility, which houses 20,000 objects – clothes, sculptures, paintings, toys, gold, jewels – including several treasures relating to King Pedro II. I saw a sculpture of the bearded man himself, a sculpture of Isabella's lips, a large coin style medal with his portrait and the words 'Dom Pedro II Imperador do Brazil' upon it, and a clock that belonged to him. Made by the official imperial clockmaker, it gives the time in Rio, Paris and New York, and is made from ebony with dragons carved upon it.

When Pedro II left his beloved country, he dug a little Brazilian soil from the ground, carried it in his bag and was buried with it when he died. His last words were 'May God grant me these last wishes – peace and prosperity for Brazil.' What a story to come out of a priceless leaf of goat eye stamps in storage.

The tools that belonged to
QUEEN VICTORIA'S DENTIST

**British Dental Association Museum
London, England**

For the first time you had to be a dentist

TO WORK ON PEOPLE'S TEETH.

BEFORE THAT, ANYONE WHO FANCIED IT

– chemists, blacksmiths and wigmakers –

HAD A GO.

PEOPLE HAD THEIR TEETH PULLED OUT

on the VILLAGE GREEN as EVERYONE WATCHED.

[Queen Victoria's dentist's tools]
This photo shows the mother of pearl-handled instruments with the Prince of Wales's crest. Hidden underneath are the instruments which are much more likely to have been used.

DOWN IN THE BASEMENT OF the British Dental Association Museum is a set of tools that belonged to Queen Victoria's dentist, Sir Edwin Saunders (1814–1901). He looked after her royal teeth for 40 years, and must have done a great job, because he was the first dentist ever to be knighted (in 1883). The tools he used on Queen Victoria's teeth are owned privately, I'm not sure who owns them – someone who likes teeth I suppose. However, I looked inside a box of tools he used to treat another royal, the Prince of Wales (later Edward VII).

The lid of the box is embossed with the Prince of Wales's feathers. Inside is a row of tools on a bed of red velvet. They're pretty fancy, with mother of pearl handles. Four have crowns and one has a rose, thistle and shamrock. One of them is a mirror, with a green stone handle. Sir Edwin Saunders kept these decorative tools for show. When he got to work he would lift up this layer to reveal his real set of tools below. I did the same. The second set of tools don't look as flashy, but they must have got the job done.

The box is surrounded by thousands of other things the museum can't fit upstairs – drawers full of false teeth, instruments, toothpaste, toothbrushes, early dentists' chairs and statues of Saint Apollonia, the patron saint of toothache sufferers.

It was during Victoria's reign, when Sir Edwin Saunders was working, that the dentistry profession started to get organized. For the first time you had to be a dentist to work on people's teeth. Before that, anyone who fancied it – chemists, blacksmiths and wigmakers – had a go. People had their teeth pulled out on the village green as everyone watched. In the 1870s leading dentists, including Sir Edwin Saunders, set up the Dental Reform Committee to regulate the profession. Dental hospitals were set up to train dentists and to treat people, and dental tools began to be mass made. There were faster drills, more fillings and anaesthetics became available. Strangely the nation's teeth got worse in the nineteenth century. Most people couldn't afford dentists, and only had one toothbrush to share between a whole family.

We take toothbrushes and toothpaste for granted every morning and evening now, but it took a long time for these basic tools to get into our bathrooms. The very first toothbrush was the most simple of all – a finger or a twig. Still today in India, neem tree twigs are popular toothbrushes – people stand around brushing their teeth with them in the morning; all you do is chew an end of the stick, to make bristles, and then brush. In Senegal, the chewing stick is called *sothiou*, which means 'to clean' in Wolof. In East Africa it is called *mswaki*, the Swahili word for 'toothbrush'. The museum has a selection of chewsticks down in the basement.

A businessman named William Addis made the first real toothbrush in 1780. It was made out of horsehair and bone, so I reckon I would have felt sick if I'd used one. They were quite popular, but it was the First World War that brought toothbrushes into everyone's home. The troops were issued with toothbrushes – some didn't know what they were for and used them to clean their boots – but most took them home to show their families. After that, the idea caught on, Boots and Woolworths started to stock them and prices went down, and then everyone could afford one.

Toothpaste was first made out of ox hooves, myrrh, eggshells or pumice mixed together; people just rubbed it straight onto their teeth with their finger. The Romans used tooth powder made

For 70 Years the
Approved Dentifrice in all Countries.

[Dentifrice]
Dentifrice came in a round block and you would scrape a toothbrush over it.

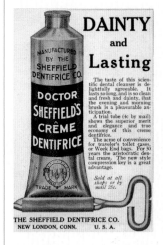

[The first tubes of dentifrice]
Dr Sheffield's son saw painters in Paris using tubes of paint and realized this would be the perfect way to package Dr Sheffield's Cream Dentifrice.

of hoofs, horns, crabs, eggshells or oyster shell, sometimes mixed with honey. You would sprinkle toothpowder on to a finger, twig or brush to clean your teeth. Then dentifrice – still the French word for tooth-paste – was invented. It came in a round block that you would scrape a toothbrush over. Usually, dentifrice was flavourless but Queen Victoria liked hers cherry flavoured. The first dentifrice to come in tubes was Dr Sheffield's Cream Dentifrice. While Dr Sheffield's son was studying in Paris he watched artists painting with tubes of paint and had a flash of inspiration – why not sell dentifrice in tubes?

Queen Victoria had a strange fascination for teeth. She wore the first milk tooth that waggled free from her seven-year-old daughter's mouth as a gold and enamel brooch, designed into the shape of a thistle (Prince Albert had pulled the tooth out when the family were in Scotland). She also had a pair of earrings with two teeth for each ear and wore a necklace Albert had made for her that was made out of 44 teeth from stags that he had shot on the Balmoral estate. She didn't go as far as a Mayan man, whose tooth is in storage at the museum, however. It has a jade stone inside it. The Mayan man would have spun a copper tube, like a straw, on to his tooth, to cut a round hole for the gem.

It's strange to think that not so long ago, false teeth were quite a status symbol. If you had fake ones, nothing could go wrong with them. George Washington had a set made from hippo ivory. Washington seems like a long time ago, but it was still a popular thing to do in recent times. When Roald Dahl sold the film rights to his first children's story, *The Gremlins* – about little creatures that caused problems with RAF planes – to Walt Disney, he gave the RAF Benevolent Fund all the proceeds except for $200. This he used to buy the best false teeth in America. Like many men his age, Roald replaced all his teeth with false ones. He urged his sister, in a rude letter – which I read in the archives of the Roald Dahl Museum – to do the same, but she would not. I'm not surprised.

We're really lucky dentists have got better and better at their jobs. Not so long ago people who could afford it used to get false teeth for their 21st birthday, or just before they got mar-ried. What a rubbish birthday present – a mouth full of false teeth.

[OBJECT 52]

SKULL of a
TAPUIASAURUS MACEDOI

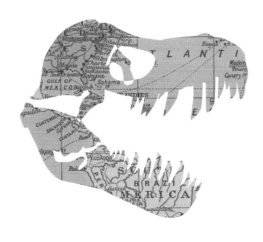

[Location]

MUSEU de ZOOLOGIA da UNIVERSIDADE
de São Paulo, Brazil

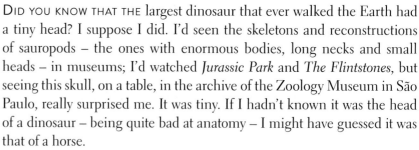

IT IS BIZARRE to THINK
that, of ALL the SAUROPODS
that ever lived in South America,
THIS is the ONLY SKULL
to have MADE IT ACROSS
the MILLIONS of YEARS.

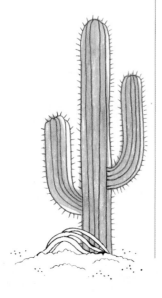

DID YOU KNOW THAT THE largest dinosaur that ever walked the Earth had a tiny head? I suppose I did. I'd seen the skeletons and reconstructions of sauropods – the ones with enormous bodies, long necks and small heads – in museums; I'd watched *Jurassic Park* and *The Flintstones*, but seeing this skull, on a table, in the archive of the Zoology Museum in São Paulo, really surprised me. It was tiny. If I hadn't known it was the head of a dinosaur – being quite bad at anatomy – I might have guessed it was that of a horse.

There are piles of dinosaur bones in museums and many more waiting to be discovered, but it's very rare to find a whole skeleton, and rarer still to find a complete skull of a sauropod. That is what makes this dinosaur skull such a precious treasure. It is the only complete skull of a sauropod ever described from South America. In scientific terms, 'describe' means it has received a description – its anatomy has been described and illustrated or photographed in a scientific paper. There are plenty of things that have been found, but not described, including a skull found in the late 1990s: so, even though it is in a museum, and people have seen it, since the discoverers have not written about it, it essentially doesn't yet exist and palaeontologists can't comment on it. This unique skull had been inside the Earth for 120 million years, and it turned up thanks to a social networking site rather like Facebook.

In 2006, a young geography student was out walking near his mother's house in northern Minas Gerais, Brazil. He saw a bone sticking out of the ground. He thought it was the rib of a giant sloth and posted a note about it on Orkut, a website popular with Brazilian students.

Students at the University of São Paulo showed the boy's post to their professor, Hussam Zaher, who realized it was unlikely to be a giant sloth, as their bones are found inside caves, not in the open. He went to meet the boy and to see the bones. As he began to dig, his jaw dropped further and further. He found a dinosaur rib, 20 per cent of its body, and then, a skull: the Holy Grail for a palaeontologist.

He assembled a team to excavate the bones and shipped them back to São Paulo. His team realized they were looking at a new titanosaur species (which includes the largest creatures ever to roam the Earth). They named it *Tapuiasaurus macedoi* ('macedoi' after a man in Minais Gerais who helped them to excavate the bones). The bones and skull were CT-scanned and briefly displayed in the museum, before being placed in the archive, where palaeontologists can study the bones in peace.

The day I visited, Jeff Wilson, a professor from the University of Michigan, was bent over the skull.

'It's hard to impress on anyone quite how rare this skull is,' he told me. 'We know of 130 sauropod species that existed across 160 million years of time, but we know them only from pieces of bone. There are only a dozen species of sauropod in the world known from their complete skulls.' The skull is really important because 'it tells how the animal interacts with the sensory world and provides important information about feeding in a huge animal that has to eat a lot. Not having the skull is a big missing piece.'

Except it's not that big. It's really rather small, for the head of a vast dinosaur. The volume of the head is about one two-hundredth of that of the whole animal. Imagine if our heads were on that same scale to our bodies. How strange we would look with heads the size of tennis balls.

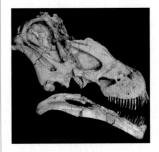

[The sauropod skull]
The only complete skull of a sauropod ever described from South America. It's really small, compared to the size of the dinosaur's body.

The skull still has a fair bit of rock on it, which is gradually being removed in the lab at the museum with a microscope and a tiny pneumatic drill. But what do we know so far about this individual dinosaur? Well, we know that 120 million years ago it was walking around in what is now Brazil. On the basis of skeletal anatomy, it seems to be a young adult, a teenager: it still has soft spots in its skull, and the joints between its backbones are really obvious. Vertebrae fuse when a creature becomes an adult. So we know that this dinosaur would have grown bigger if it lived for longer.

It had 64 teeth – 32 on each jaw. The teeth are thin and look as if they'd break easily. Their size can be explained by the necessity to pack them all into the dinosaur's small jaw. There are several generations of teeth inside this dinosaur mouth, waiting inside the gums, and this set of teeth is unlikely to be the dinosaur's first. Mammals are unusual in that they only have two sets of teeth – like sharks, dinosaurs continually replace their teeth. Sauropods, this teenager included, got a new set of pencil-like gnashers every few months.

We don't know what sex it was. With some species of dinosaur the sex can be determined from the remains, but not with sauropods. Maybe sex was evident in other ways – colours, ornamentation – it's not yet clear.

When it was born, it was alone. Some species of dinosaur – like some birds, the descendants of dinosaurs that are still living – laid eggs and left them; others cared for their young. Jeff explained, 'We've found huge nesting areas with lots of eggs and no adults. We have even found snakes inside dinosaur nests, waiting, ready to eat the emerging hatchlings.'

When this dinosaur hatched, it was half a metre long and fended for itself immediately. Then it managed to survive into its teens, before dying and resting in what became Brazil for millions of years until, one day, it became a national treasure.

It is an especially precious fossil because it allows scientists to make new discoveries about dinosaur evolution. When dinosaurs first lived on Earth, in the Triassic period, all the continents were gathered into one landmass, so we see genealogical continuity among the dinosaurs. Meat-eaters from South Africa look like meat-eaters from Arizona. Across a couple of generations, a dinosaur species could populate the whole Earth and so preserve its genetic continuity.

But then, over these millions of years, the continents began to break up. Whereas before, the sauropods roamed across one large landmass, as the continents moved apart, each island had its own distinct 'seed' for each dinosaur species. As Jeff explained, 'We're looking at the evolution of dinosaurs against the background of a fragmenting world. What we want to know is, are this dinosaur's closest relatives nearby or across the world?'

This skull looks most like that of two other titanosaur dinosaurs, *Rapetosaurus* from Madagascar and *Nemegtosaurus* from Mongolia. All three have a long snout, a nose-opening that is level with the eyes, and narrow crowns on the teeth. What has amazed palaeontologists is the discovery that this Brazilian skull is 60 million years older than the Madagascan and Mongolian skulls. Finding the skull has meant that they have had to reconsider when the titanosaurs developed their characteristics: previously, it was thought that these skull features developed after the landmass broke up, but now it seems they must have evolved when the continents were still one, which is much earlier than they had thought. Parts of sauropod evolutionary history may need to be rethought – but this is what science is about.

I was amazed at how fortunate it was that all this happened because one boy went out for a walk. The curators were less so: it happens all the time in the dinosaur world. 'We found dinosaur eggs in India thanks to a cement plant; the workers found these huge balls, called them cannon balls and kept them on their desk. Some geologists saw the balls and realized they were eggs. Chance favours only the prepared mind,' said Jeff.

Often, palaeontologists turn up in a new area to look for dinosaur bones and ask locals, such as shepherds – they're usually the ones who know of unusual bones. Sometimes, these bones have been exposed for too long to be of use. It is very rare to find a skeleton as intact as this one because sauropods were so massive the chances of the rocks they are found in staying in the same position over millennia is slim. Also, sauropod vertebrae are almost 80 per cent air, which makes the bones light. This was useful for the sauropod (a lighter neck is easier to lift) but not so handy for palaeontologists in search of bones millennia later, as they break apart easily.

Pretty much every dinosaur exhibit you have ever seen in a museum will be a cast of the original bones. Sometimes, it will be a mixture of real

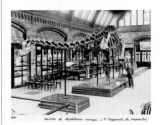

[Dippy]
The dinosaur at the Natural History Museum in London is a cast of a *Diplodocus* skeleton found in Wyoming in 1899. Copies of the head are found on dinosaurs all over the world.

bone and cast. The bones themselves are simply too precious, both for their rarity and their importance from a research perspective, to be put on display. The skull I saw was packed in foam, away from prying eyes and bright lights. Not only will dinosaur exhibits more often than not be casts, but also, often, they don't even have the right head.

In London, the dinosaur at the Natural History Museum affectionately known as 'Dippy' the *Diplodocus* (star of the 1975 Disney film *One of Our Dinosaurs is Missing*) is a cast of a *Diplodocus* skeleton found in Wyoming in 1899. It was found on an expedition funded by a Scottish-American businessman, Andrew Carnegie. It turned up on 4 July, so one team member suggested calling it the 'Star-Spangled Dinosaur'. Carnegie's friends called it 'Dippy', and the name stuck.

King Edward VII saw an illustration of Dippy and asked for a plaster-cast copy for London, now in the Natural History Museum. Other European heads of state copied him. Now, 'Dippy' or *Diplodocus carnegei*, as he is more properly known, is all over the world – Madrid, Frankfurt, Chicago and London. Its head is a cast of the original skull but, because that skull is so rare, casts from the same skull are found on dinosaurs all over the world. Museums tend to pop that head on a lot of dinosaur skeletons for show to the public. His head is one of the most viewed sauropod dinosaur heads in the world.

It is bizarre to think that, of all the sauropods that ever lived in South America, this is the only skull to have made it across the millions of years. Now it is part of a scientific collection in the busy city of São Paulo. But it's unlikely that other museums will have a cast of this dinosaur's head. It's just too precious.

[OBJECT 53]

HANDAXE
from Hoxne

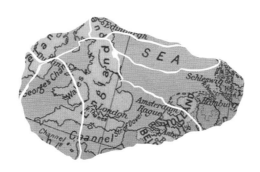

[Location]

BRITISH MUSEUM's HANDAXE STORAGE
Hoxton, London, England

YOU CAN ALMOST FEEL
the presence of the person
who made it 400,000 years ago,
CAREFULLY SHAPING IT
INTO THIS BEAUTIFUL FORM.

[The artistic handaxe]
Of all the tens of thousands of handaxes in storage in Hoxton, this symmetrical one is the curator's favourite. For some reason the creator thought to make his handaxe more beautiful than it needed to be.

'WE HAVE TENS OF THOUSANDS of handaxes in here,' said Nick Ashton, curator at the British Museum, as he opened the door to the museum's handaxe storage facility in the heart of hipster-friendly Hoxton, east London. 'They vary in shape, size, thickness and beauty.'

The storage room is lined with rows of tall cabinets. Each cabinet has a stack of slim drawers. There are 700 drawers per row and each one contains a few handaxes.

'Let me show you my favourite,' said Nick, pulling one drawer open and lifting out a stone handaxe. I could see why he liked it. There was something magical about it. The human who created it must have been something of an artist, because it is perfectly symmetrical and has an S-shaped twist on both sides. You can almost feel the presence of the person who made it 400,000 years ago, carefully shaping it into this beautiful form. It's a fully functional handaxe, but it has the X factor; for some reason, the creator thought to make this handaxe prettier than it needed to be.

Who was this artistic human being who lived hundreds of thousands of years ago? Well, he – or she – was an early Neanderthal who lived in an area now called Hoxne, on the border of Suffolk and Norfolk. He would have hunted with a spear and used this axe to cut apart the animals he killed to get meat for food and hides for clothing and shelter.

At that time, what is now the East Anglian coastline was connected by boggy marshland to mainland Europe, so this individual's ancestors would have made the intrepid journey on foot from southern Europe to Hoxne, surviving off the land as they went. The climate would have been colder, the landscape more akin to the heavily forested Scandinavian countryside of today, and there would have been lots of animals we wouldn't see in Suffolk now, including elephants, rhino and spotted hyenas.

Although this is one of the most artistic handaxes in the storage, the British Museum has an impressive range of the tools. Nick pointed some out. 'Here are the oldest ones, made 1.2 million years ago in Oldavai Gorge in Tanzania. And here are ones from Sudan and these are from the Middle East.'

The museum has lots of handaxes from Britain, mainly from Norfolk, Suffolk and southern England. The biggest in the collection of British axes is from Biddenham. Why is it so big? 'I think he was just showing off,' said Nick of the human who lived hundreds of thousands of years ago.

Each one was shaped out of a piece of rock – by banging the rock with a pebble, and then shaping it with a piece of bone or antler – into a tool that could fit into the palm of the user's hand.

We looked at a range from Swanscombe in Kent. 'These are more typical,' explained Nick. 'Look closely and you can see where a series of flakes has been removed to create the handaxe's sharp edges.' Sometimes the museum has found the flakes that were removed from the stone to shape the handaxe. We looked at some flakes from Boxgrove left behind by the maker who had walked off with his new tool tucked in his hand. Several original blocks of flint have been put back together from the flakes, leaving a hole where the handaxe would have been. Nick showed me one: 'It's like a time capsule in a way. You can see 20 minutes of someone's time, half a million years ago preserved right here.'

There is another handaxe from Hoxne that is less artistic, but very significant in handaxe history. It was the first handaxe ever to be recognized as such. John Frere (1740–1807), who lived nearby, found it near a gravel pit in 1797. He wrote to the Society of Antiquities informing them that he had found 'weapons of war, fabricated and

used by a people who had not the use of metals ... The situation in which these weapons were found may tempt us to refer them to a very remote period indeed, even beyond that of the present world ...' For six decades, no one really believed his claim that the rock was a tool made by early man. In those days the things we call handaxes were known as 'thunderbolts' because people couldn't explain them. They imagined they were created by the ether during a storm. His thinking was far ahead of its time, much like that of the artistic man from Hoxne who created a handaxe to be beautiful as well as useful.

Since John Frere's time, we've learnt more about handaxes and the people who created them. A seismic shift in our understanding of life in Britain occurred thanks to a man called Mike Chambers, who was out walking his dog on the beach in Happisburgh, Norfolk (a small seaside village right on the edge of some cliffs, which are crumbling into the sea). He spotted a handaxe lying in the mud and called the Norwich Castle Museum. The handaxe was made 700,000 years ago, some 200,000 years earlier than any previously discovered artefact. The British Museum then began excavating at two sites in Happisburgh, and found the earliest-known human settlement in northern Europe.

Palaeontologists believe these first settlers were a different species to the creative, early Neanderthal who made the stunning handaxe in Hoxne. They call this now-extinct species *Homo antecessor*, or 'pioneer man'. They think the species walked from southern Europe into the dark forests, around 800,000 years ago, never to return. They made it across the land bridge, to Norfolk which was then at the edge of the inhabited world. The land was more forested, hillier and colder than it is now (we know this because beetles found at the site are now found only in chilly Scandinavia). At the time, the River Thames was flowing through Norfolk, out into the North Sea, so pioneer man must have lived in its estuaries, hunting and fishing by the water.

Pioneer man disappeared from Britain because of an Ice Age. These occurred about every 100,000 years and, each time, Britain was depopulated. As it warmed up again, new waves of people walked from southern Europe to Britain. There were at least eight different waves of people that came in and died out before the most recent wave, which is the one that survives today: us.

Treasures excavated from the 800,000-year-old home of pioneer man are stored in the room above the handaxes. We entered a room filled with bags full of sediment waiting to be sieved – the finest sieves are for beetles; the larger ones for bones – and looked in a tray filled with flints which are more primitive tools than handaxes. As yet, no handaxe has been found at this site. Perhaps these earliest settlers didn't know how to make them.

There are so many unanswered questions about pioneer man. 'It would be nice to excavate a hairy human holding a handaxe,' said Nick, 'but, so far, all we know is they probably had smaller brains and smaller bodies. Did they know how to make fire? What about clothes and shelter? Were they the top predator?' Nick explained that it was possible they were not, and they spent their days in competition with spotted hyenas and other animals that hunt for food. Pioneer man may have survived by scavenging scraps left behind by other animals higher up the food chain. How bizarre is that?

Having spent hours looking at handaxes and talking about life on Earth millennia ago, emerging into twenty-first century Hoxton was quite a shock. These concrete city streets seemed an unnatural environment for humans to live in, after hundreds of thousands of years spent living on and off the land. Or maybe I was just unnerved as a man followed me along the road and asked me whether I was from MI5. Oh well, I thought, contending with oddballs is better than competing with a hyena for food. I nipped into a café to escape him, and looked around at people plotting ideas and creating projects over their flat white coffees. It was good to see the artistic spirit of the dreamer who lived hundreds of thousands of years ago in Hoxne still alive and well. If he were alive today, he'd probably have been an artist living here in Hoxton.

[Happisburgh]
The British Museum are excavating at two sites in Happisburgh, Norfolk. Happisburgh isn't pronounced like a happy village; in true Norfolk style, it's actually called 'hayes-bo-rough'.

[OBJECT 54]

a series of
PAINTINGS BY OZIAS

[Location]

INTERNATIONAL MUSEUM of NAÏF ART
Rio de Janeiro, Brazil

HE USED STORED PAINT THAT HAD BEEN USED FOR MAINTENANCE ON THE RAILWAYS, a chewed toothpick as a brush, or his fingers, and HE PAINTED on PAPER, WOOD, FABRIC, RUBBER – ANYTHING HE COULD FIND.

ONCE THEY'VE HIT THE BEACH to soak up some sunshine and drunk from a few fresh coconuts or drunk caipirinhas, one of the first things visitors to Rio de Janiero tend to do is make the trip to see Christ the Redeemer – the most famous symbol of Brazil, which stands, arms outstretched, on a hilltop embracing the city. On the same street as the jostling queue to catch the train up to see it there is a gem of a museum. Inside is the largest collection of naïf art in the world.

Painted a pretty pastel blue, it looks like a tumbledown former colonial home. When I visited, it had been closed for several years, after its founder, Lucien Finkelstein, passed away and the museum lost its funding (it has since reopened). When I arrived, a few dogs came to greet me, and I wondered whether I was at the right place until a curator at the museum, Tania, arrived, made delicious coffee in tiny china cups and kindly showed me around.

The walls were mostly bare, and the paintings – over 6,000 works by painters from all over Brazil, and from more than a hundred other countries, from the fifteenth century to today – were stored around the building, stacked up against walls. The former storage room was a big mess of wires and rubble, as it was in the process of being rebuilt. Added to that, they had a marmot invasion to deal with. There were several paintings still hanging, though, including

[Henri Rousseau (1844–1910)
self portrait (1890)]
The term 'naïf art' was used for
the first time at the turn of the
nineteenth century, to describe
the paintings of Henri Rousseau.

[One of the series of six
paintings by Ozias]
The series tells the story of slave
traffic between Africa and Brazil.
The founder of the museum,
Lucien Finkelstein, commissioned
them and planned to show them
at the 'right time' but that time
never came and the paintings
have never been exhibited.

the two largest naïf art paintings in the world. The bigger of the two, *Brazil, 5 centuries*, by Aparecida Azedo, is a 24-metre long fresco running along the top two walls that shows the history of Brazil; the other, *Rio de Janeiro, I like you, I like your happy people*, by Lia Mittarakis, who lived in Guanabara Bay is a 4 by 7-metre celebration of the city of Rio that hangs on the main wall. Lucien Finkelstein commissioned both.

Quotations adorn the walls, including one by the French poet Gérard de Nerval: 'The verb to love suits only the souls who are thoroughly Naïve.'

This chimes with Finkelstein's definition of naïf art, which is also hanging in the museum. In it, he explains that 'naïf' is a term that was first used to define the paintings of Henri Rousseau but it is a style of painting that has always existed and always will. Its origins are in the art of cavemen. The artists are usually self-taught anarchists, who follow no rules and are not influenced by anyone, finding their own motifs and techniques within themselves. He believed the naïf artist paints by dipping the brush in his heart.

Brazil, France, Haiti, Italy and the former Yugoslavia are where you will find the most involvement with naïf art. In each naïf art gallery around the world you will more than likely find a few creations by Brazilian artists. Brazilians, being a very expressive people, seem to love the naïf style: you find it everywhere in the country. I share their love of its colour and vibrancy and love the style. It's interesting that, despite its simplicity, naïf art often tackles complicated issues.

That is certainly true of the series of six paintings I came to see. They are the creation of Ozias (Ricardo de Ozias), a naïf artist still living in the city of Rio. They tell the story of slave traffic between Africa and Brazil in the fifteenth century through the eyes of Ozias, whose ancestors came to Brazil on slave ships.

They were created as a commission by Finkelstein, who planned to show them at 'just the right time', perhaps to coincide with an anniversary of the abolition of slavery. That date never came within his lifetime and so the paintings have never been publicly displayed. Other than the curators of the museum and Ozias and his family, I am one of very few people ever to have seen them.

The pictures are currently living in Finkelstein's former office. His desk is still there, among a collection of paintings, books, photographs and sculpted figures, including a self-portrait in clay by Ozias. One photograph shows Finkelstein with the Queen and Prince Philip. When the royal couple visited Brazil, the Queen was presented with a selection of Brazilian jewels and asked to choose one. She chose a dolphin created by Finkelstein, so he kept a photograph of the moment in his office.

We took the six Ozias paintings from the room and laid them out on the upstairs floor of the museum to get a good look. Many elements of the story are familiar. Forty per cent of Africans brought to the Americas as slaves ended up in Brazil. They were transported on ships and sold in ports along the coastline.

The scenes depicted in the paintings are shocking and tragic: men being rounded up with guns, transported in ships, herded into pens, sold by traders and led in chains. The depiction of such terrible scenes in this naïf style – childlike and almost cartoony – makes them all the more disturbing.

One curious aspect of these paintings is how Ozias paints the African people's lifestyle as if they were extremely primitive, when we know that there were a number of relatively complex and sophisticated west African societies at the time.

He also paints invading white warriors capturing tribal people and enslaving them by force. The less palatable reality is that the white traders mostly dealt with tribal kings and warriors, exchanging prisoners for guns and gunpowder. As Tatiana Levy, Finkelstein's granddaughter, explained: 'In his vision, he couldn't imagine his African ancestors enslaving their own people.'

But it was the life story of the painter Ozias that really got me interested. Born one of ten children, his family couldn't afford for him to go to school so, by the age of four, he was working in the fields pulling carts. On his way home, he passed a school where he could hear children reciting the alphabet, so he'd sit outside and listen until he'd learnt it himself. Later, an older brother explained to him how the letters created words, and he taught himself to read. Soon afterwards his family moved to Rio de Janeiro, and Ricardo worked outdoors as a bricklayer and on the railways. Then, at the age of 46, he was offered an office job at the railway company.

To begin with, he kept falling asleep. To keep awake, he began to paint, using anything he could find around the office. He used stored paint that had been used for maintenance on the railways, a chewed toothpick as a brush, or his fingers, and he painted on paper, wood, fabric, rubber – anything he could find. He still uses a chewed-up match as a brush for small details, and for his signature – which is wonderful: a curly 'O' and jagged 'S', both underlined.

His co-workers thought he was going a little mad, as he painted compulsively, on any materials left hanging around the office. The same happened at home. His wife was fed up with fingerprints in paint all over the house and thought her husband had lost the plot. He told her he knew what he was doing, and suggested she take up painting too. Years later, she also became a naïf artist.

From the moment he began, Ricardo wanted to become a painter: 'As I didn't know how to paint, I worked on many pictures at the same time, trying not to forget all ideas that came to mind. Now that I know better, I can take it slower …'

Luckily, an engineer who worked with Ricardo recognized great talent emerging in his paintings of his childhood in Minas Gerais, featuring coffee plantations, cowboys, parties and mountains. She spread the word of her frenziedly creative co-worker, and Ozias was able to mount his first exhibition in 1987. All 52 paintings were created with his fingers. He later got enthusiastic about religion and became a priest, built a temple near his house and set up an art school, in which he taught children in his community to paint.

Since I visited, the museum has reopened. I would love to have the chance to go back and see it one day. If you get to Rio first, and decide to queue to take the train up to the Christ the Redeemer statue, why not slip away and see what paintings by Ozias are on display? Several are dedicated to Brazil's love of football and to the fate of the national team.

Remember, though, that behind the scenes are more of his paintings, as yet unseen, waiting, just like their creator, for their time to come.

[OBJECT 55]

THE SPAULDING COLLECTION
of JAPANESE PRINTS

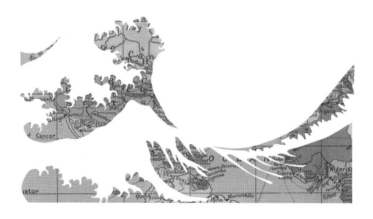

[Location]

The MUSEUM of FINE ARTS
Boston, MA, USA

They were ETHEREAL, and BEAUTIFUL,

UNLIKE ANYTHING IN WESTERN ART.

It was as thought they came

FROM ANOTHER PLANET.

THE MUSEUM OF FINE ARTS, Boston (MFA), stores more than 50,000 woodblock prints made in Japan in the seventeenth, eighteenth and nineteenth centuries. The greatest treasure of the collection is a group of 6,600 prints that are never hung on the walls of the museum. They were collected in the 1910s by two brothers, William and Henry Spaulding. The Spaulding brothers donated the prints to the MFA in 1921 on one condition: that they would not exhibit them, to protect the delicate colours from fading. So, for over 90 years they have been kept in the dark, in cupboards, in numbered portfolios, just as the Spaulding duo donated them.

I went to see the prints after hours at the museum. Everyone had gone home except for Sarah Thompson, assistant curator of Japanese art at the museum. Sarah explained that when the prints were created they were as cheap as a bowl of noodles. Most people in the city of Edo, now called Tokyo, had a couple pinned up at home. They would be ripped down and thrown away if they got tatty or a new, fashionable print took their place. Hundreds of copies of each print were made, if not thousands.

Japan had been closed to the world until the 1860s, when the country modernized and began trading with the west. When Japan opened her harbours, European ships flooded in and prints like these ones in the MFA found their way across to the west. At the time, they were virtually worthless in Japan, but to western eyes, they were mind-blowing.

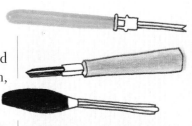

Sarah pulled swathes of images out of their drawers for me to see. You'd need months to study everything, but I got a good feel for the collection, which represents the best work of about 120 artists from the school of art called ukiyo-e (浮世絵), or 'pictures of the floating world'. *Ukiyo* was originally a Buddhist concept which suggested the sadness (*uki*) of life (*yo*). But during the peace and prosperity of the seventeenth century *uki* came to mean 'to float' and instead of connoting sadness, *ukiyo* became associated with the momentary, worldy pleasures of Japan's rising middle class and metropolitan Edo (Tokyo). The most popular prints were ones of life in the pleasurable places of Edo – scenes showing Kabuki theatre, courtesans and geisha. Later, the artists moved on to create landscapes, birds, flowers, pilgrimages and legendary heroes. No matter what the subject, the artist always used graceful lines and bright colours to depict reality in the fashionable 'floating world' style.

[*The Great Wave* by Hokusai]
The now iconic image is everywhere, however the Spaulding print of the image has never been displayed in the light. It is perfectly preserved – as though the print were created this morning.

I immediately recognized the most famous Japanese woodblock print in the western world – *Under the Wave, off Kanagawa*, also known as *The Great Wave* (富嶽三十六景　神奈川沖浪裏), by Hokusai, (1760–1849). The print shows ferocious, towering waves with foaming white heads about to engulf two stricken fishing boats. The now iconic image is everywhere, and many museums and collectors own impressions of it. However because the Spaulding print has not been displayed, the cold blue of the water, the grey and white sky and the pale yellow boats are just as they were in Japan in 1830 – it's as though the print were created this morning.

Ukiyo-e artists were the Andy Warhols of Japanese art. They mass-marketed high art: suddenly, from about 1680 on, almost anyone in Japan who wanted to own a piece of art could afford it. Whereas paintings on silk were very expensive, the ukiyo-e images were printed on paper and could be created cheaply. To make a print, an artist would design an image, then give it to a *hikkū*, or workshop assistant, who would make a tracing. A craftsman glued that on to a block of wood and cut the image into it. The block was inked and printed so as to make hundreds or thousands of copies.

[*Night Snow* by Hiroshige]
Three men are walking outside at night in the snow, wearing snow clogs or barefoot. They are bent over, to shield themselves from the bitter wind. I felt freezing just looking at them.

Every print in the collection was made like this, by hand, by men sitting on the floor at low tables in the back rooms of Edo. You may well

have done the same thing yourself: taken a stamp, pressed it on to an inkpad and pressed out the image on the stamp on paper.

One of the top artists who created prints in this way was Hiroshige. The first print the Spauldings bought for their nascent collection was one of his. Born the son of a fire-warden in Edo in 1797, Hiroshige became a prolific artist and designed thousands of compositions for ukiyo-e wood-cuts. The most popular were reprinted many thousands of times.

Sarah showed me some scenes from the work that sealed his reputation as a master, his 1833–34 *Fifty-three Stations of the Tōkaidō Road*, depicting stations along the 500 kilometres highway along the Pacific coast that linked Edo with the imperial city of Kyoto. One scene from Kanbara station called *Night Snow* (東海道五十三次之内　蒲原　夜之雪) shows three men walking outside at night, in the snow, wearing snow clogs or barefoot. They are bent over, to shield themselves from the bitter wind. I felt freezing just looking at them.

Another print I liked was *The Koto Player* (琴を弾く娘) by Suzuki Harunobu (1725–70), the first Japanese artist to design commercial prints using the Chinese method of printing with five colours. It shows a Japanese lady leaning to one side and playing a stringed instrument called a koto. Above her are built-in cabinets painted with purple iris. Behind her is a small stove with a kettle for tea on top of it. This beautiful woman is very accomplished. She reads and writes, she arranges flowers, can perform the Japanese tea ceremony, she lights incense and knows how to play the koto.

We also looked at a set of three prints that make up one design called *A Pilgrimage to Enoshima* (江の島詣り), designed in about 1789 by Torii Kiyonaga. It shows a group of women resting on the shore opposite the island which contains the sacred shrine of Enoshima. Throngs of people still visit the island today to see the shrine and the pretty island.

One Western artist who would have been in heaven leafing through the Spaulding collection was Vincent van Gogh. He first bought some Japanese prints from the docks in Antwerp and delighted in them from then on until his death, copying them and writing to his brother, Theo, about them in 1888, 'I envy the Japanese for the enormous clarity that pervades their work. They draw a figure with a few well-chosen lines as if it were as effortless as buttoning up one's waistcoat.'

Van Gogh painted his own versions of two of the prints from Hiroshige's 1856–58 series *One Hundred Famous Views of Edo* – one of delicate blossom in a plum orchard, the other a bridge showered with splinters of spring rain, called *Sudden Shower over Shin-Ohashi Bridge* (名所江戸百景　大はしあたけの夕立). I saw both of his paintings in the Van Gogh Museum in Amsterdam. They are called *Flowering Plum Orchard: After Hiroshige* and *Bridge in the Rain: After Hiroshige*. Van Gogh was was also inspired by Japanese prints to create *Almond Blossom*, in 1890, a symbol of new life, of spring, as a present for his brother Theo's newborn son, also called Vincent. Impressionist artists, including Manet, Degas and Monet – who covered the walls of his house in Giverny with more than 200 Japanese woodcuts – found the prints unusual and shocking. They were ethereal and beautiful, unlike anything in western art. It was as though they came from another planet.

The Spaulding brothers came late to the game of collecting Japanese prints: they bought collections from other people, including Frank Lloyd Wright, designer of the iconic Solomon Guggenheim building in New York, but resold any they were not in love with. They had a great eye and collected only the best, which is why their collection is so wonderful. You can see images from the collection on the museum's website, as the images were photographed in 2005, but the originals will never go on display.

Graphic arts specialists, lovers of Japan and devotees of beauty can make an appointment to visit the collection to study the prints first hand and glimpse the colours of Edo that inspired van Gogh and Impressionist artists, and which have developed into modern video games, cartoons – and the Japanese creations I like best, the delightful animated world of Studio Ghibli, a Japanese animation and film studio in Tokyo. Their film *Spirited Away* won an Oscar for Best Animated Feature in 2001, the only film that isn't in English to have done so. I'd give an Oscar to their 2008 film *Ponyo*, a brilliant interpretation of *The Little Mermaid*, with the sweetest Japanese theme song you'll ever hear.

[*Spirited Away*]
A scene from Studio Ghibli's Oscar-winning film.

[OBJECT 56]

Van Gogh's
SKETCHBOOKS

[Location]

THE VAN GOGH MUSEUM
Amsterdam, The Netherlands

HE DECIDED TO BECOME AN ARTIST INSTEAD,

as he felt he wanted to leave 'a certain souvenir' to humankind

'IN THE FORM OF DRAWINGS OR PAINTINGS,

NOT MADE to COMPLY with THIS or THAT SCHOOL

but to EXPRESS GENUINE HUMAN FEELING'.

'MY SKETCHBOOK SHOWS THAT I try to catch things "in the act",' wrote Vincent van Gogh to his brother, Theo, in 1882. That is a little how I felt, 130 years later, looking through four of the artist's sketchbooks, in storage at the Van Gogh Museum, in Amsterdam – as if I was catching him 'in the act' of creation.

There are seven of his sketchbooks in total in the museum, but only four with their original covers. These four are stored in the prints and drawings archive. Van Gogh carried each one in his pocket, at different times in his life.

Van Gogh had been all set for a deeply religious life but, aged 26, he transferred his religious zeal to art. He decided to become an artist instead, as he felt he wanted to leave 'a certain souvenir' to humankind 'in the form of drawings or paintings, not made to comply with this or that school but to express genuine human feeling'.

He moved to a rural town called Nuenen to live with his parents and begin learning his craft. I was able to leaf through pages and pages of personal sketches and observe van Gogh in the act of becoming an artist.

The first sketchbook has a royal blue, marbled inside cover and an empty pocket at the back. The first image he sketched in it was a church in Nuenen. He later painted this church in *View of the Sea at Scheveningen and Congregation Leaving the Reformed Church at Nuenen*. The painting once hung above the storage room, upstairs in the gallery, but in 2002 it

[The first sketchbook]
It has a royal blue, marbled inside cover and an empty pocket at the back. The first image van Gogh sketched in the book was a church in Nuenen.

[Jeanne Louise Calment
(1875 –1997)]

Madame Calment lived in Arles
her whole life – 122 years and
164 days. She met van Gogh
when she was 13 and found
him 'dirty, badly dressed and
disagreeable'. She sold him
coloured pencils.

was stolen. Now the museum has no idea where it is. They have only this pencil sketch – the only trace of a masterpiece that has now disappeared.

Other pages of the Nuenen sketchbook contain images of the people and places of Nuenen – people at work in the fields or weaving in workshops. In the faces of some sketches I glimpsed the faces of the family in his first masterpiece, *The Potato Eaters*. It felt very intimate to see the faces of people the artist lived amongst in such a fragile, tangible form; they seemed more real to me in the pencil sketches – more immediate – than in the paintings that hang in the galleries.

The second sketchbook has a black cover. Inside are more scenes of Nuenen, and then glimpses of Antwerp, where van Gogh next went to live. There he visited a lot of museums and indulged his new passion for Japanese woodblock prints. Van Gogh would have felt he'd died and gone to heaven if he'd been let loose among the Spaulding prints I saw in the Museum of Fine Arts in Boston.

In Antwerp, van Gogh became ill and run down, perhaps as a result of his diet, as he lived almost entirely on bread, coffee and absinthe. So, in 1886, he moved to Paris, to live with his brother. It was here that he filled the third sketchbook. It is rectangular, far wider than the others, and it has a linen cover. It's stuffed full of drawings of things he saw in Paris – faces, and sculptures in museums, as well as female nudes who posed for him. In one pencil sketch, I recognized the windmill at Montmartre – a rural village at the time – which appears in lots of his paintings. Also in this book are sketches of flowers, Theo van Gogh's laundry list and a letter from Vincent to Theo written in chalk. There is one stray sheet, which the artist tore out in order to write a note to his brother announcing his arrival in the city.

After Paris, van Gogh set off to the south of France, to Arles, hoping to see an echo of the countryside he'd fallen in love with in Japanese woodblock prints; on his way, he said he kept looking 'to see if it was Japanese yet'. When he arrived, he thought the people in Arles were like 'creatures from another world', including the 'priest in his surplice, who looks like a dangerous rhinoceros'.

One of these creatures was named Madame Jeanne Calment. She lived in Arles her whole life, and ended up breaking records: living for 122 years and 164 days, until 1997. She rode her bicycle until she was 100 years old. When asked the secret of her long life, she said she was always very calm, like her name. 'I dream, I think, I go over my life,' she said. 'I never get bored.'

According to a legend, she met van Gogh when she was 13. He came into her uncle's shop in 1888. She found him to be 'dirty, badly dressed and disagreeable'. She could remember selling him coloured pencils. Perhaps he sketched her.

Van Gogh had been lonely, and hoped to create a collective of artists, living together in Arles. Paul Gauguin came to join him. Van Gogh painted several versions of *Sunflowers*, the series of paintings of bright, wilting, yellow and brown flowers, while waiting for his friend to arrive.

The two artists lived together in the Yellow House, and a painting of sunflowers hung in Gauguin's room there. Gauguin even painted van Gogh painting sunflowers, in *The Painter of Sunflowers*. In a letter to Theo, van Gogh wrote of *Sunflowers*, 'It is a kind of painting that rather changes in character, and takes on a richness the longer you look at it. Besides, you know, Gauguin likes them extraordinarily. He said to me, among other things – "That ... it's ... the flower" ... You know that the peony is Jeannin's, the hollyhock belongs to Quost, but the sunflower is somewhat my own.'

Having never sold a painting in his life, at that moment, van Gogh would never have conceived of a time when his sunflowers would be instantly recognizable across the planet.

The artistic dream didn't work out in Arles: the artists argued and, famously, van Gogh cut off his ear. (It has also been argued that Gaugin cut it off when the two were arguing.) The residents of Arles wrote a petition asking that the '*fou roux*' – the mad redhead – be evicted from the Yellow House. Van Gogh moved into an asylum, continuing to paint there, and then ended up in Auvers-sur-Oise, where, months later, aged 32, he shot himself.

The final sketchbook has a linen jacket, a tie to keep it closed and a pocket at the back, which contains the business card of E. Walpole Brooke, a painter, who had lived in Japan and with whom van Gogh went out walking. Perhaps they discussed Japanese art and nature – the subjects that fascinated them both.

There are two sketches of sunflowers in the final book. One shows 16 sunflowers in a vase; the other 12 stems in a vase. The drawings match up with two paintings that belong to the Van Gogh Museum; they have the

[Van Gogh *Sunflower* sketch] The final sketchbook I saw contained two sketches of sunflowers. When he sketched the flowers van Gogh would never have conceived of a time when his sunflowers would be instantly recognizable across the planet.

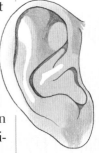

[*Self-Portrait With Felt Hat*]
This painting was in storage, waiting to be reframed and shipped to Japan. It was strange to see it, unframed, in the stacks, his piercing eyes staring out of the painting.

same number of flowers in the vases. Perhaps he was sketching and remembering happier times.

Other sketches that you'd recognize as paintings include some sketches from Daubigny's garden and sketches of irises, olive pickers and two figures in a ravine in Saint-Rémy. He called his *Irises* 'the lightning conductor for my illness'; by painting them, he thought he could ground his mind and make himself feel better. Now, the painting belongs to the J. Paul Getty Museum in Los Angeles, and is one of the most expensive paintings ever bought – for a secret sum.

Van Gogh shot himself believing that he was a failure, and a lot of his family thought the same thing. When Theo died half a year after his brother, the family washed its hands of the paintings, and it fell to Theo's wife and son to take care of the estate.

In her lifetime, Theo's wife saw her brother-in-law's work go from being worthless to being among the most prized paintings in the world. The city of Amsterdam built the museum where his sketchbooks live so as to exhibit and conserve his work. I wonder, if he had known what would become of his paintings, would he have shot himself? And, if he had not, what other paintings might he have produced?

After I had looked at the priceless sketchbooks, the curators who showed them to me let me peek into other back rooms. We went into a photography studio, where *The Harvest*, absent from its usual spot on the museum wall, was being photographed. It was at the centre of a wheel lit with nine bright spotlights. What would Vincent have made of the care and precision with which it was being recorded, or indeed of the queues outside to see his work?

Afterwards, we visited the painting storage rooms. I saw Vincent van Gogh himself. His cool green eyes stared out from a painting: *Self-Portrait with Felt Hat*. It's a small image of the red-bearded artist wearing a brown hat, a white shirt and a blue-brown jacket. His eyes are alarming, his face is serious, and seeing him reminded me of what Madame Calment had said about the man she once served in a shop in Arles.

This painting of van Gogh's face was in storage because it was about to be reframed and sent to Japan for an exhibition. I liked the idea of van Gogh going to Japan. He loved their art, and would have loved to know that they, in turn, liked his.

BOX in a VALISE
by MARCEL DUCHAMP

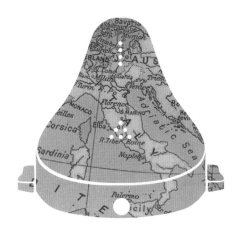

[Location]

The PEGGY GUGGENHEIM COLLECTION
Venice, Italy

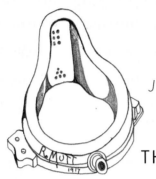

NO LONGER COULD AN ARTIST
GET AWAY WITH
JUST PAINTING AND DRAWING WHAT THEY SAW;
After Duchamp,
THEY NEEDED A CONCEPT, AN IDEA.

VENICE IS THE DREAMIEST CITY on earth. Everything there is floating, suspended. During the day, tourists crowd the city but, by night, it is eerily quiet. On the night I arrived, I walked the streets, seeing barely a soul. I felt as though I were in an enchanted city.

It's the same at the Peggy Guggenheim Collection on the Grand Canal in Venice.

By day, art lovers cram into Peggy Guggenheim's former home, drawn as much by the mystique of the lady herself as by her stunning collection of modern art. By night, only the paintings remain, and they settle down, into the quiet of the night time city, wearing their pyjamas.

Yes, most drawings and paintings in the Peggy Guggenheim Collection, and some of the sculptures, have their own pair of pyjamas. Each pair is beige and adorned with a sketch of the painting it clothes each night. They protect the works of art from the dazzling light that glitters off the canal each morning when the members of staff first arrive at the museum and pull open the blinds. Then the pyjamas are taken off, the doors unlocked and the crowds arrive.

Just outside the Pollock Room is a staircase that leads down to the basement. It is cordoned off with a metal gate and a sign that reads 'Private/Privato'. I met Grazina Subelyte, curatorial assistant at the Peggy Guggenheim Collection there. She opened the gate and we went down the stone stairs and unlocked the door to the room the staff at the museum nickname 'the bunker'.

Waiting for us inside was Siro De Boni, from Chioggia, a coastal town in the Veneto region, who has worked at the museum for decades and knows the paintings as if they were his family. Inside the bunker lives almost half of Peggy Guggenheim's collection: all the things there is no room to display, or which are too fragile to be kept in the light.

One of the most fragile pieces in the entire collection is Marcel Duchamp's Box in a Valise, a suitcase containing a box filled with 69 replicas and reproductions of the artist's works in miniature. The suitcase itself lives inside a grey box on a shelf. Siro pulled the box down and laid it on a table. He lifted the lid and revealed a Louis Vuitton case, about the size of a briefcase. Then, he opened it.

It was such fun to see what was inside. Reproductions of 69 of Marcel Duchamp's favourite works are in there, but they are all tiny. It's as if they ate the mushroom in *Alice's Adventures in Wonderland* and then were packed away out of sight.

I laughed when I saw a teeny version of his most famous work: the white urinal he called *Fountain*, put inside a gallery and called art. With this strange and bold move, he created conceptual art. No longer could an artist get away with just painting and drawing what they saw; after Duchamp, they needed a concept, an idea.

The urinal was one of a series of conceptual pieces he called Readymades. Other mini versions of those works are glued on to the lid as well, so that they hang in a vertical gallery. There is a tiny glass chemist's bottle filled with air from Paris and a small *L.H.O.O.Q.*, an artwork he created in 1919 by taking a cheap postcard copy of the *Mona Lisa*, drawing a moustache and beard on her face and then writing the letters of the title on it. These letters, when pronounced in French, make the phrase '*Elle a chaud au cul*', which was translated by Duchamp as 'There is fire down below.'

Once I'd looked at those works, Siro began unpacking the box. It's like a travelling salesman's bag: it contains a bit of everything. He pulled out a miniature *Nude Descending a Staircase, No. 1*, a work which now hangs in the Philadelphia Museum of Art. We looked at *Nude (study),*

[Box in a Valise (Boîte en-valise), 1941]
This is No. 1 of a de luxe edition of a travelling case, by Louis Vuitton, assembling 69 reproductions of Marcel Duchamp's own work. This edition has one 'original' and a dedication to Peggy Guggenheim, who assisted Duchamp financially in its production. Can you see the tiny white urinal?

[Peggy Guggenheim (1898–1979)]

Peggy moved into the Palazzo Venier dei Leoni, on the Grand Canal in Venice, which is now the museum. Here she is popping out by gondola.

Sad Young Man on the Train, a painting that hangs, full size, in the gallery upstairs.

Showing me the lot was quite a fiddly job for Siro, but we enjoyed checking out each of Duchamp's pieces and seeing what was what in his box of miniature creations, his tiny, travelling museum.

This particular Box in a Valise was made public in 1941. There are many more like it, but this is the most precious in the world, because is the first and because it was given to Peggy Guggenheim. She financed the entire project, and he wrote a dedication to her inside the box.

This box was one of 20 originals of the de luxe edition Duchamp made; they're now in museums around the world, including the MOMA in New York City. These first 20 took six years to make. Each of the boxes has one unique piece of art inside it.

Peggy was born Marguerite Guggenheim in Manhattan in 1898. She had two sisters, Hazel and Benita; she was very close to Benita. Her father died on the *Titanic* and her childhood was, as she put it, 'excessively unhappy'. When she turned 21 she inherited a small fortune, had a nose job – which didn't go well and which she regretted – and changed her name to Peggy.

She met her first husband, Laurence Vail, while working for free in a bookshop, and they had two children together. He introduced her to Duchamp, whom she would describe as 'the great influence of my life'. She left Vail in 1928 for an English intellectual, John Holmes, who died tragically young in 1934.

For many years she lived in the Sussex countryside with Douglas Garman, who, I found out in her memoirs, was a friend of a poet named Edgell Rickword, my great-grandfather Cecil Rickword's cousin. I have a book of poems by Edgell, with a dedication inside written by my great-grandfather.

It wasn't until Peggy Guggenheim left Garman and turned 39 that she decided to begin the life for which she would be remembered: she started collecting modern art. She learned as she went along, with the help of Marcel Duchamp.

In her autobiography, she writes: 'At that time I couldn't distinguish one thing in art from another. Marcel tried to educate me. I don't know what I would have done without him.' He introduced her to artists, planned her shows and gave her lots of advice.

Peggy decided to open a gallery at 30 Cork Street in London called Guggenheim Jeune. The first show consisted of works by Jean Cocteau. The only way she could speak to the artist was to talk to him while he lay in bed smoking opium. 'The odour was extremely pleasant, though this seemed an odd way of doing our business,' she said. Duchamp hung the show and made it look beautiful.

London hadn't seen anything like Cocteau's abstract, Surrealist art before, and sales were slow. Peggy bought his art under a fake name to cheer the artist up: 'That's how the collection began.'

She continued to develop her eye for modern art thanks to a brief affair with the writer Samuel Beckett: 'He told me one had to accept the art of our day as it was a living thing'.

The second exhibition at Guggenheim Jeune was the first one-man show in England of Kandinsky's work – again, Duchamp introduced her to the artist. Next up was a sculpture exhibition including sculptors Duchamp knew – Brancusi, Henry Moore, Jean Arp and Alexander Calder.

The gallery became a hip place to be. Peggy Guggenheim showed all the top contemporary artists and found talent in its embryonic stage. She even had an eye for artists who were still children. During a show of children's art, she included the paintings of her own daughter, Pegeen, and showed works by Lucian Freud. In her autobiography she says 'At the last minute Freud's daughter-in-law brought in some paintings done by Freud's grandchild Lucian,' she recalled. 'One was of three naked men running upstairs. I think it was a portrait of Freud.' Peggy also showed *Birds in a Tree*, which Lucian Freud drew in crayon when he was seven. His mother Lucie kept the drawing, which was exhibited once again in London in 2012.

As the Second World War began, Peggy Guggenheim was in Paris. As the Nazis advanced and people began to flee the city, she bought a painting a day. Some of the masterpieces of her collection – by Francis Picabia, Georges Braque, Salvador Dalí and Piet Mondrian – were bought in those days. She astonished Fernand Léger by buying his *Men in the City* on the day that Hitler invaded Norway. She acquired Brancusi's *Bird in Space* as the Germans neared Paris.

Two days before the invasion of Paris, Peggy took her whole collection to a friend's house in the south of France and stored her paintings in a

[*Birds in a Tree* by Lucian Freud] Peggy showed this crayon drawing by Lucian Freud (aged seven) in her gallery in Cork Street, London.

barn. Eventually, she shipped them to New York, and she followed them, with her family, lovers – past and present – and some friends.

In 1942, in New York, she opened her first museum-gallery in the States, called Art of This Century. The Box in a Valise I saw in Venice was shown in the New York gallery. She said of the valise, 'I often thought how amusing it would have been to have gone off on a weekend and brought this along, instead of the usual bag one thought one needed.'

It was in New York that Peggy met Jackson Pollock. He was working as a carpenter in her uncle's museum – now the Solomon R. Guggenheim Museum. She financed him, encouraged him, commissioned his biggest piece of work ever – a mural for her home – and said that helping him become a professional artist was 'by far the most honourable achievement' of her life.

After five years of parties, meeting artists and running her gallery in New York, Peggy moved to Venice and bought the white stone Palazzo Venier dei Leoni, on the Grand Canal, which is now the museum. Three afternoons a week, she let visitors roam around to look at her paintings, just as they do today.

Down in the storage room are works by all the top modern artists. I asked Siro, almost jokingly, whether he had any Pollocks there. 'Actually, yes, there are some here,' he replied. He slid one out of its slot – 'Here is the first one, it's called *Two*' – and, moving to the other side of the room, he pulled out another. 'This one is called *Bird Effort*.'

The collection's chief conservator and Siro take care of all the works in the gallery, making sure they're in a good state of conservation, packing them on to boats to go to exhibitions as loans, or to be framed if need be. Siro knows where each painting is without having to think about it for a moment.

Once he had shown me around his domain, he left, calling, 'Ciao, bella!' and winking. Grazina left for London, to pick up a Mondrian they had loaned to the Courtauld Gallery and escort it back to Venice.

I left the beautiful paintings and went out of the gallery, into the garden. There was a Wish Tree, put there by Yoko Ono. People were writing down wishes on paper and hanging them from the branches of the tree. Yoko Ono and Peggy Guggenheim spent time in Japan together, with the musician John Cage, who, Peggy complained, didn't let her go sightseeing enough. One of the wishes on the tree reads: 'That people will never cease to be astounded by the beauty and goodness of people in the world'. That felt like a great wish to make in the gardens of the beautiful palazzo in Venice, filled with the spirit of its creator, Peggy Guggenheim.

Her palazzo reminded me a little of the Isabella Stewart Gardner Museum in Boston; after all, both Peggy Guggenheim and Isabella Stewart Gardner were female collectors who loved Venice. I wrote to Hans Guggenheim, whom I met in Boston the night before visiting the Gardner.

I asked him whether he knew Peggy. He replied, saying that he did, he had gone to some of her wonderful parties and visited her in Venice, but doesn't like to visit her palazzo any more as she is nowhere to be found. He ended his email to me with a drawing of a unicorn with the tail of a fish, leaping out of the canal and the question, 'I know you know she loved her dogs, but did you know she kept a unicorn in the garden?'

[Hans's unicorn]
Hans ended his email to me with a drawing and the question, 'I know you know she loved her dogs, but did you know she kept a unicorn in the garden?'

[OBJECT 58]

MARGARET FONTEYN's
TUTU

[Location]

**The Royal Opera House Historical Costumes Store
KENT, ENGLAND**

When the prince
SEES the PRINCESS
DANCING in this LOVELY DRESS,
HE IS SMITTEN.
He DECIDES to FIND HER,
to KISS HER and so BREAK the SPELL.
The prince and princess get married,
AND THEY LIVE
HAPPILY EVER AFTER.

'I'M DEALING WITH MEMORIES,' SAID Judith Dore, conservator of the Royal Opera House's precious historical costumes as we walked through the greatest dressing-up box in the world. 'People know what they think a production looks like. If a little girl comes to the Royal Opera House and sees something magical, that is a memory she carries with her for life.'

To preserve the magic and the memories, the Royal Opera House keeps over 6,000 items – headdresses, Cinderella dresses, delicate fairy tutus, swathes of huge opera robes – hanging on rails, or packed away in tissue paper in a storage site in the Kent countryside. The humidity is controlled to keep the costumes in perfect condition; the levels are sent through to the Royal Opera House in Covent Garden every day for monitoring.

Among them is this beautiful blue hand-painted tutu worn by Dame Margot Fonteyn in 1946 when she danced the role of Princess Aurora in *The Sleeping Beauty*, the show that kissed the Sadler's Wells ballet company into stardom at its new home.

During the Second World War, the Royal Opera House was taken over by Mecca – of bingo hall fame – and became a dance hall. The American troops loved it. While they swung the nights away in Covent Garden, the ballerinas of Sadler's Wells danced, under the direction of Ninette de Valois, all over the country, to lift the spirits of their audiences with their leaps and pirouettes. Margot Fonteyn was one of the ballerinas in the company.

[Dame Margot Fonteyn (1919–91)]
Margot Fonteyn dances 'The Vision Scene', in *The Sleeping Beauty* when the Lilac Fairy shows a handsome prince a vision of Princess Aurora.

I spent an afternoon in the collection's office in Covent Garden listening to rehearsals, which are piped up from the main stage, and reading letters Fonteyn wrote during the war years to a boyfriend – 'My Dearest Patrick' – telling of how 'sad and terrified' she felt, how London was being destroyed and of her sore feet, boils in her mouth and feeling 'confused about myself and everything …' She also felt uncomfortable writing – 'I feel like a mermaid walking on land when I have to express myself in words' – just as most of us would if up on the stage at the Royal Opera House.

When the war ended, the American troops went home. The Royal Opera House floor was cleared of chewing gum, and seats were put back into the auditorium. It was decided that resident ballet and opera companies were needed. Ballet had become much more popular as an art form during the war years, and so the Sadler's Wells ballet moved to Covent

Garden and has been the resident dance company at the Royal Opera House ever since (it became The Royal Ballet in 1956). The Covent Garden Opera Company, now the Royal Opera, was created at the same time in 1946; auditions were held the length of the country. The first performance after the war was *The Sleeping Beauty* with Margot Fonteyn in the lead role.

The opening night was a Royal Gala performance. The royal family were there in their finery, and the dress code was changed so that service men and women could come in their uniform if they didn't have evening dress. Just imagine the sighs of relief as the curtain lifted, the ballet began and an audience exhausted from years of war settled down in their seats to celebrate beauty and fantasy.

This tutu worn by Margot Fonteyn shimmers with beauty. It is the dress that inspires the prince's kiss. Margot Fonteyn danced in it during Act II, 'The Vision Scene', when the Lilac Fairy – Sleeping Beauty's fairy godmother – shows a handsome prince a vision of the most beautiful girl in the world, Princess Aurora. The princess has been sleeping for a hundred years and can only be awakened by true love's kiss. When the prince sees the princess dancing in this lovely dress, he is smitten. He decides to find her, to kiss her and so break the spell. The prince and princess get married, and they live happily ever after. The production was a massive hit, and 150,000 people came to see it in that first season in 1946.

The Royal Ballet took the show to the Metropolitan Opera House in New York in 1949 for its debut performance there, and it was such a success that *Time* magazine put Margot Fonteyn on its front cover. The dress, and the production designed by Oliver Messel, made Fonteyn an international star.

Margot Fonteyn danced 'The Vision Scene' hundreds of times in this tutu. It is made from a pale blue Lurex with a bouncy silk net. The bodice is wonderfully decorated with hand-drawn shapes and stitched on cord that twirls down the front of the bodice and around the waist. It must have danced in the light as she moved.

When it was worn out, it was replaced in the 1960s with a copy, also now in storage in Kent. It's interesting to see the two dresses together. Both are made from blue Lurex – probably the exact same material kept in stock by the wardrobe team – and have crinoline straps, but, while the

[The tutu]
Margot Fonteyn danced 'The Vision Scene' hundreds of times in the pale blue, Lurex tutu, now kept carefully wrapped in tissue in the Royal Opera House's historic costumes store.

[Margot Fonteyn's tutu]
This beautiful, blue tutu has a bouncy silk net. The bodice is carefully decorated with hand drawn shapes and stitched on cord. It must have danced in the light as she moved.

1946 dress has a net skirt made from silk, the sixties' net is nylon. The earlier dress is more worn, as silk degrades over time. It is also more delicate and fine and the decorations more subtle – a lot of it done by hand, perhaps because there were fewer decorative materials around just after the war, than in the sixties. The later dress is bluer and has lovely leaf shapes – called paillettes – sewn on to the skirt and 3D sequins on the bodice.

On both, you can see grey marks around the waist where the prince lifted Princess Aurora up over and over as they danced. Part of the later tutu has been repaired because of the wear from lifts.

Judith checked the crotch of the dress to see whether it had ever been displayed – it hadn't; the crotch was still intact. 'It's the strongest piece of sewing the wardrobe does.' The 1946 dress must have been on show at some point, as the crotch has been undone to hang over a mannequin and then stitched back up again.

Neither of these two dresses will be worn again, but they are kept as memories. The last production of *The Sleeping Beauty* at the Royal Opera House, in 2006, was based on the first production in 1946, so the costumes were brought out of storage to inspire the new generation of designers. Otherwise, they are sleeping beauties themselves, lying in storage in Kent.

Brand new costumes, for new productions, are made on site in London. I visited the costume department on a behind-the-scenes tour of the Royal Opera House. It was lunchtime, and everyone was at their desk having lunch, knitting and sewing their own things.

Judith Dore, back in Kent, tells me, 'I think the wardrobe team are shocked to see the different way in which I treat their costumes. To them, they are basically a working tool.'

The costumes have to withstand enormous wear and tear while feeling like a second skin to the dancer, and still somehow look ethereal. I think it must be nice for the dancers to know their costumes are preserved so reverently once they are too worn to dance in.

Theatre is about tradition, and people like to see the show that they remember seeing, performed in the same way. Opera singers and ballerinas get superstitious about dresses, considering famous ones to be 'lucky'. The dress worn in Act II of *Tosca* by Maria Callas is one of those dresses: singers feel the fabric contains the essence of Callas in the iconic role. Margot Fonteyn was an exception: she didn't like to wear other dancers' clothes and was the only one who wore her costumes.

Only when a production is no longer in the rep will the most iconic costumes be taken into storage here in Kent. A costume becomes important when it is a significant design, or from a brilliant production (like *The Sleeping Beauty*), or when it has been danced in by a famous principal dancer. From then on very few people see the costumes other than the collections exhibition team who bring items to London for display at the Royal Opera House, or curators from other collections who ask to borrow things.

Each piece is hung on a special hanger inside a white bag made of a soft, smooth material called tyvek. Headdresses and accessories are on shelves. Everything is labelled: 'Cinderella', 'Accessories Box', 'Sleeping Beauty King', 'Sleeping Beauty Queen' ...

Only one thing is kept on a mannequin. It's a fat suit made for a rhinemaiden to wear in a nineties' production of Wagner's *The Ring*. The fat suits weren't popular with the rhinemaidens because the maidens overheated – after each performance, the suits were stored off stage with buckets underneath them to collect sweat.

The tutus are kept in boxes. The ideal way to store a tutu would be on an individual mannequin moulded to the shape of the ballerina who wore it, but this is too expensive and takes up too much space, so the tutus are kept in tissue paper, in boxes. Each tutu and costume is packed in the way that is best for it.

Some are stored upside-down with the netting on top, others with the bodice on top. Each crease is carefully packed so that it's not sharp and won't create a fold. Some tutus take an hour to pack away. The collections team make puffs and rolls out of tissue and, once they have a big pile of them, they start to pack. They use as little tissue as possible as, over time, the tissue can stress the fabric.

The Sleeping Beauty dress from 1946 was packed netside-up so, when we opened the box and lifted out the tissue paper, we saw a mass of white netting, like down. The sixties' dress was packed the right way up, with rolls of tissue paper underneath the bodice and tissue packed into the bust.

The tutus are packed two to a box. Beneath the sixties' dress is another of Fonteyn's dresses, the 'Rose Adagio' dress, and beneath her original 1946 dress is a tutu she wore to dance Odette in *Swan Lake*.

After we had put the beautiful Fonteyn tutus back to bed, we had a look at two ballet shoes. One was Margot Fonteyn's, signed in her hand, kept in its original 'Freed' box. The other, much smaller slipper belonged to Ninette de Valois, the founder of The Royal Ballet. She danced in the shoes in the 1920s and later gave them to Fonteyn, as a gift, writing inside 'Margot with love, Ninette de Valois 1954'.

We packed those away, in Judith's special way – she can tell if anyone has been in her shoe boxes, as no one folds tissue in quite the same way.

Beside the shoes was a clothes rail with three costumes hanging on it. Judith took hold of one. 'The greatest costume in here, for me, is this one,' she said, and she unzipped a white bag to reveal a dark green chiffon dress. 'It's the dress Margot Fonteyn wore to dance *Ondine* in 1958.' It was the first ballet Judith ever saw. Ondine, the sea goddess, first appears on stage shimmering in a fountain, looking like water. 'I sat with my mother, up in the gods, and when Margot Fonteyn took the stage my mother dug me in the ribs – "Look! There she is!" I said, "No, that's not her, that's the light." I'll never forget that moment. Imagine the effect on an eight year old.'

Many years later, when Judith began working as the conservator of costumes at the Royal Opera House, she was handed a box. 'I lifted the lid and I burst into tears,' she told me. 'It looked just like a piece of seaweed, but I knew it was the dress.' The green slip is now in storage. 'It keeps me happy,' says Judith.

The other two costumes on the rail beside the green Ondine slip were a tiny-waisted waistcoat belonging to Nureyev – who so often danced with Fonteyn – and a gown worn by Doreen Wells when she danced the lead role in the sixties' production of *La Fille Mal Gardée*.

I loved seeing those, because *La Fille Mal Gardée* was my first ballet, the one I remember seeing with *my* mum at the Royal Opera House.

Stanley Peach's
CENTRE COURT DESIGNS

[Location]

WIMBLEDON LAWN TENNIS MUSEUM

London, England

WHERE ONCE THERE WAS A MEADOW
COVERED WITH GRAZING COWS,
NOW there is the world famous CENTRE COURT
and the ALL ENGLAND LAWN TENNIS CLUB.

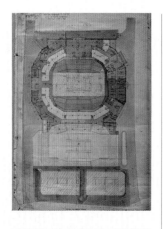

[Stanley Peach's Centre Court design]
The most striking of plans is from April 1921, drawn in ink and coloured with watercolours.

ON THE DAY I VISITED, the club had just hosted the Olympics and was filled with workmen taking down the London 2012 multi-coloured signs and reinstating the traditional purple and green colours of Wimbledon. The museum itself was closed, but Honor Godfrey, curator of the museum took me behind the scenes. In the club's museum stores are about 450 plans drawn up by architect Stanley Peach, who designed Centre Court, which opened in 1922.

Only two of the plans have been framed. The most striking is one from April 1921, which has been drawn in ink and coloured with watercolour paint. This is the plan for the creation of Centre Court, its focus that small patch of grass on which dreams come true, hopes are dashed and history is made.

The plan shows the whole of Centre Court: the court in the middle is drawn in ink; the seating areas are painted in blue and brown. The court, seats and all, is in the shape of a dodecagon – that's with 12 equal sides – with entrances to the stands from five halls around it.

On the plan, to the east of the court is the tea lawn terrace, which runs the length of the court (again including the seats) and, beyond that, the tea lawn itself. 'Taking tea was a major thing at Wimbledon,' said Honor, as she showed me the plan. 'What about strawberries?' I asked. 'Did they have those here in the twenties?' 'Oh yes,' she replied. 'Strawberries have always been here at Wimbledon.' Stanley Peach made sure that there would be enough room – about 46 by

17 metres – in the Centre Court tea room for all to enjoy the drink Britain would be lost without.

To the west of the court are three further courts, painted in brown. They were not built in the end because, two years later, in 1924, No. 1 Court opened on that site. 'I particularly like this,' said Honor, pointing to the turning circle for the grass roller. We looked really closely at the plan to make out the words written on the lawnmower's path: 'Roller Access Road' and, beneath that, it says '1 in 8 gradient'. Stanley Peach signed the plan and was involved at every stage of the process; he was skilful and meticulous, paying great attention to even the smallest of details.

Peach was described by the Royal Institute of British Architects (RIBA) as having a 'quiet clear voice', a 'sense of humour' and a 'wide knowledge of humanity'. He'd trained as a doctor and worked as a surveyor in the Rockies before joining an architect's practice at the age of 24. As well as Wimbledon, he worked on conserving St Paul's Cathedral and was part of a group that first brought electricity to homes in Westminster.

One of the things in his mind when he was working on the plans for Centre Court was to make sure that the players had the best light conditions possible throughout the day. He designed the court so that no shadow would fall on it until after 7 p.m. Another was the crowd: he put a small piece of white paper, about the size of a one-pence piece, on to the court, and made sure it could be seen from every seat in the stand. Only about a hundred seats had a view partially restricted by columns.

The other framed plan by Stanley Peach is a much smaller, coloured sketch showing the complete layout of the club. According to Peach's original design, Centre Court was not in the centre but in the far north of the ground. That is because it was first named Centre Court at its original location in nearby Worple Road, and the name stuck.

Honor showed me the most recent map of the site, and we could see that everything Peach designed remains pretty much the same now. The big change is that the club has doubled in size since 1921, and Centre Court *is* now the centre of the club, as the site has expanded northwards, on to what were once green playing fields. The tea lawn has been paved over, and is now the entrance you'll walk across if you come in from Gate 4 or 5, as I did.

[Centre Court]
Peach made sure the players had the best light conditions for play and that no shadow would fall on Centre Court until after 7 p.m.

The plans came into the museum collection only quite recently. When the new retractable roof of Centre Court was unveiled, the museum wanted to put on an exhibition about the history of the court, and wondered where the plans for it could be. The hundreds in the collection were unearthed in the cupboards of Stanley Peach's architecture firm, now called Peach and Partners, and in the club surveyor's office. The plans arrived all rolled up in tubes, some with tattered ends.

One by one, 200 blueprints and elevations, tracing cloths and photostats were taken out of their tubes, unrolled and prepared for conservation, protected by plastic covers. They are now kept in a big wooden plan chest in storage, while another 250 are yet to be conserved. The colourful Centre Court plan and the sketch of the whole of Peach's new Wimbledon hang in the same room, mounted in their frames on racks, with other posters and paintings of and about Wimbledon.

We took a few other plans out of their drawers to get a feel for the collection. I looked at a blueprint for the committee and royal box, and for the clubhouse. This was a working drawing and showed where the kitchen, bar, press room, telephones and – most importantly – tea rooms, should go. This was Drawing 11812 – originally there must have been heaps more than now survive at the museum, plans used by contractors and carried around by Peach and the team of builders and surveyors as they built the tennis club.

I saw the less glamorous side of Centre Court, too: a drawing on tracing cloth for the gas and electricity supply. It's quite dirty, as it was the original version used by the builders on the job. There are sketches of the iconic criss-cross balustrade and a photostat showing all the different columns used; the ground it was built on slopes, so all the columns are different heights. Now, there are only four super-columns instead. On other blueprints someone has drawn little caricatures of Mr Tennis and Mr Lawn.

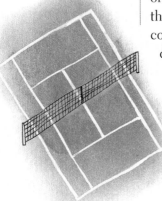

When Centre Court opened it was a hit. The *Architect's Journal* compared the court, with its 14,000 seats and standing spots, to a Roman amphitheatre, 'like the Colosseum … the "arena" is simply a rectangle of vividly green turf, but it's no less the centre of intense interest than was that other arena whose terrors provided the sport of an ancient Roman holiday.'

On day one of its opening, of course, it being England, and it being Wimbledon, it rained. People didn't mind too much as it gave them a chance to check out the new grounds. It wasn't until 3.30 in the afternoon that the King and Queen came into the royal box and the King banged a gong three times to open Wimbledon. The new Centre Court was revealed, in all its shadowless, smooth, green glory.

The first match began. The players were Colonel Kingscote and Mr Leslie Godfree. Mr Godfree served the first serve ever on Centre Court, and Colonel Kingscote whacked it straight into the net. Godfree pocketed the ball as a memento. His opponent's poor start didn't matter as he went on to win the match. The first match on the new Centre Court may have lacked the drama of some of the thousands of matches that have since been played there, but everyone was happy they'd been able to see a game at all, despite the drizzle. Due to the bad weather, only one more match was possible that day. There were a few muddy footprints on the court by sunset.

The Wimbledon museum store has plenty more treasures. There are two small storage rooms. The first one, which contains the plans, also houses paintings, postcards, greetings cards, tickets, passes, posters, sculptures and ceramics right from the early days, and up until the 2012 Olympics. There are also lots of costumes, from long white dresses and suits worn in the twenties to sexier little white dresses and men's kit from more recent times. They're all hanging in white bags, as if they were in a dry-cleaner's.

Just next door to that room is the racket store. As you'd imagine, there are rows of tennis rackets, arranged chronologically, from the old wooden style, used in the 1870s and for the next hundred years, to the modern graphite rackets. Above the wooden rackets are lots of wooden presses, which the rackets were put away in. Players kept their rackets for years back then – they'd never have imagined that, in the future, players would swap rackets several times a match. It was interesting to see the moment graphite rackets arrived in the seventies represented in the museum's collection. Some people used them right away, and others, like McEnroe, used wooden ones until the 1980s. There are some of his in the row, mixed in with the graphite.

Federer, Cash, Henman, Agassi – all of them have donated their rackets to the collection. Opposite them all, on the floor, is the biggest

[The racket store]
I saw rows of tennis rackets, arranged chronologically, according to when they were used. Modern graphite rackets replaced wooden rackets from the 1970s, but not everyone took to them right away. McEnroe used wooden ones until the 1980s.

[Centre Court's roof]
It takes about half an hour to close the roof and air condition the space inside it.

racket in the world, made for a shop promotion, and the biggest tennis ball. There was a sign on the shelf in the racket store that I liked, as it seemed so typically English – it looks like a big green table tennis bat, and it reads 'End of Queue'. 'There's always a queue at Wimbledon,' said Honor.

Honor pointed out four rackets that were used for the friendly mixed doubles match played on 17 May 2009, when Centre Court's roof was first used. After years of pondering over and then planning the roof, finally the Wimbledon organizers had an ally against the haphazard English summer. Andre Agassi and Steffi Graf took on Tim Henman and Kim Clijsters; the winners were Agassi and Graf, the husband and wife team.

It takes about half an hour to close the roof, and to air condition the space inside it – so there isn't too much condensation, which would make the grass all slippery – so the matches are played in the open whenever possible.

The museum doesn't have the architect's plans for the roof, because (of course) they are digital and stored on computer hard drives. In the future, the museum might ask for some printouts for the collection. They're adding to it all the time. 'It's easier to collect things at the time,' Honor said. I visited during the 2012 Olympics, just after Andy Murray had won his gold medal. He donated the kit he was wearing during the match to the museum. 'Did you just walk up to Andy Murray and say, "Can I have your clothes?"' I asked. 'Something like that …' laughed Honor.

[OBJECT 60]

Original Draft of
'AULD LANG SYNE',
Robert Burns

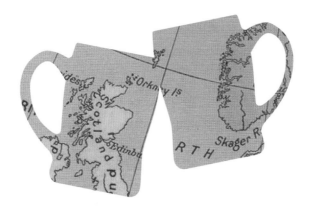

[Location]

THE MITCHELL LIBRARY,
Glasgow, Scotland

We'll take a cup o' kindness yet,
FOR AULD LANG SYNE.

[An original draft of 'Auld Lang Syne']
The Mitchell Library in Scotland keeps this original draft, written by Robert Burns, in a black, combination-lock briefcase. The traditional New Year's Eve song came about thanks to this piece of paper.

ALL OVER THE WORLD, ON New Year's Eve, we humans like to sing 'Auld Lang Syne': 'For auld lang syne, my dear, for auld lang syne, we'll take a cup o' kindness yet, for auld lang syne.' Which is a bit strange, considering how few of us know what 'auld lang syne' means ('old times' sake'), or why we cross our arms and hold hands with our neighbour while singing. Still, it is a fun thing to do and makes everyone glow with bittersweet hope and nostalgia.

The tradition all came about thanks to a piece of paper that is two centuries old and now lives in a black, combination-lock briefcase in a secret location within the Mitchell Library in Glasgow. Scotland's national poet, Robert Burns, took this piece of paper, laid it out on his writing desk and wrote the words to 'Auld Lang Syne' upon it in brown ink, using a sharpened feather. You can even see where Burns stopped to dip the quill's nib into his inkwell, as the writing is inkier and stronger in parts.

I enjoyed looking closely at the poet's surprisingly large and neat handwriting and seeing the words he immortalized on paper. As with so many of the objects I have seen in basements and cupboards, this piece of paper transported me back in time, to the moment of its creation. Although the words to the song have been set free into the world, it's nice to know the original is carefully stored in the Mitchell Library. It's best that the paper is kept out of the light, because it is already yellowed, and so fragile it looks as if it might turn into a puff of smoke if you were to blow on it. I couldn't look at it without singing the words silently in my head.

The song spread across the world as the Scottish people did; they took their traditional song with them, and it caught on. The curators of the library told me that, in Scotland, the song is sung at the end of all kinds of events and celebrations, not just at the end of the year.

'Auld Lang Syne' really only became the global New Year's anthem because of a Canadian singer called Guy Lombardo. For decades (1929–59), Lombardo performed a live broadcast from the Roosevelt Hotel in New York City on New Year's Eve. Each year, his orchestra, the Royal Canadians, would play 'Auld Lang Syne' as part of the celebration. It was thanks to radio, then television, that the song became a real 'tradition'.

[Guy Lombardo and the Royal Canadians]
For decades Lombardo performed a live broadcast of the song from the Roosevelt Hotel in New York City on New Year's Eve. Today, in Times Square, the tradition continues.

Nowadays, in Times Square, New York, New Year is celebrated by thousands of people singing 'Imagine' by John Lennon, then comes a countdown to midnight itself, and a recording of Lombardo and the Royal Canadians playing 'Auld Lang Syne' brings in the New Year. The song that always follows is 'New York, New York' by Frank Sinatra.

The Scottish song has been interpreted differently in other parts of the world. The tune of 'Auld Lang Syne' is used as a graduation and funeral song in Taiwan. In Japan it is played to usher customers out of shops which are closing for the day; there, the tune is called 'Glow of a Firefly' and uses the same melody but different lyrics. Until 1972, 'Auld Lang Syne' was the national anthem of the Maldives. The song has also been played when the Union Jack is lowered when a British colony becomes independent, and is popular in Russia, where studying Robert Burns's work is part of the curriculum in schools. In India, the melody was the inspiration for a song 'Purano shei diner kotha' ('Memories of the Good Old Days'), by the great Bengali poet and writer Rabindranath Tagore, who also wrote the Indian national anthem, 'Jana Gana Mana', sung by children across India every morning at school.

There are five other extant versions of 'Auld Lang Syne' written in Burns's hand. If you were able to see them all together, you would be able to trace the creative process at work in the writing of the song, for each version is slightly different. The Mitchell Library's version differs from the others in that the lyric generally recorded as 'For Auld Lang Syne, my dear' is, in this instance, 'For Auld Lang Syne, my jo.' I asked the curators of the library whether Robert Burns had had a girlfriend called Jo. They explained that 'jo' was a term of endearment, one that no one really uses in Scotland any more. 'My jo' means something like, 'my darling' or 'my dear'.

[An alternative tune]
In some versions of the song the tune is more nostalgic. There were several variations touted around – even Beethoven composed a version – before we got the internationally recognized tune sung at midnight each New Year's Eve.

Robert Burns said that the song 'thrills my soul', but he didn't actually write it himself. 'I took it down from an old man's singing,' he wrote in 1793. He sent it to James Johnson, the editor of *The Scots Musical Museum* (an anthology of traditional Scottish songs), saying it was 'an olden song' passed between families and friends.

As it turns out, 'Auld Lang Syne' had its origins in an anonymous fifteenth century poem that went under various names, including 'Auld Kindries Foryett', 'Old Longsyne' and, finally, in 1724, 'Auld Lang Syne'. It was also a drinking song during the Civil War. A song beginning 'Should auld acquaintance be forgot' appeared in print before Burns adopted the line: it was written by the poet Allan Ramsay, whose love of Scottish folk traditions inspired Burns; it's about two comrades parting after a battle. What Robert Burns did was to take the sentimental feeling of the poem and adapt it to an age of emigration. He universalized it, and made it far stronger and more affecting than ever before. He described what he did as 'mending' songs, giving them to the world for the future.

This version of the song, that lives in storage, doesn't break out of its vault very often. It was flown to America for a Tartan Day celebration in New York City and was on exhibition there for a little while, but most of the time it is stored wrapped in archival paper, protected by foam, in its black briefcase. Of course, anyone can see it, because this original belongs to the people of Glasgow, so the curators at the library will show it to you if you ask to see it. But preserving it out of the light is in its best interests, helping it to survive long into the future.

What I didn't know about the song is that Burns wrote the lyrics, but the tune came later. There were several versions touted around – including one by Beethoven – before we got the internationally recognized one sung at midnight on New Year's Eve. The Mitchell Library owns a copy of Beethoven's score, which it displays in its Burns Room, right at the top of the library building. The room contains all Burns's works, as well as memorabilia and other interesting treasures associated with this beloved writer. This room isn't usually open to the public, but the library does rent it out for lectures.

On show in the Burns Room was the earliest score for 'Auld Lang Syne' that they own, in that version the tune was more nostalgic, while the one we know now is more assertive and confident. The modern tune is still poignant, but it doesn't set everyone off crying at midnight each year, as the old one might have. The version we use is more suggestive of good times gone, and to come, and of the freedom of the human spirit.

Of course, Robert Burns isn't only celebrated on New Year's Eve. There is Burns Night on 25 January, that wonderful evening on which people gather together, to eat haggis (or to look at haggis and ask, 'What is in it?') and then read his poems aloud to one another while drinking whisky. Burns is also to be celebrated for giving us a word that rhymes with purple. In the last verse of a letter to Elizabeth Scott, a Scottish poetess, Burns wrote:

I'd be mair vauntie o' my hap,
Douce hingin' owre my curple
Than ony ermine ever lap,
Or proud imperial purple.

[Haggis]
Burns Night, on 25 January, is a Scottish institution: a night to celebrate the life and works of Robert Burns, eat haggis and listen to bagpipes.

Which roughly translated means, Burns would rather wear plaid over his buttocks than any ermine or posh purple cloth. Curple, in this instance, is his bottom.

People often call Burns 'Rabbie', but he never signed his name as Rabbie, Robbie – or, indeed, 'Bobbie' Burns, as some Americans call him. His signatures included 'Robert', 'Robin' and, on at least one occasion, 'Spunkie'. Neither did he ever wear a kilt, because kilts were outlawed after the Jacobite Rebellion and, if Robert Burns had put one on, he, like all Scots who wore one, would risk deportation.

But, of course, Burns's most famous work is the song we all sing in the first moments of each year: 'Auld Lang Syne'. Next New Year's Eve, when you begin singing, 'Should auld acquaintance be forgot and never called to mind,' you might remember the piece of paper that lives quietly, in a foamy bed inside a briefcase, in the library in Glasgow. I know I will.

INDEX

Page numbers in *italics*
denotes an illustration

A

Abernathy, Barbara 275
Ablett, Jon 120
Addis, William 291
Afro-Brazilian museum
    (Salvador de Bahia) 173–8
Agassiz, Louis 135
Akkadian language 76
Albarn, Damon 153
Albert I of Monaco, Prince 114–15
albino quail 127
Alert (Nunavut) 172
Alicia (Artigas and Miro) 198–202
Allende meteorite 30
Altona, synagogue in 263
Amelin, Olov 244, 247
Amundsen, Roald 164–5
Angel, Roger 29
Angivranna 168, *168*, 170
anglerfish couple 117–22, *118*
Anne Frank House (Amsterdam) 254–60
Antoinette, Marie 218
Apollo 17 22–3, 37
Aramaean gods 240–1
Archie, the giant squid 120–1, *120*
Arctic 172
argillite 63
Ark, The (Lambeth, London)
    52–3, *53*, 54
Armstrong, Neil 36
    spacesuit and boots of 24, *24*
Artigas, Josep Lloréns
    Alicia 198–202
Ashmole, Elias 54
Ashmolean Museum (Oxford) 54
Ashton, Nick 300, 301, 303
Ashurbanipal, King of Assyria
    school exercise book
        belonging to 72–7
astronauts 36–7
    spacesuits 21–5
Atlantis Space Shuttle 34–5
Attenborough, David 204
Auden, W.H. 87
'Auld Lang Syne' (Burns), original draft
    of 339–43, *340*
Aung San Suu Kyi 246–7
Auster, Paul 87
Avicenna 41
Azedo, Aparecida 306
Aztecs 191, 194, 196, 197

B

Babylonians 76
Bagge, Peter 42
Bahia (Portugal) 58
Ballard, Robert 107
ballet 328–32
ballet shoes 332
balloon gondola, Piccard's
    100–5, *103*
bananas 43
Banks, Joseph 40
Barbary Lion Project 235
Barefoot Carmelites, Order of 58
Bata, Mrs 228–31
Bata Shoe Museum (Toronto) 227–31
bathyscaphe 103
Beagle, HMS 68
Bean, Alan 23
Beauharnais, Joséphine de 127
Beckett, Samuel 323
bees, golden 222–6, *223*
Beethoven, Ludwig van 16, 342
beetles
    use of to clean up specimens
        153–4
bejewelled cross 56–9
Bell, Alexander Graham 283
Berg, Albert and Henry 86
Bernaud, Mark 214–15
BESM-6 104
Bible, Gutenberg 14–19, *19*
binomial nomenclature 39
bio-piracy 49
black emu 127
Blake, William
    *Songs of Innocence and
        Experience* 87
Blaschka, Rudolph and Leopold 134,
    134
Bletchley Park (Buckinghamshire)
    270–5, *271*
Blood, Colonel Thomas
    dagger belonging to 232–6, *234*
'Blue Marble, The' (photo) 22
Blue Whale 41, 149–54
Blythe House (London) 61, 62, 63
Boni, Siro De 321, 324
book(s)
    Diamond Sutra 210–15
    Gutenberg Bible 14–19, *19*
    unopened 203–9, *206*
Boston Library 18
'Box in a Valise' (Duchamp)
    319–25, *321*
Brazil 174, 176
    end of slavery 287

and naïf art 306
seeds from 49
use of postage stamps 286
Breazeal, Cynthia 110
British Dental Association Museum
    (London) 289–92
British Library (London) 210–15
British Museum (London) 68, 130,
    196, 226
    Handaxe Storage (Hoxton) 299–303
    Tablet K.143 72–7
British Postal Museum and Archive
    (BPMA) (Essex) 276–9
Brontë, Bramwell 148
Brontës 147
Brooke, E. Walpole 317
Brooks, Linda 40
Brownstone, Arni 189, 192
Buckingham Palace switchboard
    280–4, 282
Buddha 211, 212–13
Buffon, Comte de 127
Burke and Hare 150
Burma 224
Burns Night 343
Burns, Robert
    'Auld Lang Syne' 339–43, *340*
Burton, Sir Richard 182
buttercups 41
Butterfly Genitalia Cabinet,
    belonging to Nabokov 78–82, *80*
butterfly pea 41
Byström, Lars 142

C

'cabinet of curiosities' 130
Callas, Maria 330–1
Calment, Jeanne 316–17, *317*
camari 224, 225
Cameron, James 103–4, 108
Canadian Arctic Expedition
    (1913-18) 168
Canadian Museum of Civilization
    (Ottawa) 167–72
candiru (catfish) 121
Candomblé, religion of 174–5, 176,
    177–8
cannon, world's smallest 148
Cannonball jellyfish 135, *136*
Carnegie, Andrew 298
Casco Ltd 120
Castlereagh, Lord 274
cats
    Dickens' feline cat opener
        83–8, *84*
Cernan, Eugene 6, 22, 23

Challenger Deep 103
Chambers, Mike 302
Champley, Robert 131
Channel Islands, pillar box
    276–9, 277
Chapman, Eddie (Agent Zigzag)
    270–5, 273
Charles II, King 234
Charles, Prince 140
Checketts, Sir David John 283
Chilean miners 231
China 18
Christie, Agatha 239
Churchill, Winston 271–2
    sketches of 248–53, 252, 253
Clarke, John 218
classification system 39–41, 43
clay tablets 73–7, 75, 76
Clifford, George 43
Cocteau, Jean 323
codebreakers (Second World War)
    271–5
Coixtlahuaca 189, 190, 191
Collingwood, Cuthbert 146
Collinson, Nika 64
Collinson, Vince 64
Columbia (ship) 185–6
Con Tiki Viracocha (sun-king) 156
Consolmagno, Brother Guy 28–9,
    30–1, 31
Convent of Saint Teresa de
    Avia 58
Cook, Captain James 187
Cook, James 164
Cope, Edward Drinker 40
Coram, Eunice 89–90
Coram, Thomas 89–90
corsets 151
Cortés, Hernan 196, 197
Cousteau, Jacques 114
Covent Garden Opera Company
    (Royal Opera) 329
Crick, Francis 68–71, 69
Crimmen, Ollie 119, 122
cross, bejewelled 56–9
Crown Jewels 234
Culhuacán 196
cuneiform 73–7, 75

D
dagger, belonging to Blood 234–6, 234
Dahl, Roald 95–9
    The BFG 96, 99
    Charlie and the Chocolate Factory 96
    The Gremlins 292
    Matilda 97

and RDMSC RD 1/11 94–9, 98
Dalai Lama
    13th 218–19, 218, 220–1
    14th 221, 221, 247
dance-houses, Inuit 170–1
Dark Knight Rises, The 36
Darwin, Charles 68, 121
date palm seed 46
Davis, Wade 172
Debussy, Claude 16
Delft, Lilian van 260
delphinium 41
dentifrice 291, 292
dentistry 290–2, 290
Diamond Sutra 210–15, 212
Dickens, Charles 84–7, 86
    A Christmas Carol 85
    David Copperfield 87
    feline letter opener 83–7, 84
    and Foundling Hospital 90
    Little Dorrit 90
    Oliver Twist 91
    public readings and prompt
    copies of his work 84–6
dinosaurs 293–8
    Dippy the Diplodocus 298
DNA 69, 70
    Crick's sketch of 66–71, 68
Dore, Judith 328, 330, 332
drinking chocolate 69
Duchamp, Marcel 322
    'Box in a Valise' 319–25, 321
Dunant, Henry 246
Dunhuang, Caves of 213, 214
Dupont, Inge 17
Dürer, Albrecht 16, 147
Dutton, E.P. 86
Dylan, Bob 16

E
Easter Islands 156, 160
Edwards, Talbot 234
egg, great auk 128–32, 129
Egyedi, Kitty 256, 260
elephant, Indian 154
Eliot, T.S.
    The Waste Land 87
Elizabeth I, Queen 228, 229
Elizabeth II, Queen 140, 283, 283,
    284, 307
emu, black 127
Enigma machine 271, 272, 272, 275
Epic of Gilgamesh 74
Essex, Earl of (Robert Devereux) 229
Evans, Ronald 22
Exu Boca de Fogo 173–8

Exxon Valdez oil spillage (1989) 65
Eze, Anne Marie 206–7

F
Fairhurst, Fiona 121
Fastskin® swimsuit 121–2
feather helmet, Hawai'ian 184–7, 185
Fiennes, Sir Ranulph 164
Finkel, Irving 73, 73, 74, 75, 76, 77
Finkelstein, Lucien 305, 306–7
fish 118–22
flag, from Battle of Trafalgar 143–8, 145
floorboards, things beneath the 51–5
folk charms 62
Fonteyn, Margot 328
    tutu belonging to 326–32, 329
Forester, C.S. 98
Foundling Hospital 89–91
Foundling Museum (London) 88–93
Fowler, Lottie 136
France
    first giraffe in 123–7, 125, 126
Frank, Anne 254–60, 259
Frank, Otto 257, 257–8
Franklin, John 147–8
Franklin, Rosalind 69, 70
French Revolution 125
Frere, John 301–2
Freud, Lucian 323
    'Birds in a Tree' 323, 323
Friedlander, Michal 264
Friendship Book 254–60

G
Gardner, George 208–9
Gardner, Isabella Stewart 204–5, 204,
    206, 325
Garman, Douglas 322
Gauguin, Paul 317
Gemini 9 36
German Secret Service 273
Germplasm Bank of Wild Species
    (Kunming Institute of Botany,
    China) 49
Gewirtz, Isaac 84, 86–7
Ghosh, Amitav
    The Glass Palace 225
Gies, Miep 257
Gieves & Hawkes 181
giraffe, first (in France) 123–7, 125, 126
glass jellyfish 133–6, 136
Glass Palace (Burma) 224
    Bee Throne 223–5
    Lion Throne 224, 225
    pageboy 224, 225, 226

Glaucomys volans
   (flying squirrel) 41
goat eye stamps, leaf of 285–8, 286
Godfree, Leslie 337
Godfrey, Honor 224, 335, 338
golden bees 222–6, 223
gondola, Piccard's balloon 100–5, 103
Goodale, George 134–5
Gordon, John 86
Gostner, Martin 268
gravity 34, 35
Gray, Captain 185–6, 186
great auk egg 128–32, 129
Great Fire of London 281–2
Great Pacific Garbage Patch 160–1
Great Wave, The (Hokusai) 311, 311
Gregorian calendar 28
Guggenheim, Alicia Patterson 199, 200
Guggenheim, Fromet 263
Guggenheim, Hans 325
Guggenheim, Harry F. 199–200, 199
Guggenheim Museum (New York City)
   98–202
Guggenheim, Peggy 322–5, 322
Guiraud, Michel 124, 126–7
Gustav Adolf II, King of Sweden 138, 141
Gutenberg Bible (on vellum) 14–19, 19
Gutenberg, Johannes 17–19, 17
gynandromorphs 81, 81

H

Haida Gwaii (Queen Charlotte Islands)
   63, 63, 64, 65
Haida people 63–5
Haida Repatriation Committee 64
Haida Shaman's rattle 60–5, 62
Haida totem pole 65, 65
Halley, Edmund 36
Hamilton, Emma 147
handaxe (Hoxne) 299–303, 300
Handel, George Friedrich 90
Happisburgh (Norfolk) 302, 302
Harunobu, Suzuki 312
Harvard University
Museum of Comparative Zoology
   78–82, 133–6
Natural History Museum 17
Peabody Museum of Archaeology
   and Ethnography 184–5
Haskell, Susan 185
Hasselbalch, Kurt 108, 109
Haugland, Knut 160
Hawai'i 187
Hawai'ian feather helmet 184–7, 185
heart token 88–93, 92
herbal 68

herbalism 68
Herbert, Sir Wally 164, 165
   sledge 162–6, 164
Hergé 102
Hewitt, Captain Vivian 131
Heye Foundation Museum
   (New York City) 195
Heye, George Gustav 195
Heyerdahl, Olav 160
Heyerdahl, Thor 156–7, 156, 158,
   159, 160
Hiroshige 311–12
Hitler, Adolf 267–8
Hocker, Fred 139, 140
Hockney, David 44
Hogarth, Georgina 84, 86
Hogarth, William 90
Hokusai 311
Homo antecessor (pioneer man) 302–3
Hope Entomological Collection
   (Oxford) 181
Hope, Frederick 181
hot chocolate 130
Houdini, Harry 283
house mouse (Mus musculus) 41
Howison, Thomas 35
Hoxne handaxe 299–303, 300
Hubble space telescope 36
Huet, Nicholas 126
Humboldt Current 160
Hurley, Selina 62, 63

I

Ice Ages 302
Illustrated London Zoo 115
Incas 156
Indian elephant 154
International Museum of Naïf Art
   (Rio de Janeiro) 304–8
Inuit 164, 168–72
Isabella Stewart Gardner Museum
   (Boston) 203–9

J

James, Henry 205
Japan 310
Japanese prints, Spaulding Collection of
   309–13, 311, 312, 313
Jardin des Plantes (Paris) 125, 127
Jason Junior 106–10, 107
jellyfish, glass model of 133–6, 136
Jenness, Diamond 168–72
Jersey, first British letterbox 277–9, 279
Jewish Museum (Berlin) 261–4
Jews, escape from Germany 263–4

Johnson, James 342
Johnson Papyrus 68
Judaism 263

K

Kalmia 41
Kandinsky, Wassily 323
Kapara (Aramaean ruler) 239
Kapitsa, Pyotr 247, 247
Ketellapper, Juultje 256, 259–60
Kew Gardens, Millennium Seed Bank
   45–50
Kingscote, Colonel 337
Kiyonaga, Torii 312
Knox, Dr. Frederick John 150–2, 153
Knox, Robert 150
Kon-Tiki expedition logbook 155–61,
   158, 161
Kon-Tiki Expedition, The 159
Kon-Tiki Museum (Oslo, Norway)
   155–61
Koto Player, The (Harunobu)
   312, 312
Kum raj va 212

L

Lamourouxia viscosa 45–50, 46
Lane, Heather 165, 166
Lapland 42
Lenoir, Michelle 124
Leonardo (robot) 109–10
letterboxes 277–9
Levy, Tatiana 307
Lewis, Cathleen 21
Lienzo of Tlapiltepec 188–92, 190
Linnaea borealis 41, 41
Linnaeus, Carl 39–44
   Iter Laponicum 42–3
   Systema Naturae 43, 43
Linnean Society (London) 38–44
Lister, Joseph 62–3, 62
Livingstone, David, hat of 180–3
Lodoicea maldivica 46
Lombardo, Guy 341
London Metropolitan Archives 91
Lovell, Jim 36

M

McCormick, Robert 68
McDonald, David 220
MacFarlane, Ross 68
MacGibbon, Rab 251
Maclaine, James 119, 122
Malagasy Traveller's tree 47

Marc, Franz 267
  The Tower of the Blue Horses
  265–9, 267
Margaret, Princess 283
Marquesa Islands 160
Mars, three pieces from 26–31, 29
Martin, Lutz 240, 241–2
Mason, Gillian 272–3, 274
Massachusetts Institute of
  Technology *see* MIT
Matson, Harold 97, 98
Mebots 110
Mendelssohn, Moses 263
Messel, Oliver 329
Messer, Thomas M. 200–1
meteorites 29, 30–1
Miescher, Johann Friedrich 69
Millennium Seed Bank (MSB)
  (Kew Gardens) 45–50
Milton, John
  Paradise Lost 16
Miro, Joan
  'Alicia' 198–202
MIT Museum (Massachusetts
  Institute of Technology) 106–10
Mitchell Library (Glasgow) 339–43
Mittarakis, Lia 306
Mixtec people
  and Lienzo of Tlapiltepec
    188–92, *190*
  turquoise shield 193–7, *194*
Moctezuma II, Aztec ruler 196
Modern Art Museum (Stockholm) 142
Mondrian 142
monks 18
Montezuma II *197*
moon, globe of 30
moon landings 22–5
Moore, Keith 33, 36
Moreton, Dr. Tim 249
Morgan, J.P. 16
Morgan Library and Museum
  (New York City) 14–19
Morgan, Pierpont 16, *16*, 19
Mozart, Amadeus 16
Murray, Andy 338
Musée Océanographique de Monaco
  111–16
Museu de Arte Sacra (Salvador de
  Bahia, Brazil) 56–9, *59*
Museum of Comparative Zoology
  (Harvard University) 78–82, 133–6
Museum of Fine Arts (Boston) 309–13
Museum of Garden History 53
Museum of the History of Science
  (Oxford) 51–5
Museum of London 280–4

Muséum Nationale d'Histoire
  Naturelle (Paris) 123–7
museums 16, 55

N

Nabokov, Vera 81, *81*
Nabokov, Vladimir 79, *81*, 87
  Butterfly Genitalia Cabinet
    78–82, *80*
  Lolita 81
  Speak, Memory 81
naïf art 304–8
NASA 22, 30, 37
National Air and Space Museum
  Storage Facility (Suitland) 21–5
National Gallery, The (Berlin)
  266, 267
National Historical Museum (Rio de
  Janeiro) 285–8
National Maritime Museum
  (Greenwich) 143–8
National Museum of the American
  Indian (Washington DC) 193–7
National Museum Collections Centre
  (Granton) 152–3
National Museum of Scotland
  (Edinburgh) 149–54
National Portrait Gallery (London)
  248–53
Natural History Museum (France)
  123–7
Natural History Museum (Tring)
  128–32
Natural History Museum (London),
  Spirit Building 117–22
Nazis 263, 268
  'Degeneration Art' campaign
    (1937) 266, 267–8
  resistance to by White Rose
    group 268–9
Neitfield, Pat 195
Nelson, Horatia (daughter) 147
Nelson, Horatio 145, 146–7
  shoe buckles belonging to 230, *230*
neurobiology 71
New York Public Library 83–7
Newton, Sir Isaac 32–7, *34*
  apple tree 32–7, *37*
  Principia 36, *36*
Nexi (robot) 109, 110, *110*
Night Snow (Hiroshige) *311*, 312
Nile, source of 182
Nineveh (Kuyunjik) 74, 75
  King's Palace at 77
  library at 74, *74*, 75–6
Nobel, Alfred *244*

will of 243–7, *245*
Nobel Museum (Stockholm) 243–7
Nobel Peace Prize 245, 246–7
Nobel Prize 244
Nola, Fra Girolama da 207, 208
North Pole, Herbert's expedition
  to 163–5
Nunavut 172

O

Oates, Captain 165
Oceanographic Museum (Monaco)
  111–16
oceans 108–9
Oludumaré (god) 175
'Ondine' (ballet) 332
Ono, Yoko 324–5
Oppenheim, Max von 239, *239*, 240
orangutan 127, *127*
orixás 175, 176, 177, *177*
Oxum 178
Ozias, Ricardo de
  paintings by 304–8, *306*

P

paintings
  by Ozias 304–8, *306*
  Pritchard's underwater
    111–16, *115*, *116*
Parmenter, Ross 191
Passy, Frédéric 246
Peabody Museum of Archaeology
  and Ethnography (Harvard
  University) 184–7
Peach, Stanley
  Centre Court designs 333–8, *334*
Peale Museum (Baltimore) 186
Peale, Rembrandt 186
pearls, first cultivated 38–44, *42*
Peary, Robert 164
Pedro II, King of Brazil 286–8, *287*
Peggy Guggenheim Collection
  (Venice) 319–25
pelicans 43
penguins 132
Pepys, Samuel 36
Pergamon Museum (Berlin) 237–42
Phelps, Michael 121, *121*
Pi Sheng 18
Picabia, Francis, 'The Acrobat' 142
Picasso, Pablo 16
Piccard, Auguste, balloon gondola
  100–5, *103*
Piccard, Bertrand 104
Piccard, Jacques 103

Pilgrimage to Enoshima,
   A (Kiyonaga) 312
pillar box, Channel Islands
   276–9, 277
Pinto, Gilcelia Oliveira 177
pioneer man (*Homo antecessor*)
   302–3
Pitt Rivers Museum (Oxford) 64, 226
Plastiki (boat) 160, *161*
Pluto 29
Pocohontas 53
Pollock, Jackson 324
Polynesian islands 156
Polyommatus blue butterflies 82
Ponting, Herbert 165
Ponyo (film) 313
Portugal, Francisco 57
Portuguese man of war 135, *135*
Post Office 277–9
Post Office Underground Railway
   (Mail Rail) 279
Powhatan's mantle 53, *53*
Prins, Erika 256–7
printing press, invention of
   17, 18–19
Pritchard, Zahr
   underwater paintings by
   111–16, *115*, *116*
puffins 63
Purpus, Carl Albert 194

Q

Quetzalcoatl (god) 190, 196

R

Raaby, Torstein 160
Ramsay, Allan 342
Ranunculus 41
rattle, Haida Shaman's 60–5, 62
Ray, John 36
RDMSC RD 1/1/1 94–9, 98
reflecting telescope, Newton's
   35–6, 35
Reid, Bill 65
Rejewski, Marian 272
Remotely Operated Vehicle
   (ROV) 107
Rickards, Constantine 191
Rickword, Cecil 322
Rickword, Edgell 322
Rinpoche, Demo 219
Roald Dahl Museum
   (Great Missenden) 94–9
robots 108–10
Roman votive offerings 62

Rothschild, Leo 263
Rousseau, Henri 306, *306*
Royal Academy of Arts 90
Royal Ballet, The 329, 332
Royal Geographical Society
   (London) 179–83
Royal Ontario Museum (Toronto)
   188–92
Royal Opera House Historical
   Costumes Store (Kent) 326–32
Royal Society (London) 32–7
Rutan, Burt 101
Rutherford, Ernest 33–4

S

Sadler's Wells 328–9
Saint-Hilaire, Geoffrey 125
Salk Institute 71
Salmon, Narii 113
Salvador de Bahia 173–8
Samoan wood rail egg 130
San Ildefonso (ship) 146, *147*
San Juan Nepomuseno (ship) 147
Santa Maria dell'Arco, convent
   of 207, 208
Sargent, John Singer 205, *206*
Saunders, Sir Edwin 290–2
Saunders, Wally 99
sauropods 294–8, *295*
Saville, Marshall H. 195
Schmitt, Harrison 37
   spacesuit of 20–5
Scholl, Hans 268–9, 268
Scholl, Sophie 268–9, 268
Schuttes, Richard Evans 136
Science Museum 61
   Large Object Store
   (Wroughton) 100–5
scientific names 40–1
Scorpion, USS 107
Scott, Captain Robert Falcon
   164–5, 166, 183
Scott Polar Research Institute
   (Cambridge) 162–6
Scottish Suttie letterbox 278
sculptures, Tell Halaf 233–42
Secchi, Father Angelo 28
   Sistema Solare 28, 29
Second World War 271
Sedgwick Museum of Earth
   Sciences (Cambridge) 68, 165
seed bank (Kew) 45–50
Sellers, Piers 37
Seneca Iroquois log cabin 195
sGaaga 63, 64
Shackleton, Sir Ernest

balaclava belonging to 182–3, *183*
sharks 121
shield, Mixtec turquoise 93–7, *194*
slap-soled shoes 227–31, 228
slavery 85
   end of in Brazil 287, *287*
sledge, Herbert's 162–6, *164*
'Sleeping Beauty, The' (ballet) 328,
   328, 329, 330
Sloane, Sir Hans 68–9, 130, *130*
Smith, James Edward 40
Smith, John 53
snowsuits 163
Sohlman, Ragnar 245–6
solar system, age of 30
Song 21 167–72
South Pole
   Scott's *Terra Nova* expedition
   164–5, 166
spacesuits
   Apollo 21–5
   Mars 23–4
Spallanzani, Lazzaro 131
Spanish conquistadors 190–1, 196
Sparks, Peggy 115–16
Spaulding Collection of Japanese Prints
   309–13, *311*, *312*, *313*
Spaulding, William and Henry
   310, 313
species 40
spectacled cormorant 131
Speedo 121
Spirit Building (Natural History
   Museum) 117–22
Spirited Away (film) 313, *313*
squid, Archie the giant 120–1, *120*
stamps, leaf of goat eye 285–8, *286*
Stan Winston Studios 110
Stanley, Henry Morton *182*
   hat of 180–3
starfruit 47
Stein, Sir Marc Aurel 214
Stoker, Bram 283
Stopes, Marie 165
stratosphere 101, 103
Studio Ghibli 313
Stukeley, William 34
Stuppy, Wolfgang 46, 47–8
Subelyte, Grazina 320–1
Sullivan, T.R. 205
Sumerian language 76
Sunshine, Jenny 168, 169,
   171, 172
Supayalat, Queen 225
Sutherland, Graham 250, *250*,
   251–2
Swan, Katherine 97–8, 98

Swedish Museum of Natural
    History 235
swimsuits 121–2
switchboard, Buckingham Palace
    280–4, 282
Syrian ostrich 131

T

Tablet K.143 72–7
tabloids 61
Tagore, Rabindranath 341
tandem bicycle 105
Tangaroa expedition 160
tapeworm 136
Tapuiasaurus macedoi skull
    293–8, 295
taxidermy 127
telephone 232CB 284, 284
telephone directory, first 283
telephone exchange, first 283
television sets 284
Tell Halaf sculptures 237–42
Tengye Ling monastery (Lhasa)
    218–19
tennis rackets 337–8
Terra Nova expedition
    164–5, 166
Thames Whale 153
Thibaw, King 225
third law of motion 36
Thompson, Sarah 310
Thornton, Frank 183
Thresher, USS 107
Tibet 220
    Tibetan Abbot's costume
        216–21, 217
Tintin 102
Titanic 104, 107, 108, 108
titanosaurs 297
Tlapiltepec, Lienzo of 188–92
Tli'cho (Dogrib) tipi 195
tokens, Foundling Hospital
    89–93, 91
Tomlinson, Barbara 145, 148
toothbrushes 291
toothpaste 291–2
Torah Ark Curtain 261–4, 263
totem poles 195
    Haida 65, 65
*Tower of the Blue Horses,
    The* (Marc) 265–9, 267
Tower of London 232–6
    menagerie 235, 235
    ravens 236
Tradescant, John, the elder
    52, 52, 53

Tradescant, John, the younger
    52, 52, 53
Tradescantia virginiania 53
Trafalgar, Battle of, flag from
    143–8, 145
Travelling Post Offices (TPOs) 279
Troctolite 76535 23
Trollope, Anthony 277, 278
    The Eustace Diamonds 278
    He Knew He Was Right 278
tsetse fly 181
Turing, Alan 275
Turvey, Peter 104
Twain, Mark 19
Twirl, Benjamin 93

U

Ukiyo-e 311
undersea exploration 108–9
underwater paintings, Pritchard's
    111–16, 115, 116
UNESCO Memory of the World
    list 161
unopened book 203–9, 205

V

Valois, Ninette de 332
Van Gogh Museum (Amsterdam)
    314–18
van Gogh, Vincent 312–13, 318
    Irises 318
    sketchbooks 314–18, 315
    Sunflowers 317
VASA Museum (Stockholm)
    137–42
Vasa (ship) 137–42, 138, 140
Vatican Advanced Technology
    Telescope 29
Vatican Observatory (Castel
    Gandolfo, Rome) 26–31
vellum 19
    Vellum Collection (Natural
    History Museum of France)
        124–5
Venice 320
Victoria and Albert Museum
    (London) 216–21
    Object Storage 222–6
Victoria Falls 181, 181
Victoria, Queen 148
    fascination with teeth 292
    tools belonging to dentist of
        289–92, 290
Victory, HMS 145, 146, 147
Virgin Galactic 101

Virginia 53
Voyager 101

W

Wainwright, Jacob 182
Walsh, Don 103–4
Walsingham, Frances 229
Walsingham, Sir Francis 229
Ware Collection of Blaschka Glass
    Models of Plants 135
Washington, George 292
water lilies 41
Watson, James 69–70, 69
Watzinger, Herman 159–60
WDT valve 95–6
weather forecasting 103
Wellcome Collection
    (London) 60–5
Wellcome, Sir Henry 61–2
Wellcome Library (London) 66–71
Wellcome Trust 61
Wellington, Duke of 230–1, 235
Wells, Doreen 332
Westwood, John 181
White Rose 268–9
Wilkins, Dr. Maurice 70
Willughby, Francis 36
Wilson, Jeff 295, 297
Wimbledon
    Peach's Centre Court designs
        333–8, 334
    Wimbledon Lawn Tennis
    Museum (London) 333–8
Wollaton Hall 36
Wood, Frances 211, 212
Wood Press 104–5
Woods Hole Oceanographic
    Institution (WHOI) 107
Woolf, Virginia 86, 87
Woolsthorpe Manor
    (Lincolnshire) 34
Wright, Frank Lloyd 313

X

Xerces blue butterfly 81

Y

Young, Lisa 21

Z

Zigzag (agent), Christmas telegram
    from 270–5, 273
Zoology Museum (São Paulo) 293–8

ACKNOWLEDGEMENTS

I'd like to say a huge thankyou to everyone who helped to make this book.

I couldn't have written it without the help of so many fantastic curators and museums. Thank you for your generosity, and for showing me around the backrooms, basements and storage cupboards of your collections. I've had the most wonderful time learning from and exploring with you all.

Thank you John Mitchinson – the brightest shining star ever! Since the evening we broke down in your car, on the way back to Great Tew, and talked about the idea whilst walking to your friend's house to get petrol you've been so kind and wonderful. Thank you, thank you, thank you for all your amazing advice and help. Thanks also to Rach.

Thank you to Hennie Haworth for bringing this book to life with your beautiful illustrations, firstly from Kyoto, when we'd only met via Skype, then from your home in the British Museum, and later with Theo toddling alongside you. Sending you chapters and then receiving back beautiful illustrations of things I'd seen was really magical. Thank you.

A massive thanks to the fabulous Zoë Waldie for great advice, encouragement over cups of tea, and for taking my book proposal to just the right place. Thank you to Ele Simpson for introducing me to Zoë.

Thank you Hannah MacDonald for believing in the book. Your ideas and input have been invaluable, and I've so enjoyed working with you and your team at Collins. Thank you Craig Adams for spot-on advice and Georgina Atsiaris for juggling all the different things that went into making this book – I'd probably still be thinking about finishing this book if it wasn't for your excellent plans of action. For the beautiful design I have Martin Topping and Lucy Sykes-Thompson to thank – I couldn't have imagined it turning out as perfectly as it has, thank you so much.

Thank you to Giulia Hetherington for sourcing the perfect photographs,

Spitzbergen

C. Chelyuskin

Sarah Day for copy-editing – even when on holiday – and Sarah Patel and the publicity team. Thank you all so much for making it happen.

Thank you John Lloyd for giving me such a fantastic job at *QI* from day one. I knew I wanted to do something 'interesting' but that was all, so thanks a million for finding me and allowing me to do just that. Thanks to James Harkin for coming to museums with me, when the book was just an idea, high fives also to Dan Schreiber, and Justin Pollard - thanks guys – and to Flash, Sarah L, Sarah C, Liz and everyone at *QI*.

Thank you to my mum, dad, family and grandparents. I've loved writing lots of this sitting beside you, Grandpa, with you asking questions and reading bits and pieces. Thanks to my lovely friends, especially Jarad and Francesca for checking in on the book's progress, and to Charlotte for endless chats, fun times and inspiration – I'm glad you've been just around the corner.

Thanks to everyone who had me to stay: Seb and Katie in NYC, Ches and Gabe in Boston, Paul in Toronto, Nyasha in Paris. Thank you to everyone who gave me advice, including: Ute for all the amazing help and fun times in Berlin and Boston, Cley and John P for Brazilian tips, Laura Z for hooking me up to the Morgan Library, Kath for Guggenheim connections, Martin for Swedish ideas, the fish curators at the Natural History Museum for suggesting my first ever behind-the-scenes trip, James MacLaine for contacts to other museums, Burgs, Alexa, Deana, Sophie D, Claus, Tor (for introducing me to Hennie), Shan and Emily.

Finally a massive thankyou to Olly for great ideas, delicious snacks, coming to museums, taking photos, adding geeky 'amendments' and for so much more besides.

Oh, and thank you for picking up and reading this book.

Amsterdam I.

PICTURE CREDITS